Patterns of Epiphany

Martin Bidney

Patterns of Epiphany

*From Wordsworth to Tolstoy,
Pater, and Barrett Browning*

Southern Illinois
University Press

Carbondale and Edwardsville

PR468
. E65
B54
1997

Library of Congress Cataloging-in-Publication Data
Bidney, Martin.
    Patterns of epiphany : from Wordsworth to Tolstoy, Pater, and
Barrett Browning / Martin Bidney.
       p.   cm.
    Includes bibliographical references and index.
    1. English literature—19th century—History and criticism.
2. Epiphanies in literature.   3. Browning, Elizabeth Barrett,
1806–1861—Criticism and interpretation. 4. Wordsworth, William,
1770–1850—Criticism and interpretation. 5. Tolstoy, Leo, graf,
1828–1910—Criticism and interpretation. 6. Pater, Walter,
1839–1894—Criticism and interpretation. 7. Romanticism.
I. Title.
PR468.E65B54   1997
820.9′1—dc20   96-38623
ISBN 0-8093-2116-5 (alk. paper)   CIP

for dearest Sarah

Contents

Acknowledgments

Some chapters of this book incorporate previously published material from the following sources: "Radiant Geometry in Wordsworthian Epiphanies," *The Wordsworth Circle* 16 (1985): 114–20; "The Structure of Epiphanic Imagery in Ten Coleridge Lyrics," *Studies in Romanticism* 22 (1983): 29–40; " 'A Dream' as Key to a Reverie Pattern in Matthew Arnold: Interactions of Water and Fire," *Victorian Poetry* 26 (1988): 45–60; "Water, Movement, Roundness: The Epiphanic Pattern in Tolstoy's *War and Peace*," from *Texas Studies in Literature and Language*, 23. 2, pp. 232–47, by permission of the University of Texas Press; "Diminishing Epiphanies of Odin: Carlyle's Reveries of Primal Fire," *Modern Language Quarterly* 44 (1983): 51–64.

The December 1987 MLA panel on epiphanies, in which I participated with Professors Carol T. Christ, Morris Beja, Ashton Nichols, Jay B. Losey, and Robert Langbaum, proved a stimulus to clarify my thinking on epiphany. I thank Professor Nichols for organizing this panel and for inviting me to present a paper.

I am grateful to the administration of the State University of New York at Binghamton for computer help, and to Lisa Fegley, Carol Fischler, Arlene Nowalk, and Chris Storrs for generous computer assistance. I also want to thank poet/fictionist Patricia Wilcox and Professor John T. Wilcox for their unfailing kindness, friendship, and support.

My late parents, David and Evelyn Bidney, to whose treasured memory I dedicated *Blake and Goethe* (1988), remain my constant helpers.

My warm thanks to Twin Oaks Indexing; to Jim Simmons, Tracey J. Sobol-Hill, Carol Burns, Connie Fritsche, and Kyle Lake of Southern Illinois University Press; and to my very helpful colleagues David Bartine, Nancy Henry, Robert Micklus, Robert Mooney, Francis X. Newman, Lucy R. Olson, Philip Rogers, and Alvin Vos.

Patterns of Epiphany

Introduction

How Epiphanies Are Made

This is a book about puzzling but privileged moments, sudden gifts of vision, when one's feeling of aliveness intensifies and the senses quicken. In a world with few metaphysical guarantees, poets and fiction writers and literary essayists for two hundred years now have tried to locate meaning in enigmatic but vivid instants—impulsions of dreamlike power that, brief as they may be, resonate with a riddling intensity. Wordsworth called these ultimate poetic moments "spots of time"; James Joyce dubbed them "epiphanies," and Joyce's term has been widely adopted among English speakers.

There is general agreement that the modern epiphanic tradition begins with Romanticism, and specifically with Wordsworth. Ashton Nichols, in his valuable *Poetics of Epiphany*, cites Abrams, Frye, Beja, Langbaum, and Hartman to this effect. These writers further agree: beginning with the Romantic movement, epiphanies have been crucial organizing principles of modern poetry and imaginative prose.[1] Indeed, the combined effect of influential studies by the critics just mentioned has made the word "epiphany," in its modern secular sense, an accepted analytical tool, which we may employ freely in literary discussion without a preliminary review of its religious history or of the ways it was used by James Joyce (though fine accounts of both topics may be found in Nichols' first chapter).

Literary epiphanies are felt as aesthetically privileged. They are moments of imaginative or poetic intensity, comparable in imaginative power to traditional theophanies or appearances of the divine. Given their intensity, their import for writers favored with the ability to generate them, literary epiphanies have received surprisingly little systematic attention. In this book I will propose a method for the systematic study of epiphany, and I will apply the method to a series of literary epiphanies ranging chronologically from Wordsworth to Pater.

1

A) THE NATURE OF EPIPHANY

What are the criteria that qualify a poetic moment as an epiphany? Nichols, again, comes to our assistance. In his *Poetics of Epiphany* we find three criteria: "expansiveness," "atemporality," "mysteriousness."[2] For Nichols, the privileged or epiphanic moment is an expansive, timeless mystery.

I accept the first and third of these qualities—expansiveness and mysteriousness—as defining criteria for a literary epiphany, provided they are understood subjectively (as Nichols seems to intend): an epiphanic moment feels expansive and seems mysterious. But I would reject the criterion of "atemporality" because of the metaphysical assumptions it might presuppose, for I do not think that epiphanies are necessarily felt to abolish time. "Expansiveness" implies that the moment in question seems to mean far more than its limitedness in time and space might warrant (the word "resonance" is a roughly equivalent way to indicate this sense of expanding imaginative meaning). "Mystery" indicates the inexplicability at the heart of the epiphanic experience: the inner power that the vision conveys, a seemingly expansive power enabling the epiphany to resonate beyond the scope of its immediate spatial and temporal setting, is felt as vivid but rationally unaccountable.

In this study I will seek to avoid ontological or metaphysical entanglements. In a famous essay, "The Rhetoric of Temporality," Paul de Man mounted an attack on the widespread use of the ideologically weighted term "symbol" by Romantic poets and their twentieth-century admirers as implying an unspoken theology of the "translucence" of the eternal in temporal objects; de Man charged the promoters of the "symbol" concept with "ontological bad faith."[3] But, as Frank Lentricchia has shown, de Man here reveals his own Sartrean philosophical preferences (gradually replaced in de Man's later attacks on "symbol" by a Derridean set of equally controversial assumptions).[4] I intend to keep my own study of epiphanies free of unannounced presuppositions, whether Coleridgean, Sartrean, or Derridean. To ensure an empirical method I want to define "epiphany" in a way that assumes no ontological commitments.

So my proposed addition to Nichols' two epiphanic criteria of expansiveness and mystery is the most emphatically subjective of all: heightened intensity. The intensity criterion is crucial to any description of literary epiphanies as, I think, most readers understand them. Nichols, too, at one point speaks of "psychic intensity and emotional importance" as characterizing the "epiphanic imagination,"[5] though he does not single out intensity as a defining attribute of each epiphany.

A literary epiphany, then, is a moment that is felt to be *expansive, mysterious, and intense*. Can we go farther than this in creating conceptual tools for analyzing epiphanies? Nichols has tried to do so by introducing a distinction: the epiphanic moment (to quote from my review of Nichols' book) "transcends its momentariness either by transforming the past or by seeming to point beyond itself during the moment it appears."[6] This distinction between past-transforming and self-sufficient epiphanies may seem promising, but in practice it unfortunately proves of little use. It did not help Nichols organize his book, and after initially introducing it, he rarely mentions it again. It may well be that the very mysteriousness of the epiphanic moment's expansive resonance precludes any clear distinction between epiphanies that transform the past and those that don't. So this particular pathway does not help us: we need to look elsewhere.

Before opening up new questions to take us in new directions, however, I want to situate the definition of epiphany just arrived at. How does our threefold definition (expansiveness, mystery, intensity) relate to the earlier attempts at definition presented by Morris Beja and Robert Langbaum? In *Epiphany in the Modern Novel* Beja introduces as chief defining attribute for epiphanies the "Criterion of Incongruity: that when the cause of the illumination is clearly important, there is no epiphany unless the revelation is not strictly relevant to whatever produces it." Beja adds: "Another way of saying much the same thing would be to use the term Criterion of Insignificance," an insistence on the triviality of the epiphanic occasion that Beja finds prominent in Joyce.[7]

The insignificance requirement (though applicable to Joyce) seems too rigid. For example, it would rule out Walter Pater's red-yellow fire flowers, dazzling and brilliant in themselves, and manifestly epiphanic to Pater. The criterion of incongruity is equally problematic. It defines epiphanic power by context. But why should an epiphany have to arise in an irrelevant or incongruous context? Our "expansiveness" concept preserves the sense of disproportion between the moment and its extensive meanings but more appropriately situates this disproportion within the epiphanic experience itself.

In "The Epiphanic Mode in Wordsworth and Modern Literature" Robert Langbaum proposes four more criteria to add to Beja's: "Psychological Association," "Momentaneousness," "Suddenness," and "Fragmentation or the Epiphanic Leap."[8] Unfortunately, the criterion of psychological association (as Nichols' experience confirmed) is problematized by what we have called the "mysteriousness" of epiphanies: in most cases one simply cannot establish chains of mental association that would account for the perceived power of epiphanies. "Momentaneousness" and "Suddenness" seem valid; rather than calling them defining criteria I simply interchange the terms "epiphany" and "epiphanic moment" as a matter of course: that epiphanies are brief and surprising is noncontroversial. But the criterion of "Fragmentation" is unduly restrictive: Carlyle's eruptive epiphanic fires are destructive but complete, not fragmentary.

I do want to agree with Beja, however, in emphasizing what epiphanies are *not*. They are not insights that can be called "simply results of direct statement," of knowledge arrived at in a "rational, straightforward" manner.[9] Mere rhetorical description is not epiphany, nor is discursive psychological analysis. The study of Paterian epiphany, for instance, has been impeded by the critical practice of considering as epiphanies those passages in which Pater merely *states* that something wonderful happened but dissolves the meager imagery of the moment in languid discursive commentary. The best way to avoid such critical traps is to attend carefully to the criterion of intensity.

B) ANALYZING EPIPHANIES

Now that we have a clear sense of what an epiphany both is and is not, two practical questions will open up new directions for inquiry. (1) How are epiphanic moments made, constructed, put together? (2) Since almost every author capable of epiphany making produces more than one epiphany, what distinguishes the epiphanic moments of author A from those of author B?

The first question may sound paradoxical: how can something epiphanic—that is, mysterious in its expansive intensity—be spoken of as "made"? Yet the question is not only meaningful, it is forced upon us when we start to observe distinctive recurrent patternings in epiphanic experiences, patterns of structure that mark a mysteriously intense and resonant moment as recognizably Coleridgean or Wordsworthian or Tennysonian. Unfortunately, in most current criticism we get no clear sense of what distinguishes, say, a Tolstoyan epiphany from a Carlylean one, or of how we may distinguish a privileged moment in Arnold from one in Pater or Elizabeth Barrett Browning. But if we had an overall sense of how epiphanies are made, we could then acquire a more particular understanding of how the characteristic epiphanies of any given literary artist are constructed.

The hypothesis to be tested throughout this book—a theory to be judged, like any other, by its results—is twofold. I want to show, first, that epiphanies tend to be composed primarily of *elements, motions, and/or shapes* (I am using the word "elements" in its ancient meaning, to indicate earth, air, fire, and water). I should add that epiphanic writers may envision these elements, motions, and/or shapes together with closely related additional features (such as a red-yellow color scheme for a fire epiphany, or a bird in an epiphany of air—though the bird might equally well be considered as a concrete "shape").

Second, I want to show that any given epiphany maker is likely to present a distinctive, recognizable, *recurrent combination* of one or more elements, motions, and/or shapes (and closely related features as exemplified above). The epiphany-making process of a writer may be largely unconscious, felt by the literary artist more as a revelation granted than as a product constructed. But even though an epiphany may be experienced by the creative writer as a given—as something perceived and not consciously created—it has certainly been put together on some level of the psyche. And the total constructed epiphany, as perceived by the literary artist and as presented by that artist on the written page to be re-perceived by the reader, can very often be articulated into its component parts: elements, motions, shapes, and a few other closely related features called up by the main element(s) in the epiphany.

The kind of thinking I am proposing here is partly based on the work of the French philosopher-critic Gaston Bachelard. I will be applying to the study of (chiefly British) epiphanies an approach that Bachelard used to investigate what he called reveries—and I do this because I consider the two terms, "epiphany" and "reverie," as for practical purposes equivalent.

Indeed, this volume took shape when I realized that critics in the French tradition stemming from Bachelard had been studying the same kind of resonant intensities that had attracted readers of British and American literature. Only the labels differed.

Investigation of individual writers' structures of reverie/epiphany (the kind of study Bachelard does) is called phenomenological criticism—an approach used in major works by such critics as Geoffrey Hartman and J. Hillis Miller. Phenomenology is the study of structures of perceived experiences. Regrettably, in the vigorous competition of literary methods that we are currently witnessing, phenomenological analysis is the one approach that suffers the most unmerited neglect in Britain and the United States. Gaston Bachelard, the phenomenologist whose approach I have newly revised for this book, has inspired writers ranging from Roland Barthes to Luce Irigaray, yet his works are still only partially available in English.[10] Through the wide variety of examples offered here, I want to show the potential of this newly revised approach, which I call the "paradigm method."

First, however, we must look at certain objections that have been raised against phenomenological method in general: in replying to these queries I can show in each case the advantages of my phenomenological approach. Then, in the fourth part of the introduction (section d), I will explain the "paradigm method" to be used here. Finally (in section e) I will outline briefly the structure of this study, showing how it helps us transcend restrictive boundaries as we study epiphanies of what is conventionally called the nineteenth century (though it begins with Wordsworth and Coleridge in the 1790s)—epiphanies both Romantic and Victorian.

C) THE APPEAL OF PHENOMENOLOGY

Four queries need to be addressed regarding the value of the phenomenological project in general. (1) Given the fact that phenomenology, popular in the 1960s, has dwindled to near invisibility on the American theoretical scene, why do we need to rethink the method now? (2) How can the phenomenological project of isolating for analysis individual structures of perception be reconciled with the verbal or rhetorical nature of literary epiphanies—the fact that epiphanies are things made out of words and therefore conditioned or shaped by language? (3) How can the phenomenological attempt to study individual authors' structures of perception be reconciled with the intertextual nature of every literary work? (4) Lastly, how can phenomenological method reply to the charge that it is oblivious of history?

In sum, I would like to show that phenomenology, as I practice it here, offers rich possibilities for innovative research; it focuses on the verbal text, on product rather than process; it illuminates both influence and intertextuality; and it clarifies the ways in which history is imagined and conceived.

Phenomenology is generally ignored in America now. In *Modern Criticism and Theory: A Reader*, edited by David Lodge, a work widely studied in university theory courses, there is no section on phenomenology; nor does *Introduction to Scholarship in Modern Languages and Literatures*, edited by Joseph Gibaldi, contain any essay devoted to this approach. I do not fault these editors and essayists, who have conscientiously surveyed the current methodological landscape. Yet I see good reason for trying to alter that landscape.

But wasn't phenomenology popular at one time, and hasn't its potential been explored? The answer to the first question is that *one* kind of phenomenology, that of Georges Poulet, chief representative of the "Geneva school" (a group whose achievements Sarah Lawall surveyed in *Critics of Consciousness* [1968]), was influential in America during the 1960s through the brilliant works of his then disciple J. Hillis Miller: *The Disappearance of God: Five Nineteenth-Century Writers* and *Poets of Reality: Six Twentieth-Century Writers*. (Geoffrey Hartman's phenomenologically influenced *The Unmediated Vision: An Interpretation of Wordsworth, Hopkins, Rilke, and Valery* and *Wordsworth's Poetry: 1787–1814* are harder to categorize, as Hartman "worked to remain independent" of perceivable enrollment "in any school."[11]) Then, as Vincent B. Leitch explains, "In 1970 Miller dropped Geneva phenomenology [mainly Poulet] in favor of deconstructive criticism—a telling event signaling a new wave of philosophical criticism."[12] Poulet, then, was once admired and later dropped.

But the potential of a quite different phenomenology, the Bachelardian kind, has remained virtually ignored in the United States. What I want to show here is that Bachelard's writings may serve as the basis for a new method that will prove invulnerable to the objections raised against Poulet—objections of a linguistic or rhetorical nature.

To show this, I must answer the second question I raised a moment ago: doesn't phenomenology limit or distort critical perceptions by directing attention away from the verbal nature of literary epiphanies, from their status as linguistic constructs? The answer is that while Pouletian thinking may be partly vulnerable to this charge, Bachelardian method—in the form in which I have newly revised it—is not. Poulet, and the Geneva school generally, were indeed critics of "consciousness"; for them, literature was to be considered "an act, not an object."[13] In *The Interior Distance* Poulet shows us how each of the writers whose *oeuvre* he describes shapes a personal conception of temporal process; we get a picture of Hugolian time or Baudelairean time. Temporal consciousness, in such an interior portrait, becomes a unitary process subsisting beneath individual literary works, a formative dynamic substratum, a consistent consciousness-shaping force.

Poulet's works do not have much to say about language as a constitutive power or determinant of vision, and they do rely on intuitive reconstruction of an inevitably hypothetical process of time-structuring. Part of the reason why J. Hillis Miller criticized Poulet for ignoring the "systematic interplay of elements which is the ground of the mind, rather than the other way around"[14] is that Miller objected to the hypothetical or unprovable nature of Poulet's supposed (possibly prelinguistic) structures of consciousness.

But such objections do not apply to my method here; unlike Poulet, I do not engage in hypothetical reconstruction of complex mental processes (prelinguistic or otherwise), nor do I presuppose any underlying multi-stage temporal unities of consciousness. It is true that Bachelard—my mentor—likes to talk about mental processes; he characteristically called one of his books *The Poetics of Reverie*, emphasizing process over product. But in the new method I have worked out for this book, I have redesigned Bachelard's approach so as to accomplish the reverse aim: to emphasize the *concrete literary, verbal product* and not to speculate about hypothesized interior processes. Thus, Bachelard's process-oriented terms—"waking dreamers" or "dreamers" or "*rêveurs*"—will be replaced here by "epiphanists" or "epiphany makers," terms that focus not on process but on product. My emphasis will be on the structural components of intense moments verbally presented.

So my newly revised Bachelardian method, far from ignoring the verbal nature of literary epiphanies, requires close attention to the words on the page, words that describe elements, motions, and shapes—things mentioned by the writer and not hypothesized by the reader or treated as manifestations of some "deep" process whose temporal stages are to be intuitively reconstructed, as Poulet might recommend. Thus, we will resolutely avoid Pouletian hazards.

We will avoid Husserlian hazards, too. For Edmund Husserl, the most influential modern formulator of phenomenological method, "self-present being, pure being, preceded language"[15]—a Platonic-sounding assumption from which Derrida has famously dissented. Also, Husserlian *epochē* or "bracketing," the phenomenological isolation of a given object of consciousness for the contemplation of its pure structure, was somehow meant eventually to reveal "an unchanging and universal essence (*eidos*),"[16] again a kind of Platonism to which Derrida, or somebody else, might react skeptically. Finally, Husserl's "acts of intention," though designed to be more dynamic than Kantian categories, still ran the danger of positing invariant structures of human consciousness-processes, categories of awareness that might imply another, subtler kind of metaphysical essentialism than the Platonic or even the Kantian sort. There are, then, three Husserlian hazards: trying to get at a prelinguistic purity, seeking for unchanging universal essences, and positing invariant processes of consciousness. All three of these hazards, like the Pouletian ones mentioned above, are ruled out by my new method, with its emphasis not on hypothesized structures of consciousness but rather on *observed structures of epiphanic literary products*. (Briefly put, the aspect of Husserl I value in this book is exclusively the Humean Husserl—the empiricist, the concrete observer.)

In sum, elements, motions, and shapes (plus closely related attributes, for example, the colors of elements) as constitutive components of literary epiphanies—epiphanies that are products of the verbal imagination and that recognizably appear on the printed page—are the objects of study in this book. Metaphysical essentialisms or assumptions are not posited or entertained; for our purposes it is not necessary to believe that Walter Pater ever "really" saw a red-yellow fire flower bloom and burn, or that Coleridge ever watched the fitful trembling of a flat or rounded object in some posited hypothetical place called the "real world." That these Paterian or Coleridgean epiphanies appear on the literary page is enough; verbal constructs are the objects we will "bracket," describe, and study.

But the very notion of "bracketing," the isolation of the verbal epiphany for the unhindered consideration of its structure, raises another question: does phenomenological method threaten in any way to limit our awareness of either intertext or influence? Quite the contrary. The method used here can extend and enrich our sense of both of these historical factors.

In "Figures in the Corpus: Theories of Influence and Intertextuality," Jay Clayton and Eric Rothstein note that although both terms have received multiple definitions, in general "influence has to do with [personal] agency, whereas intertextuality has to do with a much more impersonal field of crossing texts."[17] How should the phenomenology of literary epiphanies relate to these questions of influence and intertext? It can contribute clarifying discoveries in both areas. A writer's epiphanies, being products of the verbal imagination, are influenced by the writer's language, readings, and general culture. After we have "bracketed" a given writer's literary epiphanies and analyzed their shared structure pattern, we will be prepared to spot resemblances as well as contrasts between this pattern and the patterns or imagery of other epiphanies by other writers. This perception of resemblances and contrasts will be a welcome opportunity for discovering illuminating contexts. And if we find not only the personal influence of a mentor but also, or alternatively, a more general intertextual or cultural mediation, that too will be our gain. The discovery of epiphanic influences and intertexts will enrich our awareness.

The last major objection to phenomenology has been raised by Terry Eagleton, who says that "phenomenology begins and ends as a head without a world"; "its stance" toward "reality as actually experienced" is said to be "contemplative and unhistorical," so that it imposes upon its practitioners "the sacrifice of human history itself."[18] Eagleton's account of phenomenology in *Literary Theory: An Introduction*, an eight-page attack on Husserl (whose phenomenological project is said to have "refurbished the old dream of classical bourgeois ideology"[19]), never mentions Bachelard. Still, it deserves a reply since the question it implies is central. How does my method for the phenomenological study of epiphany relate to our understanding of how history is perceived?

So far from being oblivious of history, I end this book with a unit on epiphanies *of history*. These are visions—presented respectively by Carlyle, Tolstoy, and Barrett Browning—in which an intense, expansive, mysterious moment of literary or verbal power is thought to contain meanings not just for the writer, or for his or her fictional or poetic persona, but for our understanding of historical process. Of course, in line with the empiricism of the present study, I will not claim that such epiphanies reveal the "true" meaning of "real" history; but from such imaginative achievements as these epiphanies represent we do learn how a vision of history's meaning or structure may come to form the basis of an entire "philosophy of history," such as those extrapolated from their respective visions by Carlyle, Tolstoy, and Barrett Browning. So the last section of this book, containing its final three chapters, is a refutation of Eagleton, a sequence of demonstrations that epiphanic structures matter, and matter greatly, to the shapers of written history.

The phenomenological study of epiphanies has profound implications for literary study no matter what one's theoretical orientation. If New Historicists will be interested in the consequences of epiphanic vision for historiographical practice, feminists will find it revealing to contrast the fiery feminist epiphanies of Barrett Browning with the more traditionally "male" epiphanic pattern of Carlyle, with its exclusively masculine flames. Psychological critics may be surprised by the rootedness of Paterian and Tennysonian epiphanies in paradigmatic scenarios of indelible guilt. And students of the history of critical theory should be interested in our findings as we investigate the relation of Coleridgean epiphanic structures to Coleridgean critical ideals, of Arnoldian epiphanic structures to Arnoldian critical pronouncements and recommendations. (In the case of both these men, we find that the implications of their epiphanic practice are wholly at odds with the basic spirit of their critical practice.) Phenomenological bracketing—the isolating of an epiphanic pattern for structural analysis—is a necessary starting point but never an endpoint for the reader who is aware of the contemporary world and of the range of diverse concerns in critical theory. Phenomenology as I intend to practice it here is no dead end. Instead, it offers a series of beginnings.

So phenomenology, as a method for studying verbal epiphanies, is forward-looking and linguistically aware, interested in influence and attentive to history. It also has implications for our understanding of literary feminism, of psychological determinants of vision, and of the relation of critical theory to epiphanic practice.

Thus every chapter of this book will have two concurrent aims. (1) It will disclose a recurrent epiphanic structure in the work of a nineteenth-century writer—a structure unsuspectedly pervasive though ingeniously varied. (2) It will at the same time show the central contribution the epiphanic pattern makes to our understanding of the writer's other creative concerns and interests—to intertexts and influences as well as to the writer's critical theorizing, psychological explorations, feminist outlook, or philosophy of history.

Having countered possible objections to phenomenology by discussing them in a context that instead shows the advantages of this approach, we can look next at the newly revised Bachelardian methodology I will use in the nineteenth-century studies that constitute this book.

D) REVISING BACHELARD: THE PARADIGM METHOD

Working primarily but by no means exclusively with francophone writers,[20] Bachelard devoted decades to the structural study of reveries/epiphanies. In doing so he inspired masterworks ranging from Jean-Pierre Richard, *Poésie et profondeur* to Roland Barthes, *Michelet* to Luce Irigaray, *Amante marine de Friedrich Nietzsche*.[21] In this section I would like (1) to outline Bachelard's postulates that we will be using as guides, (2) to explain the "paradigm method" that I have worked out to make the Bachelardian approach more effective in discovering epiphany patterns, and (3) to distinguish my new method from psychoanalytic, New Critical, and deconstructive approaches.

Bachelard concentrates on imaginative experiences of earth, water, air, and fire. If for the pre-Socratic philosophers (cosmological speculators) these four elements were the determining constituents of the physical universe, for the French philosopher they are rather the chief activators of our reverie-world. They are intense and expansive, not bounded or delimited; fire is fiery, earth earthy, in its smallest as in its largest part; shifts from the microscopic to the cosmic induce the most varied sorts of poetic vision. So the most expansive, mysterious, and intense moments, according to this hypothesis, focus on absorptive, encompassing, fluxile, or explosive elements—not on images of objects.

Since an element has a less definable shape or boundary than an "image" and is in this sense more "abstract," element-study encourages us to look for other semi-abstract determinants of epiphanic experience: patterns of motion, or geometric shapes that may take on special meaning irrespective of what fills them. (I have found that it sometimes pays to take even the idea of elements somewhat abstractly—to watch the emergence of the broader category of "light" as it develops from "fire," say, in the radiant geometry of Wordsworth.) Elemental epiphanies are endlessly varied; for example (as Bachelard shows), no two air epiphanists could be more unlike than Nietzsche, with his aggressive, arrowy ascents, and Shelley, with his soft, flowery floatings.[22] But only a prolonged imaginative absorption in the respective air epiphanies of Nietzsche and Shelley can clarify these contrasts. We never know what kind of pattern we will find in the next elemental epiphanist we study.

In speaking of "elemental" epiphanists, I acknowledge that in my analyses, as in Bachelard's, elements tend to receive the primary emphasis. Bachelard usually thematizes elements much more pervasively and explicitly than either motions or shapes. In some of my own case studies (Coleridge, Tolstoy), the three components are coequal. But often elemental emphasis tends to predominate (as in my studies of fire-water interchange in Arnold, or the turning of stones to fire in Barrett Browning).

As I noted earlier, we must also admit into the analyses of recurrent epiphanic structures certain features closely linked by the epiphany-maker to the element(s) that the writer continually reintroduces. In the epiphanies I study here, the "shape" component will not always be geometric or semi-abstract but will sometimes be quite concrete. Wordsworth and Carlyle like to associate fire (or fiery light) with movement from the center to the circumference of a geometric sphere, but Pater and Tennyson prefer to join fire to the concrete forms of flowers. Bachelard sets the example for an inclusive, flexible approach to the use of analytic categories by including in his analyses of elemental reveries a wide variety of related features. For instance, in his book on "air" he contrasts the odorlessness and silence of Nietzschean air reveries to the perfumes and music of Shelleyan ones (see note 22 above). In order to give this book a reasonable unity of focus, in my own analyses I have treated only writers who privilege elements, motions, and shapes.[23] Yet I have found it necessary to give the notion of "shape" a flexibly inclusive (concrete as well as abstract or geometric) interpretation and have thus not hesitated to include fire flowers and birds as well as circles and spheres.

I have found that the diverse epiphanies presented by each writer vary greatly in the degree of their completeness or elaboration, relative to what seems to be the *fully developed paradigm* of the writer's epiphanic pattern. When a given epiphany is fragmentary, the function of the fragments only begins to make sense when we see them as parts of the larger paradigm. When some features of an epiphany are a bit attenuated or indistinct, we see them more clearly as variants of more boldly and vividly developed features in the complete paradigm.

For investigative efficiency, I have therefore devised a "paradigm method," which I will use consistently throughout. In each of the case studies that constitute this book I will begin by locating and describing a given writer's epiphanic paradigm—that is, the writer's most complete, intense, and fully elaborated epiphany. I will then use that paradigm as guide to more fragmentary or attenuated versions or variants of the writer's recurrent epiphanic pattern of elements, shapes, and/or motions.

Where may such a developed, elaborated paradigm be found? Surprisingly often, it is presented in a work that is given the clear name of "vision" or "dream," almost as if the poet or fiction writer were determined to offer the phenomenological investigator or paradigm seeker an unmistakable guidepost. "Look here," the writer seems to tell us, "this is what I have been hinting at, working toward, throughout my collected epiphanies: here, in this 'vision,' this 'dream,' you may focus on the one moment when the total epiphanic pattern became clear at last, all at once and fully formed." The vision may indeed have been a waking dream rather than a sleeping one—in fact, when turned consciously into literature it becomes a verbally embodied and verbally transformed waking vision in any case. The point of using words like "vision" and "dream" is to stress the exemplary *mys-*

terious intensity and completeness of the *paradigmatic verbal epiphany*, its quasi-involuntary and overpowering character.

"Visions" or "dreams" that provide the phenomenologist with fully elaborated and intense paradigms for epiphanic study are strikingly abundant in the nineteenth century—the period of literary history I have chosen for this set of studies. So, for example, we find the ultimate Wordsworthian apocalyptic epiphany of fiery light in "The Pilgrim's Dream." Coleridge's paradigm epiphany is "Melancholy: A Fragment," a poem that started out to be a sonnet but was interrupted in the middle of the thirteenth line with the words "Strange was the dream— . . . ." Matthew Arnold likewise reveals the riches of his epiphanic world most fully in "A Dream." Tolstoy's paradigm epiphany is Pierre's water-sphere dream; Carlyle's historical heroes all vary his purely imaginary and unhistorical epiphanic vision of Odin. Tennyson's epiphanic world is contained in "The Vision of Sin," Pater's in a remembered vision of a childhood house, Barrett Browning's in an extraordinary vision seen simultaneously by a blind man and a sighted woman. An explicitly labeled "dream" or "vision" is very frequently the key to the epiphany pattern of any given writer.

A special benefit of the method employed in these case studies is that it highlights neglected works of major aesthetic merit and psychological interest. Tennyson's "Rosalind" is a lyric of great psychological complexity and visionary power; yet it never appears in anthologies, and its deep interest was only disclosed to me when I began searching for variants of the phenomenological paradigm that requires Tennysonian lovers to descend from (often dismayingly) distant heights. Coleridge's "Melancholy: A Fragment" is, I think, one of his ten supreme lyric achievements, but—again—only a Bachelardian search led me to it. In the secondary literature it is ignored.

Although Bachelard, uninterested in "unconscious" determinants of vision, distinguishes his method from that of Freudian depth psychology, his structure studies—and mine in the present book—have their own kind of depth: phenomenological depth. Phenomenology— once again—is the study of structures of perceived experience. But the experiencer may not be consciously, discursively aware of the structure of what he or she perceives. The depth involved in the phenomenologist's concentration depends on the ability to see structures that are not obvious, not entirely on the surface. In Tolstoy's epiphanies, we must train ourselves to see structures of oscillatory, symmetrical pendular motion, regardless of what it is that moves. When we look at Walter Pater's flames, we must notice their juxtaposition with fire-colored flowers and with imperiled birds: we will then see how the natural ascent of fire is resisted by the countervailing quick descent of airy creatures and earthly glories. Tennysonian skyblooms take meaning from the associated semi-abstract circular motions that impel us toward them. It takes a deep, penetrative, absorbed, empathetic contemplation to perceive these half-hidden structures. The phenomenological critic is at once structural analyst and empathetic re-describer.

My neo-Bachelardian approach differs from the structure studies of New Critics or formalists in that Bachelardian analysis is not chiefly concerned with the formal unity of a poetic work. Rather, the epiphanic pattern constitutes the imaginative preoccupation from which the larger encompassing work arose. A couple of examples from Matthew Arnold will make this clear. If, say, a sudden picture of Moses responding to a flashing fire, or a sketch of the meditative Rebecca guarding a "spring of feeling" within herself, proves to be bound up with a recurrent Arnoldian pattern of water-fire epiphany, such an image or episode will be of more intense interest to the neo-Bachelardian critic than the remainder of the poems where these heightened moments are found. The prime object of critical interest, from this standpoint, will be the beguilingly insistent imaginative patterns—primarily of elements, motions, and shapes—conveyed by the epiphanic writer.

Since each author's epiphanic paradigm—whether a self-contained brief lyric or a passage in a larger work of verse or prose—is a crucial literary text, we will always need to attend very closely to that text. Deconstructionists, like the formalist New Critics, are also close readers of texts, though deconstructionists find aporias and "black holes" where New Critics discovered organic unities and ironic tensions. In contrast to both New Critics and deconstructionists, my phenomenological close readings of epiphanic paradigms have a very different focus, a Bachelardian focus on elements, shapes, and motions. But fascination with the literary text remains basic to my interpretive approach—fascination with the epiphanic paradigm and with its multiple ingenious variations.

A final note on definitions as used in this book: it is useful to distinguish, as Nichols does, between "epiphany" and "theophany"; and it is equally important to follow Nichols' wise example in not pushing the distinction too far. Epiphanies are resonant moments that seem to mean more than any explanation can justify; these modern moments of intense, expansive mystery—unlike traditional theophanies or clear signs of God—are typically unaccompanied by theological endorsement. To quote once more from my review of Nichols' book:

> Epiphanies as understood by modern poets are dearer for their mystery. They come without guarantees: "modern magi bear a message only as valid as their ability to tell its truth" (34). . . .
> The result is "a new form of meaning in which the moment of inspiration is absolute and determinate, while the significance provided by the epiphany is relative and indeterminate" (4).[24]

In practice, though, Nichols recognizes that epiphanic moments whose subjective qualities are their only guarantee of authenticity while they are being experienced can later be fitted into a traditional religious framework by the writer who has experienced them. G. M. Hopkins, as Nichols shows, has epiphanies of varied types: some are presented without theological comment, while others, which affect both poet and reader in the same way as the uninterpreted ones, are also supplied with a religious moral or allegory.[25] The distinction between epiphanies and theophanies becomes, in practice, impossible to define sharply. Instead, it is best to think of a gradual continuum connecting the two polar concepts.

Nineteenth-century epiphanies encourage us to think of such a continuum. For example, Barrett Browning's epiphanies of rock-transforming crystalline fire are mysteriously expansive in themselves. Because she is a professing Christian, she sometimes appends theological commentary to them, in a Hopkins-like manner. But it is impossible to classify some Barrett Browning resonant moments as modern epiphanies while insisting that other such moments, because of their commentaries, are traditional "theophanies" with traditional divine certification. For whether interpreted or uninterpreted, Barrett Browning's fires, like those of Carlyle, are presented as *prima facie* manifestations of poetic power: their "imaginative temperature" or intensity, along with their expansiveness and mystery, is their primary test of value. They are subjective first and foremost.

So this book of nineteenth-century studies will deal with epiphanies that speak for themselves—intense, expansive moments that behave like mysterious or riddling revelations, moments whose meaningfulness seems inexplicably out of proportion to their observable features. And we will not disqualify them from consideration as epiphanies even when their originators, on occasion, add traditional types of interpretation or comment.

E) STRUCTURE OF THE BOOK

This book is the most thoroughgoing systematized[26] application of Bachelardian phenomenology to literary epiphanies that has yet been attempted in English. The book's three parts, unified by their nineteenth-century time frame, also have specific goals, as do the individual studies within each group—goals beyond merely illustrating the range and diversity of case studies to which the method may be applied. In this final part of my introduction I want to outline briefly how the three subdivisions are respectively designed to show the ways neo-Bachelardian phenomenology of epiphany can bestir us to rethink traditional investigative categories by crossing restrictive boundaries of periods, genres, and disciplines. I will also indicate how, within the several sections, each individual study puts the epiphanist's work into a new perspective with implications extending beyond phenomenology.

Part 1, "Elemental Diversity and Conflict," crosses period borders as well as genre limitations by bringing together two Romantics (Wordsworth and Coleridge) and a Victorian (Arnold), and by studying the latter two figures as both epiphanic poets and critics. Conflicts and contrasts are central: Wordsworth's vivid fiery lights introducing an apocalyptic urgency into an often tranquil world; Coleridge's elemental combats and perturbations; Arnold's perception of duplicities in both water and fire. We will also explore the conflict between critical ideals and poetic epiphanies in Coleridge and in Arnold.

Each author will be put into a new perspective transcending purely phenomenological considerations. The study of a Wordsworthian epiphanic pattern based on an explicit, detailed apocalypse—which we undertake in my first, "Radiant Geometry" chapter—brings to the foreground a neglected aspect of the Romantic poet's achievement. We discover Wordsworth's capacity for a much more assured, even violent and blazingly defiant, epiphanic presentation than he has been given credit for.

The Coleridge and Arnold chapters each bring out an unnoticed paradox or contradiction in the legacy of a great poet-critic. As critic, Coleridge proclaims the gospel of organic unity in the work of literary art, the ideal interrelation of parts in the integral aesthetic whole. But my phenomenological study of Coleridgean epiphany discloses a pattern of sudden, frenzied impulsions having more in common with a fever or seizure than with a healthily functioning plant or animal. Arnold, Victorian inheritor of the Coleridgean mantle as critical *éminence grise*, offers a contradiction of equal interest between the ambivalent import of the elemental epiphanies he produces in his role as poet and the contrasting pure nostalgia expressed by the imagery in his criticism.

Part 2, "Elemental Deaths and Illuminations," focuses on the two writers I consider the most powerful epiphanists of the Victorian Age. Tennyson and Pater—the subjects of this genre-crossing unit—are not often viewed together, and it is not obvious that Tennyson's verse and Pater's prose have anything central in common. But Bachelardian study discloses in the work of both writers a shared (and unusual) recurrent pattern of epiphanies: the flower of fire. Tennyson's fire flowers expand into the sky while Pater's are consumed into ash or "mould," but the very contrast is clarified and given significance by the surprising similarity. As elemental fire-flower seers, Pater and Tennyson share a preoccupation with aesthetic ecstasy and death. Moreover, the two men's fire-flower paradigms originate in contexts of self-castigation and deep-rooted guilt. Guilt means that, for Tennyson as for Pater, ecstasy will always be the herald of death—in an epiphanic pattern that tragically embodies and announces both.

Pater's work is the chronological endpoint of this study, but chronology is less important for my purposes than thematic organization. And it is appropriate to conclude these investigations with the most "expansive" epiphanies, the ones by which their authors claim to shed light on history as a whole. So in the last part of this book, dealing with epiphanies of human history, we backtrack to consider three earlier nineteenth-century epiphanists. Epiphanies have social and even historical consequences. This requires us to cross yet another boundary—the border separating the disciplines of literature and history—as we conclude with a unit on "Elements, History, and Heroism." Tolstoy's philosophy of history and heroism (or anti-heroism), like those of Carlyle and Barrett Browning, is in large measure an expanded epiphany. That, of course, need not persuade us of its validity as a theory of history. But phenomenological study of the structure of epiphanies in the works of history's interpreters—whether in fiction (Tolstoy), poetry (Barrett Browning), or history lectures (Carlyle)—can help us understand how the interpretations in those works arose. Then we can stand back and view, in the broad perspective that juxtaposition affords, Tolstoy's historical currents or tides, Carlyle's fire-god heroes, and Barrett Browning's apocalypses designed to allow her poet-hero to transform the stoniness of matter (and materialism) into the rarer, intenser element of fiery spirit.

Each of the three chapters constituting Part 3 of this book will use the phenomenological scrutiny of epiphanic imagery to suggest an alteration in the current dominant perspective on the given writer's work. The epiphanic pattern of Carlyle's lectures on hero-worship will open up a new, disturbing perspective on his even better known *Sartor Resartus*. The study of Tolstoyan epiphany in *War and Peace* will suggest an insufficiency in the influential perspective of Gary Saul Morson, who claims the book has "no center." (Tolstoy is the only non-British author in this book, but he is crucial to any discussion of epiphanies of history. More: he is fully aware of western European developments in this area and, in *War and Peace*, implicitly argues with Carlyle.) Finally, Barrett Browning's masterly *Aurora Leigh* is being increasingly recognized as the feminist work of genius that it truly is, but only a detailed study of the epic's epiphanic structure can reveal the apocalyptic boldness of its vision.

In sum, the three groupings of author-studies that constitute this book loosen categories and expand critical perspectives by helping us cross boundaries: in Part 1, the boundaries of literary periods (Romantic, Victorian); in Part 2, the borders of genre (Tennyson's verse, Pater's prose); and in Part 3, the limits of a single discipline (as we cross over the line customarily separating history and literature). Further, every chapter in the book shows that the phenomenological scrutiny of epiphanies will put the work of any given author into a new perspective whose importance extends beyond phenomenology. Whether we discover a new apocalyptic dimension in Wordsworth and Barrett Browning, or reveal crucial discrepancies between the critical thought and epiphanic practice of such poet-critics as Coleridge and Arnold, or disclose in Tolstoy's *War and Peace* the powerful epiphanic center that earlier criticism failed to find, in all my studies I will seek to show that phenomenology yields results that matter to critics and readers generally. I will sum up my findings in "Conclusion: Fifteen Theses."

This is above all a book designed to show how critical perspectives on epiphanic products of the verbal imagination can be expanded through the locating of structural paradigms and the tracing of their variants throughout a writer's work. Various writers' contrasting imaginative constructions, juxtaposed, provide implicit mutual criticism: each points up the limitations of the others. Phenomenological scrutiny promotes empathy as well as distance. It encourages comparative understanding and critique. It shows us the diversity of epiphanic patterns.

Part One:
Elemental Diversity
and Conflict

ONE

A Pilgrim's Dream
of Apocalypse
Radiant Geometry in
Wordsworthian Epiphanies

William Wordsworth devoted most of his finest poems to the exploration of epiphany. His chief masterwork, *The Prelude*, is a verse autobiography whose major moments—the main plot events of the lyrical life story—are epiphanies. So a fully adequate treatment of Wordsworth's epiphanic discoveries as embodied in his lyric and epic works would require a book by itself. In this chapter I will carry out a more immediately practical, smaller-scale project: to study an unsuspected epiphanic pattern of fiery light. Wordsworthian epiphanies of radiant geometry (illuminated circles, spheres, radii, and fiery points of light) are paradigmatically embodied in a vision that is powerfully dramatic—indeed, consciously "apocalyptic" or world-transforming.

Wordsworth's apocalypse-related epiphanies vividly demonstrate how the phenomenological scrutiny of an epiphanic paradigm, and then of its less complete or less fully elaborated manifestations, can provide a salutary shift in focus, significantly altering our view of a poet. In *Wordsworth's Poetry: 1787–1814*, Geoffrey Hartman, three decades ago, set the tone for much that has been most useful and probing in subsequent Wordsworth criticism with his emphasis on the burden of self-consciousness in the development of this relentlessly introspective seer. Hartman stresses the " 'broken windings'," the endless "doubts, revisions, and vacillations"[1] attendant on the Wordsworthian project of retrospective mental exploration, the anxieties, hesitations, and diffidence that often impeded the poet's progress in his epic-scale work.

Hartman is right about all this, but it is also true that his portrayal can benefit from a corrective balance. By studying in detail a previously unexamined vision in which the poet's powers are manifest in an outburst of visionary defiance on a cosmic scale, we will be looking for the first time at poetic data that show us, with rare force and forthrightness, the Wordsworthian persona in a mode of unencumbered confidence and pride in the transformative power of his epiphanic attainments.

Let us first note another thing Hartman has taught us about Wordsworth's peculiar strategies of concealing his apocalyptic motives and motifs in many instances. Wordsworth's epiphanies are often puzzling because they seem half-hidden, suppressed, or muted, so thoroughly are they blended with the landscapes that seem to have taken over imagination's activity while the poet quietly watches. As Hartman pointed out, the archaic religious resonance of these experiences has its source in the "omphalos feeling." The omphalos, the world navel or "place of places," as Hartman describes it, is "at once breach and nexus, a breach in nature and a nexus for it and a different world." The Wordsworthian seer is a "borderer": "With rare exceptions Wordsworth's poetry stops short of the supernatural and draws its energy from boundary images," which have their being at the "border between natural and supernatural." Since Wordsworth scrupulously blends natural and supernatural worlds, accentuating their continuity even as he feels awe at their point of juncture, his characteristic epiphanies are frequently enigmatic, and their underlying structures are not always easily discernible. The poet's insistence on stopping short of the supernatural often seems a reluctance to own up to the full extent of his imagination's own world-transforming powers—its apocalyptic powers. It is as if Wordsworth feared apocalypse.[2]

But if we are willing to go excavating among the often unregarded "lesser" lyrics of Wordsworth, we come upon a delightful and phenomenologically valuable rarity in the poet's *oeuvre*: an undiluted apocalyptic epiphany. In "The Pilgrim's Dream, or, The Star and the Glow-Worm," the poet for once proves himself willing to cross the tabooed boundary into the frankly and unapologetically supernatural. With the poet-pilgrim, we see the final subjugation of a force that is compared to "Lucifer"; we witness, in a strange new version, the resurrection of the dead (in elemental form, as fiery lights). We are present at the destruction of the starry universe and its replacement by "New heavens" of light emanating from "Transfigured" souls.[3] The influence of the Book of Revelation upon these apocalyptic matters is indisputable—whether directly or as transmitted through services and sermons; we have here an intertextual epiphany of the most vivid kind.

Yet it *is* an epiphany, not a theophany. For, as we will see, the apocalyptic action is initiated not by God or by his divine or angelic emissary, as we might have expected, but rather by the visionary power and pride of a glow-worm, the poet's delegate in this world-transformative tale. For, in the course of the mythic drama, the dreaming pilgrim learns that the humble glow-worm's central light is in no way subordinate to the more imposing lights of the larger surrounding starry sphere with which the worm spiritually communicates through light. Indeed, the glow-worm's power of light is infinitely greater than that of the fiery stars and at length defeats them all. God is not the victor here, as in a traditional theophany. Rather, the glow-worm's (or Romantic poet's) visionary power is what initiates the epiphanic transformation of the perceived universe.

Wordsworth's epiphanic originality here is twofold, and in both respects it is paradoxically linked to the intertextual indebtedness of his imaginings. First, as just noted, the glow-worm epiphany is strongly influenced or mediated by the apocalypse in the Book of Revelation. But, to an equal extent, it may be seen as a dramatic variant of another standard western *topos*: the figure of a sphere whose center is everywhere, or *sphaera cuius centrum ubique*, traditionally used as a metaphoric definition of God. Georges Poulet has traced the varied history of this metaphor from its original use as a definition of God in a "pseudo-hermetic manuscript of the twelfth-century," through Dante and Jean de Meung and Ronsard and Ramus, to Campanella and Traherne. But by the time it reaches these last two seers, the figure has also turned into a figure for the individual soul: "The infinite sphere has now become the symbol, not only of God, but of man. The infinite sphere is now nothing but the field encompassed by human consciousness."[4] Poulet says nothing of Wordsworth in his historical survey-analysis,[5] but we may draw the intertextual consequences.

The originality of Wordsworth as geometric-apocalyptic epiphanist of the central light and spangled sphere is that he combines and reshapes, in a wholly unique synthesis, two intertextual determi-

nants: biblical apocalypse and philosophic-allegoric traditional metaphor of the divine sphere whose center is everywhere. The result of
this synthesis is an epiphany of the world-transforming effect of a
glowing central power resident within the poet or within his metaphoric delegate, the glow-worm. And this epiphany, in turn, serves
as the most fully elaborated version of an epiphanic pattern that, in
its more fragmentary variants, gives unexpected apocalyptic resonances to a series of epiphanic moments scattered throughout the
poet's *oeuvre*.

But let us begin at the beginning. First we need to retrace briefly
the apocalyptic narrative of "The Pilgrim's Dream" to bring out the
visionary psychology that the story implies. Then we can look at the
lyric, from a phenomenological standpoint, as a paradigm of Wordsworthian epiphanies of radiant geometry—of fiery lights, of spheres
and circles and radii, of motions linking center and circumference in
a dramatic spiritual interchange of light. "The Pilgrim's Dream, or,
The Star and the Glow-worm" will illuminate the structure of a surprising variety of Wordsworthian "spots of time."

1

As we begin reading this paradigmatic epiphany-lyric, we see the
Wordsworthian wanderer unkindly spurned by a prospective host—a
snub that induces resentment (in light of later developments, we
might call it suppressed rage) that will soon find its fiery expression
within the pilgrim's "dream":

> A Pilgrim, when the summer day
> Had closed upon his weary way,
> A lodging begg'd beneath a castle's roof;
> But him the haughty Warder spurn'd;
> And from the gate the Pilgrim turn'd,
> To seek such covert as the field
> Or heath-besprinkled copse might yield,
> Or lofty wood, shower-proof.
>
> (*PD* ll. 1–8)

In the original manuscript the inhospitable castle was a "Convent,"
and the ungenerous Warder was an "Abbot."[6] Wordsworth's initial
impulse had been to subject not only social but religious institutions

to apocalyptically allegorical critique, showing that the houseless pilgrim rejected by church authorities was really their superior in spiritual merit. Some readers may regret that the poet stifled this rebellious impulse, since the fable in its published version has forfeited some of its force.

As the outcast wanderer continues his search for shelter, he canvasses the area from top to bottom:

> He paced along; and, pensively
> Halting beneath a shady tree,
> Whose moss-grown root might serve for couch or seat,
> Fixed on a Star his upward eye;
> Then, from the tenant of the sky
> He turned, and watch'd with kindred look,
> A glow-worm, in a dusky nook,
> Apparent at his feet.
>
> The murmur of a neighbouring stream
> Induced a soft and slumb'rous dream,
> A pregnant dream within whose shadowy bounds
> He recognised the earth-born Star,
> And *That* whose radiance gleam'd from far;
> And (strange to witness!) from the frame
> Of the ethereal Orb there came
> Intelligible sounds.
>
> (*PD* ll. 9–24)

But there is no music from this starry sphere. It refuses to avow its fiery consanguinity with the "earth-born": it is like the Abbot rejecting the Pilgrim.

> Much did it taunt the humbler Light
> That now, when day was fled, and night
> Hushed the dark earth—fast closing weary eyes,
> A very Reptile could presume
> To show her taper in the gloom,
> As if in rivalship with One
> Who sate a Ruler on his throne
> Erected in the skies.
>
> (*PD* ll. 25–32)

The sky-born star promotes himself to Deity, while rhetorically degrading his earthly cousin to the status of Devil, the primal serpent ("Reptile") of pride. The star rebukes the glow-worm for presumptuously daring to compete with him in what seems an attempted rivalry of nocturnal incandescence. The worm replies that the star's pride is not only "unbecoming" (*PD* l. 34) but unjustifiable:

> "Exalted Star!" the Worm replied,
> "Abate this unbecoming pride,
> Or with a less uneasy lustre shine;
> Thou shrink'st as momently thy rays
> Are master'd by the breathing haze;
> While neither mist, nor thickest cloud
> That shapes in heaven its murky shroud,
> Hath power to injure mine."
>
> (*PD* ll. 33–40)

The logic of this is itself rather foggy, since the glow-worm's light would surely be dimmed as effectively by earthly as by heavenly mists and vapors (also, dimmed from whose point of view?). While criticizing the "uneasy lustre" (*PD* l. 35) of the star, the glow-worm appears at least mildly uneasy about the merits of his own reasoning, for he hastens to add that he does not really want to enter a competition of light-power but simply to show, in the face of arrogant challenge, "What favours do attend me here, / Till, like thyself, I disappear / Before the purple dawn" (*PD* ll. 46–48). He ends his speech on a note of modesty and with a gesture toward equality.

But the apocalyptic poet will not leave it at that. Instead, he shows us the modest glow-worm becoming the fiery center whose power expands to traverse and transform the visible world. The universe proves to be a *sphaera cuius centrum ubique*, a sphere whose center can be anywhere, even in the minute fiery glow of a worm. And this glowing center, apocalyptic in its transformative force, suddenly and eruptively rises till it reaches and reconstitutes the stellar circumference:

> When this in modest guise was said,
> Across the welkin seem'd to spread

A boding sound—for aught but sleep unfit!
Hills quaked—the rivers backward ran—
That Star, so proud of late, looked wan;
And reeled with visionary stir
In the blue depth, like Lucifer
Cast headlong to the pit!

Fire raged,—and, when the spangled floor
Of ancient ether was no more,
New heavens succeeded, by the dream brought forth:
And all the happy Souls that rode
Transfigured through that fresh abode,
Had heretofore, in humble trust,
Shone meekly mid their native dust,
The Glow-worms of the earth!

This knowledge, from an Angel's voice
Proceeding, made the heart rejoice
Of Him [the dreaming pilgrim] who slept upon the open
    lea:
Waking at morn he murmur'd not;
And, till life's journey closed, the spot
Was to the Pilgrim's soul endeared,
Where by that dream he had been cheered
Beneath the shady tree.

                            (PD ll. 49–72)

One can easily imagine the deep psychological pleasure Words-worth must have felt in penning this apocalyptic epiphany. If both the harshly rejected Pilgrim and the rudely rebuked Worm are sur-rogates for the poet, his fiery (indeed, fierily "raging") dream-revenge is now complete. Pilgrim-Worm-Poet is now higher than the angels. His erstwhile opponent in the dream-debate, now unmasked as Lu-cifer, has been banished to the lower depths. Though the apocalyptic typology might suggest that all these changes were wrought by God, the poem pointedly never says this—not "God raged" but rather "Fire raged." The creation of "New heavens," newly filled with ascended pilgrim-worm-poets who have rightly displaced the Luciferian angelic hosts, is not ascribed to God's miraculous supervention or to His righteous wrath. Rather, these new heavens were quite simply—and breathtakingly—"by the dream brought forth," the dream envisioned by the pilgrim poet. It would appear that the dream-faculty itself, Romantic Imagination in general and the Wordsworthian imagination in particular, is more than a little higher than the angels.

The message of this endearing evangel is that inward power displaces outward show; that pride dims—indeed, extinguishes—spiritual luster far more radically than any material mist can do; that cosmic favor is truly shown to the central inner light, however unimposing its radiance may at first appear. Central power at length expands to fill the world sphere with its light.

The geometric pattern of the poem's epiphanic motion is clear. As each glow-worm, or ascending soul, rises from its tomb to a new dwelling in the heavens, it traces a path of pure light from a subterranean enclosure to a higher or larger starry sphere: this path resembles a radius from a center to a circumference. The universe fills with fiery light as glow-worms rise from the earthly center to radiate outwards and upwards to the celestial circumference. Here we have, in full glory, the complete Wordsworthian epiphanic paradigm of apocalyptic fiery light.

Let us look more closely at the pattern's component parts. The "elemental" component of the paradigmatic epiphany is fire, and by extension, light. Often, in Wordsworthian epiphanies, the light will be concentrated in small points or sparks, as in glow-worms, glistening rocks, or sudden gleams of sunshine on the hills or among the clouds. The power of these concentrated sparks or points of light can be immense: they communicate with kindred lights, sometimes at huge distances, and the strength of one such central spark may be enough to determine the fate of worlds.

The formal component of the Wordsworthian epiphany pattern we are looking at is strikingly geometric: it includes the formal categories of center, sphere, circumference, and radius or straight line. Generally we find a center connected with a larger or higher sphere or circumference by means of a straight line or radius. While we already knew (from *The Prelude*) of Wordsworth's deep respect for mathematical science, it is rather surprising to find geometric patterns so recurrently central to the poet's most valued epiphanies.

Finally, the pattern of motion that gives life to Wordsworthian epiphany is most frequently a communication of movement between widely separated lights, generally the movement between a radiant center and a higher, lighted sphere or myriad-lighted circumference by means of a path or line of light. Since the combined motifs of center and light often suggest, in Wordsworthian epiphanies, the poet's inner light as well as a spiritual light-force emanating from nature's own center, the effect of these epiphanies is to convince us that the poet, as world-center, feels at one with the outer reaches of the natural-spiritual universe. And since there is often a two-way communication of power or light, from center to circumference (or higher sphere) and back again, the poet as world-center appears equally receptive to forces directed inward from the extreme outer reaches of the world. Though this effect is generated in full force only when all components of the epiphany pattern (light, geometry, and motion) are fully and explicitly present, something of its power is felt also in those epiphanic episodes where one of the component parts may be absent or only implicit. We will look first at the most dramatic manifestations of the pattern and then use them to clarify the less elaborate illustrations of the same world view.

2

In a related glow-worm passage of *The Prelude*, the apocalyptic values are, as usual, somewhat muted, but with "The Pilgrim's Dream" in mind, we see the pattern of that passage more clearly. Here the glow-worm reminds the poet of "a hermit's taper,"[7] a point of connection with the religious "Pilgrim" in the dream-poem, and here too, the light is diffused from a glowing center to irradiate a larger expanse. The difference is that this time the expansion of the spiritual energy is temporal rather than spatial:

> . . . the child
> Of summer, lingering, shining by itself,
> The voiceless worm on the unfrequented hills,
> Seemed sent on the same errand with the quire
> Of winter that had warbled at my door,
> And the whole year seemed tenderness and love.
>
> (*P* VII.43–48)

A moment projects its joy-giving power outward in time, filling the year with its light. The glow-worm in "The Pilgrim's Dream" is more apocalyptic, more Blakean in its uncompromising supernatural victory (one thinks of Blake's line, "If thou chuse to elect a worm, it shall remove the mountains."[8] But both "Dream" and *Prelude* glow-worms relate to the same epiphanic pattern.

Incidentally, the dialogue of light between the center and the stars in "The Pilgrim's Dream" also clarifies the remarkable image-cluster (not an epiphany but a telling metaphor) that Wordsworth offers as a sketch of his own "soul": "A rock with torrents roaring, *with the clouds / Familiar*, and a *favourite of the stars*" (*P* XIII.228, 231–32, emphasis added). The glow-worm felt favored insofar as his light, if less powerful than the star's, was less veiled by clouds and so could claim at least equality, if not superiority, in a dialogue of light. The stars in the *Prelude* passage evidently show their favor to the poetic "rock" in a quite similar way, by reflecting their light on its wet surface and thus dignifying the rock's spiritual power through a dialogue of light: there is no doubt that a "rock with torrents roaring" would be very wet indeed and could reflect a good deal of starlight.[9] Once again we have an implied communication between a shining center-image and a supernal myriad-lighted sphery vault.

A shepherd scene in a peaceful valley and a Druid vision at Stonehenge, two of the epiphanic high points of *The Prelude*, provide a pair of mutually corroborating variants of this same basic pattern of communication or motion from a lower center to a higher sphere or circumference through a path of light (though in these two episodes one misses the explicit illumination of the center). As the shepherd's dog chases the sheep "upwards" from the shepherd's central position at the bottom of the valley, the upward path of the fleeing sheep is given a typically epiphanic illumination. Again we start to see golden radii emanating from a center toward a higher, outer circumference:

> A shepherd in the bottom of a vale,
> Towards the centre standing . . .
> Gave signal to his dog, thus teaching him
> To chace along the mazes of steep crags
> The flock he could not see . . .
> . . . while the flock
> Fled upwards from the terror of his bark

> Through rocks and seams of turf with liquid gold
> Irradiate—that deep farewell light by which
> The setting sun proclaims the love he bears
> To mountain regions.
>
> (P VIII.105–19)

The circumambient world, the concavity of the valley, is blessed with loving light, which here particularly illumines the pathways of the sheep, chased by the dog that runs from the deep center to the raised circumference and back again. The dog's paths (and consequently those of the directed flock), though geometrically irregular when observed one at a time, are in a larger perspective variations on the theme of a radius from the "centre" (Wordsworth's own term), near which the shepherd stands, towards the rounded valley's outer rocky rim. One may say that the center communicates with the higher circumference of the epiphanic sphere through radii of light.

The Druid vision of Stonehenge on Salisbury Plain involves a central mythic microcosm (symbolizing the zodiac) that communicates with the larger, macrocosmic starry sphere through the symbolic motions (up and down, advancing or retreating) of lines of light in the form of "white wands":

> Three summer days I roamed, when 'twas my chance
> To have before me on the downy plain
> Lines, circles, mounds, a mystery of shapes
> Such as in many quarters yet survive,
> With intricate profusion figuring o'er
> The untilled ground (the work, as some divine,
> Of infant science, imitative forms
> By which the Druids covertly expressed
> Their knowledge of the heavens, and imaged forth
> The constellations), I was gently charmed
> Albeit with an antiquarian's dream,
> And saw the bearded teachers, with white wands
> Uplifted, pointing to the starry sky,
> Alternately, and plain below, while breath
> Of music seemed to guide them, and the waste
> Was cheared with stillness and a pleasant sound.
>
> (P XII.338–53)

The "breath" of music strengthens the idea that the alternate up-and-down movement of the bright wands indicates a harmonious communication—indeed, a life-giving one—from the central heart (source of "breath") to the Pythagorean poetic music of the higher sphere. Though the center-image here (the microcosmic Stonehenge circle) is unillumined, we are to see it as metaphorically or analogically star-spangled, for in the poet's view it is a tool of that early "science" whereby the Druids allegedly expressed their star-knowledge "covertly" through "imitative forms."

3

Another pair of epiphanic visions from *The Prelude*—one serious, one delightfully parodic—varies the pattern of light expanding from a center to a larger sphere by presenting this expansion—with less typological completeness—as a circular diffusion, omitting the more customary element of a connecting line or radius. In the first of these visions, the poet presents two closely related images, those of the "eyelet" and "island" (islet?) of light. Sphere and center are so intimately allied in Wordsworthian epiphanies that they are often difficult to distinguish. Eyelets and islands of light are tiny circle- or sphere-signs that represent centrality as well as fullness of being—what we might call microcosmic circularity. When the central microcircle unfolds or expands to form a larger circumference, the accompanying epiphanic light is diffused from an initial gleam to a wider day. Wandering amid the mountain mist, the poet sees

> . . . gleams of sunshine on the eyelet spots
> And loopholes of the hills, wherever seen,
> Hidden by quiet process, and as soon
> Unfolded, to be huddled up again—
> Along a narrow valley and profound
> I journeyed, when aloft above my head,
> Emerging from the silvery vapours, lo,
> A shepherd and his dog, in open day.
> Girt round with mists they stood, and looked about
> From that enclosure small, inhabitants
> Of an aerial island floating on. . . .
>
> (*P* VIII.88–98)

The unfolding, emergence, diffusion of the widening isle of light must be a natural epiphanic process. What happens when a city-bred shepherd tries to duplicate this natural supernaturalism through calculated artifice may be seen in another *Prelude* passage, a mock-epiphany that implicitly satirizes the vision just described. The same cluster of motifs appears: a shepherd—this time metaphorically, as a pastor—is associated with a central eyelet or tiny circle that expands into a wider circle through a diffusion of radiant light. But now the epiphanic pattern is parodied. The poet bemusedly watches a London preacher, after a "toilette of two hours," ascend the pulpit with "seraphic glance,"

> And, in a tone elaborately low
> Beginning, lead his voice through many a maze
> A minuet course, and, winding up his mouth
> From time to time into an orifice
> Most delicate, a lurking eyelet, small
> And only not invisible, again
> Open it out, diffusing thence a smile
> Of rapt irradiation exquisite.
>
> (*P* VII.550–57)

Thus the mincingly artificial "pretty shepherd, pride of all the plains, / Leads up and down his captivated flock" (*P* VII.565–66): the guiding of the flock "up and down" amusingly recalls, and parodies, the shepherding dog in the valley-vision we looked at. The mechanically modish, Ossian-quoting pastor unwittingly travesties the natural process by which an "eyelet" of sunlight expands into an aerial circle of "irradiation exquisite" amid the shifting mist.

Perhaps the most intriguing variations of the pattern whereby a center is linked to a radiant higher sphere or circumference by a connecting linear path are found in a pair of passages (one from "The Ruined Cottage," the other from *The Prelude*) that offer epiphanies of consolation. In both cases, we see little more than slender blades of dew-tipped grass overarching a suffering woman and somehow indicating a reconciling transcendence, both of the woman's sufferings and of the poet's sympathetic melancholy. Since Wordsworth does very little to elucidate directly the roots of the power these images hold for him, an attempt to relate them to the recurrent epiphanic structure pattern we are examining here may be particularly useful. For they do indeed fit the pattern, only with this most notable variation: the higher illumined sphere to which the center is joined by the linear path is in these two cases a microsphere—what we might call the symbolic sign of the sphere.

The first of these somewhat oblique but beautiful epiphanies culminates "The Ruined Cottage." At the end of his narrative of Margaret's death from poverty and grief (after the equally tragic death of her baby), Armytage says of Margaret:

> She sleeps in the calm earth, and peace is here.
> I well remember that those very plumes,
> Those weeds, and the high spear-grass on that wall,
> By mist and silent rain-drops silver'd o'er,
> As once I passed did to my heart convey
> So still an image of tranquillity,
> So calm and still, and looked so beautiful
> Amid the uneasy thoughts which filled my mind,
> That what we feel of sorrow and despair
> From ruin and from change, and all the grief
> The passing shews of being leave behind,
> Appeared an idle dream that could not live
> Where meditation was. I turned away
> And walked along my road in happiness.[10]

Margaret is the deep center of this vision in the most literal sense; though not irradiated or illumined (as the center so often is in this pattern of Wordsworthian vision), this central figure sleeps in a "calm" that is conveyed upward to the tall plants and crowning "silent" raindrops, giving the whole scene the "calm and still" serenity and immobility of Margaret. Since it has been raining, the tall grasses assuredly glisten: they are the radiant connectors of the center too deep for tears with the "silver'd" sphere-signs above, presented by the raindrops resting on the slightly bending tops of the high, straight spears. Conformity (with variation) to a recurrent epiphanic pattern may well explain why this unimposing landscape should convey to Wordsworth's narrator the peace that passes understanding.[11]

In sum, a tragically victimized mother rests below the shining sign of the sphere, to which she is allied by a glistening connecting line, slender and straight but curving slightly at the top. A typologically identical image cluster appears in *The Prelude*, with similar effect:

> . . . when the foxglove, one by one,
> Upwards through every stage of its tall stem
> Had shed its bells, and stood by the wayside
> Dismantled, with a single one perhaps
> Left at the ladder's top, with which the plant
> Appeared to stoop, as *slender blades of grass*
> *Tipped with a bead of rain or dew*, behold,
> If such a sight were seen, would fancy bring
> Some vagrant thither with her babes and seat her
> Upon the turf beneath the stately flower,
> Dropping in sympathy and making so
> A melancholy crest above the head
> Of the lorn creature, while her little ones,
> All unconcerned with her unhappy plight,
> Were sporting with the purple cups that lay
> Scattered upon the ground.
>   (*P* VIII.544–59, emphasis added)[12]

To furnish what his epiphanic imagination requires, the poet elides the single remaining foxglove bell with a bead of rain or glistening dew, accentuating the necessary element of the shining sphere-sign. Again the woman is the center, surrounded by her children and by the purple cups: one thinks of Wordsworth's comparison of his own mother to a hen forming "A centre of the circle" made by its hungry chicks (*P* V.252; for the larger context of comparison see *P* V.246–60). Once again, the connection of a bright, raised sphere-sign with a pitiable woman, by way of a tall, slender plant-stem, mitigates for the Wordsworthian imagination the melancholy of her unhappy fate. The plant, bending slightly at the top to support the raindrop or dewdrop, seems to bow in sympathy with the woman's sadness, but it also bears the victorious sign of tranquil faith, the sphere-sign, and so forms a "crest" (a crest can mean a plume or tuft of feathers affixed to a helmet or headdress—this relates nicely to the "plumes" in the "Ruined Cottage" epiphany). The foxglove plant is "Dismantled," as Margaret's cottage was "ruined," but the sole remaining rounded bell is "stately": it symbolically protects the woman as she protects her babies. As the top of the tall, slender plant bows gently over the mother's head we have a sense of a higher-order maternal embrace, a circumambient, enclosing world of protective concern.

The last pair of epiphanic moments to be looked at may seem far removed from the star-and-glow-worm vision with which we began. But when taken together—and they are in fact juxtaposed in Wordsworth's *Prelude*—they combine to form an experience that manifests the same basic pattern. The glow-worm's "spark of local fire" (*PD* l. 42) bears an analogy to the "Slight shocks" of "love-liking," which the youthful poet experiences at an all-night dance, and like that apocalyptic "spark," these germinal "shocks" are centers of joyful energy and tokens of manifest "favour" indicating a high and privileged destiny. The poet tells of having spent

> The night in dancing, gaiety and mirth—
> With din of instruments, and shuffling feet,
> And glancing forms, and tapers glittering,
> And unaimed prattle flying up and down,
> Spirits upon the stretch, and here and there
> Slight shocks of young love-liking interspersed
> That mounted up like joy into the head,
> And tingled through the veins.
>
> (*P* IV.320–27)

The slight shocks of love-liking, pleasant shocks of mild surprise, are like sparks allied with the glittering tapers, diffusing light as they mount up joyfully "into the head" and tingle "along the veins"— having issued, obviously, from the central heart. "Spirits upon the stretch" provides a strong hint of a long, straight line—the recurrent motif that so often in Wordsworth is associated with a center-circumference connection. And when the poet issues at daybreak from the dance-hall, he carries with him the epiphanic intimations he had felt within:

> The sea was laughing at a distance; all
> The solid mountains were as bright as clouds,
> Grain-tinctured, drenched in empyrean light;

And in the meadows and the lower grounds
Was all the sweetness of a common dawn—
. . . .
Ah, need I say, dear friend, that to the brim
My heart was full? I made no vows, but vows
Were then made for me: bond unknown to me
Was given, that I should be—else sinning greatly—
A dedicated spirit. On I walked
In blessedness, which even yet remains.

(P IV.333–37, 340–45)

Again the fullness of joy extends outward and upward from deep center to outer circle (brim) in the poet's inner world, as light diffuses itself throughout the upper sphere (blending mountains and clouds in heavenly or empyrean light) in the larger cosmos. Here too, as with the stretched spirits in the dance-hall, the associated theme of an extended, connecting line is hinted at, this time by the "bond" that connects the poet with the radiant world he joyously approaches (the word "bond" still carries something of its formerly more concrete meaning of "string, band, tie"—*OED*). Slight shocks of love have deepened and extended themselves into a state of beatitude. Here two chronologically sequential episodes mutually confirm each other's epiphanic geometry and outflowing, diffusing motion.

One could relate this pattern in a more tenuous way to other *Prelude* epiphanies. We might mention the "track / Of sparkling light" connecting the stolen boat with its central home in the adventure illustrating Nature's punishment of theft (*P* I.393–94). Or one might note, in the poet's Don Quixote dream, the "glittering light" that advances with the waters from the central abyss as they try to recapture those stolen microcosmic sphere-signs, the rock and shell (*P* V.129). But the epiphanic episodes that repay the closest scrutiny in this context are those we have already examined, for in them the pattern manifests, with only moderate variation, its basic elements: illumined center, illumined wider circumference or higher sphere, illumined line or radius or path.

To view these epiphanic indicators as parts of an informing paradigm is to reveal phenomenologically an unsuspected center of Wordsworth's sensibility, of his changing but constant "pilgrim's dream," with its ever-present though sometimes fragmentary intimations of visionary apocalypticism expressed through visionary geometry. It is true that, as Hartman claimed, Wordsworth most often prefers to stand at the "border." He would rather offer repeated intimations of glory than risk reimagining the full blaze of elemental apocalypse. But our neo-Bachelardian study discloses a startlingly complete apocalyptic world-transformation serving as paradigm for all the lesser lights, the radiant geometries. The Wordsworth we come to know from this perspective is a less diffident, more dramatically assertive epiphanist than the Wordsworth we had seen before.

TWO

Fitful Motions, Fragile Forms
Elemental Conflict in Coleridge

Every chapter of this book is designed to show that phenomenological analysis of epiphany patterns matters to students of literature generally, not just to phenomenologists. Epiphanies of radiant geometry clarify the tension between apocalypticism and diffidence in Wordsworth—an issue central to an understanding and appraisal of that poet. In this chapter and the next, dealing respectively with Coleridgean and Arnoldian epiphanic structures, we may be surprised at the light shed by neo-Bachelardian epiphany analysis on the roles of these two men as poet-critics. Coleridgean epiphanies, like Arnoldian ones, suggest that the structures of perception embodied in the poetic works bear implications wholly at variance with the metaphors used in the critical writings. Coleridge (or Arnold) conveys one attitude in poetry and another, strongly contrasting attitude in criticism. This inner schism gives a quite distinct application to the theme of "Elemental Diversity and Conflict," the overall rubric of the first group of studies in this book.

Coleridge's critical pronouncements repeatedly portray the poetic imagination, and likewise each work of art that it creates, as an organic unity whose parts and functions reciprocally interact—a smoothly functioning dynamism, an enlivening and flowing harmony. This faith in the vital harmoniousness of the imagination and of its works, a principle extremely congenial to the formalist practice called New Criticism, is still maintained in James Engell's history of the "creative imagination"—a history culminating in Coleridge. As Engell explains, in Coleridgean imagination

> All experience is drawn up under one "living copula." The Dynamic becomes a moving, vital, and all-informing process. . . . The imagination is, in the original Greek sense of the word "organic," an instrumentality unifying and touching all parts of a

living and autonomous composition. . . . The synthetic process is constant, a "combination or transfer of powers," which involves what might be called continuous feedback.[1]

The parts of the poet's mind, and of the poetic work, are unified by imagination as by a circulatory system. Engell continues:

This explanation of the imagination as one organic and harmonious process helps to clarify Coleridge's short and characteristic descriptions: the imagination is "modifying," "co-adunative," and "fusive"; it is "unifying" and "esemplastic"; it shapes or "forms into one." A lowest common denominator exists in these characteristics: they suggest . . . a vital and lifelike process. The faculties of the mind affect each other; they mix and transfer power. . . .[2]

In *Biographia Literaria* Coleridge sums up his doctrine of vital organicism: "In every work of art," he says, there is "a reconcilement of the external with the internal," a synthesis accomplished because imagination is able "to make the external internal, the internal external, to make nature thought, and thought nature,—this is the mystery of genius in the Fine Arts."[3]

A "mystery" indeed: Coleridgean organicism is more metaphor than practical criterion. Yet Coleridge's own epiphanies, his own created poetic moments of highest intensity and expansive mystery, do not conform at all to the requirements of the organic image. These epiphanies do not in any way embody the harmonious unity, the reciprocal interaction of vital parts as in the healthy growth and motion of an animal, that Coleridge in his criticism uses as metaphor for the poetic ideal. Rather, Coleridgean epiphanic moments are disjunct, nervous tremblings, fevered flushings or flashings. They do not suggest a healthy circulatory system. Instead, they convey motions that are sudden and hectic, frenzied and overwrought, implying the opposite of vital health: extreme sensitivity, frailty, fragility, subject to ungovernable motions, to seizures or nervous fits.

To show this in detail, we will study the epiphanic structures of ten Coleridge poems, including the three great supernatural poems, the six most celebrated conversation poems, and an early dream-lyric called "Melancholy: A Fragment" (neglected in the critical literature, just like our Wordsworth paradigm, "The Pilgrim's Dream"—but a masterwork nonetheless), which will serve as an epiphanic paradigm. The poems will be surveyed in roughly chronological order.[4]

Because the epiphanic structure we will be studying here unifies all the most celebrated lyric works that Coleridge produced, the pattern is an indispensable tool for any critic who hopes to find a common imaginative source for the poet's two vividly contrasting types of lyrics: (1) the "supernatural" group ("Kubla Khan," "The Rime of the Ancient Mariner," and "Christabel") and (2) the "conversation poems" ("The Eolian Harp," "This Lime-Tree Bower My Prison," "Frost at Midnight," "The Nightingale," "Dejection: An Ode," and "To William Wordsworth"). Other attempts have certainly been made to find such a common denominator: the most effective traditional unifying rubric—a commonplace of Coleridge criticism—is the tension between solipsism and dialogue, between self-absorption and empathetic response, to be found in all nine of the poems. I would not dismiss this idea entirely. Yet such a tension is hardly unique to Coleridge.[5] And this moral-psychological schema is further weakened by its generalized abstractness; it is not nearly so individually distinctive as the epiphanic pattern that gives Coleridge's masterworks their uncanny, trancelike power.

Patterns of motion, geometric shapes, and the dynamism of elemental substances are all equally crucial to the epiphanies of Coleridge. The unifying pattern of motion in these moments is remarkably constant: Coleridgean epiphanic motion is typically tremulous or fitful. Depending on what it is that moves, this tremulous or fitful motion may be manifested as glittering, flashing, flushing, trembling, shuddering, bubbling, fluttering, or any combination of these. Often the motion will be felt as something induced or superimposed or invasive, not inherent in the nature of the moving object, and consequently unsteady or unstable.

The shapes of the objects thus moved are of three kinds. They may be rounded (eye, bubble, dome, tear, cheek, coil of a snake, convex boss of a shield), or flat (film, flake, dead or dying leaf, thin dry sail of a ship), or elongated (harp string, vocal cord, twig). They may also belong to more than one of these categories, for example, a long lank leaf (elongated and flat), a coiled snake (elongated and rounded). The cause of the motion induced in these objects is an encounter of elements: any combination or number of these (earth, water, air, fire) may set off the epiphanic moment. This elemental encounter gives Coleridgean epiphanic motion a dramatic intensity that is closely connected with its frequent instability, ephemerality, and resistance to control.

Coleridgean epiphanies contrast with the Wordsworthian visions we have looked at. It is true that the apocalyptic "Pilgrim's Dream" paradigm that sets the pattern for Wordsworth's epiphanies of light and motion manifests a Coleridge-like dramatic force. Yet despite all the violent apocalypticism and world-transforming suddenness manifested in the "Pilgrim's Dream" paradigm, Wordsworth's epiphanies of fiery lights and radiant geometry also offer a strong feeling of "center." In Coleridge, all such centrality, all feeling of deep-rootedness, has vanished. What remains is shakiness, literal shaking or fluttering, flushing or glittering—nervousness and extreme instability felt as inseparable from epiphanic vividness and force. Wordsworthian patterns of radiant geometry imply a connectedness: center is linked to circumference, frequently by a line of light. Coleridgean epiphanies, lacking this pattern of connection, are unrooted, feverish, disjunct.

In the early "Melancholy: A Fragment" the basic pattern is already clearly and richly developed. No fragment at all but the whole key to Coleridge's epiphanic method, this powerful lyric deserves to be quoted in full:

> Stretch'd on a moulder'd Abbey's broadest wall,
>   Where ruining ivies propp'd the ruins steep—
> Her folded arms wrapping her tatter'd pall,
>   Had Melancholy mus'd herself to sleep.
>   The fern was press'd beneath her hair,
>   The dark green Adder's Tongue was there;
> And still as pass'd the flagging sea-gale weak,
> The long lank leaf bow'd fluttering o'er her cheek.
>
>   That pallid cheek was flush'd: her eager look
> Beam'd eloquent in slumber! Inly wrought,
>   Imperfect sounds her moving lips forsook,
> And her bent forehead work'd with troubled thought.
>   Strange was the dream—[6]

The "fluttering" motion of a thin, elongated shape ("long lank leaf") conveys a fitful ("flush'd") motion of warmth and light to the dreamer's rounded cheek. Both motions are intermittent, though continually ("still") repeated, and they result in two related fitful motions: the "moving" of the dreamer's lips and the troubled nervous working of her forehead. An encounter of elements is responsible for this ensemble of fevered flutterings since it is a "flagging sea-gale weak" (air and water) that, stirring the leaf of the "dark green Adder's Tongue" (earth, with the special associated earthiness of the adder), momentarily inflames the pallid cheek of the melancholy dreamer. Yet though her thought is "troubled," the dreamer's look beams "eloquent in slumber!" Her thoughts, though she may express them in "Imperfect sounds," are animated by complex visionary vibrations of external damp coolness and inward dry heat, by trembling or nervous motions both frustratingly intermittent and reassuringly recurrent. As Keats's goddess Melancholy embodies all the paradoxes of the Keatsian vision in the odes, so too does Coleridge's "Melancholy" express the basic ambivalence of all Coleridgean epiphanic motion: the fitful, undependable manifestation of its aweful power.

The special feature of the quivering epiphanic motions in "The Eolian Harp" is the skill with which the poet symmetrically arranges their expressions alternately in sound and in light. Such an arrangement is appropriate in a poem that speaks of "A light in sound, a sound-like power in light" (l. 28). First we hear the "sweet upbraidings" and "delicious surges" that sink and rise in a "soft floating witchery of sound" on the aeolian harp (ll. 15–20); though air is the predominantly active element, words like "surges" and "floating" and "sink and rise" make one think of water too, accentuating the theme of an encounter of elements. Next we see "The sunbeams dance, like diamonds on the main" (l. 37), a tremulous motion of light. Many "idle flitting phantasies" flutter across the poet's brain as sound takes over once again: "random gales" (compare the "sea-gale" of "Melancholy") "swell or flutter" on the aeolian harp, suggesting that all living beings are likewise earthly harps that "tremble" into thought (ll. 42–46) when animated by an aerial or a spiritual breeze (encounter of elements).

Light next appears in a sudden flashing motion as the "eye" of the poet's beloved "Darts" a "mild reproof" against the poet's heterodox pantheism.[7] Chastened, the poet blends light and sound imagery as he admits that his revelations may well be only "Bubbles that glitter as they rise and break / On vain Philosophy's aye-babbling spring" (ll. 56–57). Glitterings, like bubblings, are tremulous motions (glitter: "To shine with a brilliant but broken and tremulous light; to emit bright fitful flashes of light; to gleam, sparkle"—*OED*). And indeed the poet's self-descriptive metaphor of "babbling" (related in sound to "bubbling") sounds quite intimidated: the whole poem quivers with excitement but also with guilty fear. Shapes both elongated (harp strings, sunbeams) and spherical (eye, bubbles) participate in this fluttering or flashing. Sound and light finally merge, recurrently but in an unstable form, as fire meets water and air (elemental encounter) in the glittering bubbles of the lazily meandering philosophic stream.

By contrast, "This Lime-Tree Bower My Prison" and "Frost at Midnight" are each organized around one central epiphany of trembling or quivering motion. In both cases, this epiphanic motion is imparted to objects both flat and frail. As he describes in "This Lime-Tree Bower"

> . . . that branchless ash,
> Unsunn'd and damp, whose few poor yellow leaves
> Ne'er tremble in the gale, yet tremble still,
> Fann'd by the water-fall! and there my friends
> Behold the dark green file of long lank weeds,
> That all at once (a most fantastic sight!)
> Still nod and drop beneath the dripping edge
> Of the blue clay-stone
>
> (ll. 13–20)

what strikes the poet is the elemental encounter whereby the dying ash leaves and frail slender weeds (according to Coleridge, they are "Adder's Tongue" plants; cf. "Melancholy") are kept in constant visionary motion, in continual, gently shaking nervous ecstasy, by breezes from the waterfall. In "Frost at Midnight" the thin, quivering leaves are replaced by a fluttering film of soot on the grate, likewise an extremely thin and frail, almost two-dimensional form subjected to a powerful animating force. The elemental encounter here is that of air with the residue of fire.

An epiphany of this quivering "stranger" film of soot in "Frost at

Midnight" makes the young poet's book seem to swim before his eyes (l. 38), much as the epiphany of trembling leaves in "This Lime-Tree Bower" has made the poet stand "Silent with swimming sense" (l. 39). In the former poem Coleridge is led to envision the "Great universal Teacher" communicating with his son (l. 63); in the latter, the poet is led to envision the "Almighty Spirit" imparting wisdom to his friend Charles (l. 42): in both works, Coleridge overcomes a sense of initial deprivation through a vision of empathetic dialogue. Yet the extreme frailty inherent in the flattened object that is the quivering recipient of grace (weak or dying, dry leaves; thin film of soot) dramatizes the precariousness of the poet's ideal, the disquieting instability of its sources in his own past moments of tremulous vision, of nervous apprehension mixed with nervous joy.

Incidentally, Coleridge had originally intended to treat us to still another delightful epiphanic moment in the conclusion to "Frost at Midnight." An earlier version of the poem had ended with a six-line passage later excised. In this version, after the description of "silent icicles, / Quietly shining to the quiet moon" (ll. 73–74)—an admittedly beautiful scene of dialogue that now ends the poem—Coleridge had added these lines:

> Like those, my babe! which ere tomorrow's warmth
> Have capp'd their sharp keen points with pendulous drops,
> Will catch thine eye, and with their novelty
> Suspend thy little soul; then make thee shout,
> And stretch and flutter from thy mother's arms
> As thou wouldst fly for very eagerness.

The pendulous drops and eager responding eye are mutually mirroring epiphanic spheres. The verb "stretch" gives the feeling of a long, straight line. The impulsive, irresistible fluttering motion, trying to turn itself into flight, is a wild, nervous epiphanic movement of the best Coleridgean kind. Richard Holmes values this original conclusion to "Frost at Midnight" for the tenderness of the scene and its biographical implications, yet he approves, on aesthetic grounds, of Coleridge's later decision to omit the lines.[8] Here I would disagree. By deleting the original concluding epiphany, Coleridge lost something of real value. I think the excised epiphany—the portrayal of the icicles' glittering drops mirrored in the child's eager eye, of the child's stretching arms and fluttering hands—is excellent, its loss regrettable. Even from the standpoint of strictly formal unity, the excision of this fine passage was no improvement: the fluttering of the child from its mother's arms nicely counterpoints the fluttering of the "stranger" on the grate.

"The Nightingale" has a crescendo-decrescendo structure, with the nervous shaking motion and elemental encounter strongest in the central epiphanic climax. Fitful or frenzied motion in sound is introduced in the early description of a nightingale's "fast thick warble" (l. 45); intermittent motion of light is then revealed as the flickering glow-worms light up their love torches while other nightingales' eyes glisten. In the climax, the moon's sudden emergence from behind a cloud makes a choir of birds frenziedly "burst forth" as if "some sudden gale had swept at once / A hundred airy harps" (ll. 81–82). Everything sways shakily, unsteadily: the nightingales perch "giddily," the twigs are seen "swinging from the breeze," and "tipsy Joy . . . reels with tossing head" (ll. 83–86). Fire and air and earth, light and breezes and birds, create in their elemental encounter the effect of a hundred wind-harps' trembling strings. A moment earlier we saw the pronouncedly circular forms of the birds' eyes ("their eyes both bright and full" [l. 67]); now we imagine the long forms of harp strings, metaphoric of the birds' vocal cords, along with the light of the spherical moon.

The light-sound unity of this epiphanic climax divides in the poem's two final visions as we see Hartley first raising his finger to his ear as the birds sing, then, in a separate vision, suspending the sobs of his infant dream, "While his fair eyes, that swam with undropped tears, / Did glitter in the yellow moonbeam!" (ll. 104–5). His father has brought Hartley out to see the moon so he can associate joy with nighttime, but the reader's final feelings are mixed. The tremulous glitter, the unstable semi-suspension of unshed tears, the elemental encounter of eye-moisture with moonlight, the round, mutually mirroring forms of eye and moon—all these are unmistakable imaginal components of a fine Coleridgean epiphany. But the joy of the encounter is inseparable from the "inward pain" of the infant's dream that made his father hurriedly carry him outside. Joy and the results of nervous fright are blended in a beautiful but disquieting visionary moment, an unstable, tearful eye-glitter.

In "Kubla Khan" every component part of the typical Coleridgean epiphanic structure is expanded and intensified. The spherical shape becomes a large, inclusive pleasure-dome, though this unstable dome, whose shadow floats on the waves of the sacred river, is but a giant bubble, both in its extreme visionary instability and in its intimate association with water and bright shining ("sunny," "ice"). The shaking or intermittent, jerky motion becomes here a sequence of chthonic labor pangs, with the earth giving birth to a "mighty fountain" in "fast thick pants" (ll. 18–19; compare the "fast thick warble" of the birds in "Nightingale"). The elemental encounter (of water and fire) becomes a cosmic wonder, a "miracle of rare device, / A sunny pleasure-dome with caves of ice!" (ll. 35–36). Of course the more pairs of contraries are unified (life-death, order-immensity, birth-harvest, fertile-sunless, fountain-cave), the more unstable the structure becomes: Kubla hears prophecies of destruction, the damsel's dulcimer is now mute (a dulcimer looks just like that notoriously undependable instrument, the aeolian harp), and the poet-as-shaman's round eyes flash their dread fire only after the poet imbibes risky liquids (honeydew, milk of Paradise). But the elongated shape of the dulcimer with its vibrating strings and the frenzied flashing of the shaman's eyes are additional Coleridgean epiphanic indicators.

Even greater epiphanic power comes forth in "The Rime of the Ancient Mariner" from the transfiguration of the water-snakes (ll. 271–85), an experience that precipitates the mariner's conversion to cosmic love. Here, too, as in "Kubla Khan," the encounter of elements becomes a "miracle of rare device," as "golden fire" is juxtaposed with frostlike "hoary flakes": fiery tracks appear on the water in an interaction of opposites that anticipates Goethe's water-and-fire vision of Homunculus' surrender to the power of Galatea, another victory of visionary Eros. Indeed, Coleridge's elemental interaction here is actually threefold since water and fire combine with the primal serpent, associated traditionally with earth. And just as the elemental encounter is multiple, so too is the assemblage of Coleridgean epiphanic shapes: flattened "flakes" accompany elongated "tracks" of "shining white" and of "golden fire" and the rounded, "coiled" shapes of the long, thin snakes.[9] And there are likewise contrasting expressions of the Coleridgean fitful or frenzied motion: the snakes' sudden rearing cuts a fiery "flash," and this "flash of golden fire" arouses an equally impulsive, sudden outburst of metaphoric water-motion within the poet's heart ("A spring of love gushed from my heart, / And I blessed them unaware" [ll. 284–85]). Within the realm of motion, too, it is a fire-water union of rare device.

Air enters the elemental encounter in the hardly less epiphanic sequel to this conversion experience, as a "roaring wind," through sound waves alone, shakes the sails of the mariner's ship, "That were so thin and sere" (l. 312) like fluttering, flattened stranger-films. Somehow this wind-sound makes the "upper air" so "burst into life" that "a hundred fire-flags" begin to move fitfully back and forth ("To and fro they were hurried about"—see ll. 309–25 for this section). Though "flag" makes one think at first of the flattened shape of the thin, dry sails, a "fire-flag" is actually a "meteoric flame" (*OED*), another elongated fiery track. The ever-louder wind makes the sails mournfully "sigh like sedge" ("grassy, rush-like, or flag-like" plants— *OED*), much as the sea-gale stirred the long lank leaf in the early "Melancholy: A Fragment." Finally, just before the temporary resurrection of the corpses, "Like waters shot from some high crag, / The lightning fell with never a jag"—undeterred, undeflected in its impulsive flash.

The whole two-part epiphany is a masterly patterning of Coleridgean elemental encounters, flat or elongated or rounded shapes, and fitful or tremulous motions. Coleridge was right to downplay the importance of the poem's "moral," taken simply by itself, but he perhaps exaggerated the poem's supposed irrationality when he likened it to the illogic of the blinding of the genie's son by date-shells in the Arabian Nights tale.[10] There is an integral coherence in the "Ancient Mariner," the coherence of the image structures of epiphanies. There may be a half-maniacal look in the mariner's "glittering eye" (ll. 3, 13) as he tells his purgatorial tale, but the instability or possession it conveys is of a piece with the disquieting electrical flashings and flutterings he makes us see and feel.

"Christabel," too, offers the deep clarity of a consistent epiphanic image pattern. True, "Christabel" infuses power with guilt and despair, revelation with the threat of doom. But any pattern of epiphany based on unstable, quivering, or intermittent, frenzied motion may well call into question easy ideals or simple distinctions between good and evil. "Christabel" only brings out with special force the darker implications[11] that are never wholly absent from any Coleridgean epiphanic image structure. We find one such epiphanic structure in Part 1 of the poem, two more in Part 2, and yet another in the odd "Conclusion" to the second part, unifying it with the rest of the poem to a greater extent than has been realized.

Rounded shapes pervade and unify the four epiphanies in the poem—as is fitting in a story featuring characters named Christabel (bell) and Geraldine (eyne)—and in the first two of these passages elongated forms are also prominent (compare Sir Leo*line*). As the two women pass the hearth in Christabel's home, suddenly a long serpentine "tongue of light, a fit of flame" (l. 159) illuminates simultaneously Geraldine's "eye" and the rounded "boss" ("central convex projection"—*OED*) of Sir Leoline's shield, which hangs in a "murky old niche in the wall" (ll. 160–64). The placing of this shield in a dark recess within the wall gives the shield's suddenly illuminated boss the appearance of a flashing eye within a deep eye socket, and the consequent similarity of Leoline's rounded shield-boss to Geraldine's round flashing eye suggests the occult resemblance between Geraldine and Christabel (via Christabel's father). Elemental encounter is less clear here than usual; but liquid eye, metal shield, and frenzied fire are certainly unified, if only by supernatural "action at a distance" (*Wirkung in die Ferne*). And the "fit of flame" is one of the most strikingly effective expressions of Coleridgean epiphanic motion.

In the next epiphany, Bard Bracy's vision, a long green Geraldine-snake is suddenly seen "Coiled" around the neck of the Christabel-dove among the elongated "grass" and green herbs that at first had camouflaged the snake's form (ll. 550, 540). The dove is twice described as "fluttering" (ll. 535, 544), as well as heaving and stirring (l. 535). And the dream of this imprisoned fluttering, says Bard Bracy, "seems to live upon my eye!" (l. 559)—a phrase that takes on special meaning in the context of Coleridgean epiphanic motions, shapes, and elemental encounters. The encounter of dove and snake, of air and earth, expressed in the fitful struggling motions of Christabel, is alive "upon" the "eye" of the Bard: i.e., the encounter and the fluttering are not simply seen by, but are inseparable from—they "live upon"—the visionary sphere. And the next epiphany develops further this integral relation of spherical shape and tremulous motion as Geraldine's snaky eyes make Christabel shudder aloud: because Christabel is in a "dizzy trance" as she shudders (ll. 589–91), her unsteady, unstable motion is communicated to the whole world she sees.

The elemental encounters in this poem so far have been traumatic, but the poet has nevertheless found it salutary to "force together / Thoughts so all unlike each other" (ll. 666–67) as are fire and water, or earth and air. The final epiphany, in the Conclusion to Part 2, illuminates the use of such confrontations in an application to Coleridge's relation with his son. Rounded forms communicate through frenzied motion. The "red round" cheeks of the poet's singing, dancing "fairy" child parallel the father's light-filled eyes (ll. 658–61); the pleasures he takes in his son's joy "flow in . . . thick and fast" (l. 622), like the "fast thick pants" of the earth's birth pangs in "Kubla Khan" or the "fast thick warble" of the birds in "Nightingale." But here, too, as in those earlier visions, the "giddiness" (l. 675) of fitful motion betokens a disquieting instability (the nightingales of the earlier lyric, we recall, perched "giddily," and their "tipsy Joy" led us quickly to a troubled infant's dream). In this instance, giddiness of heart and brain indicates "love's excess," inseparable from "rage and pain" (ll. 664, 676). Though the poet's words were "wild," the "recoil" was sweet (ll. 671–72). Yet one sees the snake's "coil" even in the poet's "recoil" of excessive love and pity.

One sees a recoil of excessive love, too, in "Dejection: An Ode" as the poet counteracts depression through a series of panicky compensatory wishes for his innocent lady friend/anima to feel joy and yet more joy. Yet here, too, is a dark-bright epiphany. Its elements are all present in the first stanza: flat "flakes" of cloud, long "strings" of the aeolian harp and the long, rounded "silver thread" that circles the moon, a wind that intermittently, impulsively "moans and rakes" the vibrating harp strings, and an elemental encounter both explicit in the contact of wind and harp strings and implicit in the moon's reflected fire-light, which is yet both watery ("swimming") and palely frostlike ("winter-bright," "phantom light" [ll. 9–11]). Yet the motion, the central but frustratingly cunctative component, is still "dull," muted, torpid, apathetic. Coleridge wants the wind to "startle this dull pain, and make it move and live!" (l. 20). And despite the poet's modest disclaimers, this is exactly what happens. The epiphany, which builds throughout stanza 7, has two phases: the first tremulous, the second fitful. First the rushing of the wind among the "timorous" leaves (l. 107) evokes the vision of a fleeing army, who "groan with pain, and shudder with the cold," with a "noise, as of a rushing crowd, / With groans, and tremulous shudderings" (ll. 113–16). Then the poet seems to hear a lost child, who "now moans low in bitter grief and fear, / And now screams loud, and hopes to make her mother hear" (ll. 124–25). During these dramatic episodes, brief though they are, one cannot doubt that the poet feels as well as sees. In his shudderings and fitful fears, he awakens, he revives, he moves and lives.

The last epiphany to be found in the great conversation poems of Coleridge is brief but rich. In "To William Wordsworth" Coleridge recalls how,

> In silence listening, like a devout child,
> My soul lay passive, by the various strain
> Driven as in surges now beneath the stars,
> Fair constellated foam, still darting off
> Into the darkness; now a tranquil sea,
> Outspread and bright, yet swelling to the moon.
>   (ll. 95–101)

Moon and water provide the elemental, tidal encounter; the fair foam of gleaming starlike bubbles is the epiphanic shape; and the motion of "darting off" into the darkness is the sudden flash that betokens the ephemerality of Coleridgean revelation. We recall the darting of Sara's glance in "The Eolian Harp" or the "Bubbles that glitter as they rise and break / On vain Philosophy's aye-babbling spring" (ll. 56–57). A sense of passivity had plagued Coleridge in that earlier poem, and it haunts him here. As a sea, he is driven, or upraised, by another's power, by the moon's motive force; only bubbles, mere transient reflections of the eternal stars, are acknowledged as "of my own birth" (1.98). Yet these bubbles are constellated, and as such, fair: they are the glittering, rounded shapes of the poet's transcendence, mirrorings of his pleasure-dome. This parallel with "Kubla Khan" is made in Coleridge's note:

'A beautiful white cloud of Foam at momentary intervals
coursed by the side of the Vessel with a Roar, and little stars of
flame danced and sparkled and went out in it; and every now

and then light detachments of this white cloud-like foam darted off from the vessel's side, each with its own small constellation, over the Sea, and scoured out of sight like a Tartar troop over a wilderness.' —*The Friend*, p. 220

Kubla Khan was a Tartar prince; his troops are mirrors of him, and their visionary shapes mirror his. These Tartar bubbles are stars of flame, sunny domes with something, too, of the coldness of stellar distance as they hang in air, midway over the waves. Innumerable tiny glitterings and sudden myriad bubblings—in less than a moment they go out. The end is sudden darkness.

The significance of this study's findings is summed up in my initial thesis: however strong the emphasis, in Coleridge's critical writings, on the organic unity of parts, their balanced interrelationship within a durable and vital whole, Coleridge the lyricist offers epiphanies that suggest a far different and more problematic picture. Here we find instead contrasting elements whose powerful confrontation focuses upon weak objects. This sudden or intermittent influx of forces proves at best transient, unstable, ephemeral, at worst ominous and potentially destructive. One sees and feels flutterings and shiverings and tremblings, frenzied flashes, vanishing flakes and films and bubbles. Yet these experiences are Coleridge's epiphanies, his moments of highest intensity and most expansive mystery. The fitful or tremulous movement that gives them their troubled life brings to mind the words of Faust: "Doch im Erstarren such' ich nicht mein Heil, / Das Schaudern ist der Menschheit bestes Teil" ("I seek no salvation in stasis. The best aspect of humanity is shown in shudderings" [of awe]).[12]

One might argue that Coleridge produces "organically harmonious" presentations of his hectic and trembling epiphanies, but what would that mean? The "organic" ideal, as Coleridge describes it, is less a clear conceptual criterion than a "mystery" heavily dependent on its embodiment in the imagery of a healthy creature—while the imagery of the epiphanies is decidedly nervous and fevered. We find mainly a contrast in imagery. To be sure, the image of a healthy vital functioning set up by Coleridge as critic is not invalidated by Coleridge's own epiphanic portrayals of hectic tremors: as a metaphoric ideal, Coleridgean organicism is not discredited by one set of *realia*. But Coleridge as critic seems to be evoking the way he thinks imagination really operates when it produces great poetry, so we may wonder why the powerful, disturbing epiphanies he creates do not fit his own metaphorics of organic harmony. The theories presented by Coleridge as critic may actually constitute a *Wunschbild*, a fantasized ideal, rather than a description of literary reality; Coleridge's theoretical formulations, like Engell's summaries of them, have a distinctly utopian sound. In any case, the rift between the image repertories of Coleridge the critic and Coleridge the epiphanic poet concerns not only phenomenologists. It is central to any accurate portrayal of Coleridge the conflicted human being.

THREE

Duplicitous Welcomers

Water-Fire Epiphanies in
Arnold

The conflict between the imagery employed by Arnold as critic and the paradigmatic vision of Arnold as epiphanic poet is as remarkable as the conflict we studied in Coleridge; here too, phenomenological scrutiny focuses on a problem of interest to readers seeking to understand the dual mentality of a major cultural figure. The tension between Arnold's activities as poet and as critic is obvious: we remember the embarrassment felt by the author of *Empedocles on Etna* in having to admit that this highly Romantic work sharply contravened the classicist principles of the 1853 preface to *Poems*; and we remember (or try to forget) the deadness of *Merope*, where Arnold *did* try to carry out his own classical program—and failed. That Arnold the poet battled Arnold the classicizing critic is well known. My neo-Bachelardian study will suggest that Arnold's inner conflict is rooted in a tension between two kinds of imagining.

As classicizing critic Arnold presents an elemental metaphor that idealizes origins, bygone perfections, the freshness of the early (Greek) world. As epiphanist, Arnold offers a paradigm that undermines all nostalgic ideals, a vision of the duplicity of early glories and early promise.

Though the full resources of Bachelardian method have never been mustered for the study of Arnoldian epiphany, patterns in Arnold's poetic landscapes have been analyzed. A. Dwight Culler based a book on a three-part analysis of Arnold's River of Life, as it flows from the upper "forest glade" (youthful innocence) through the traumatic "Gorge" of threatening transition to the "burning plain" (antithesis of the forest glade, conflict with the father instead of unity with the mother), to issue at last in the "wide-glimmering" sea of "reconciliation."[1] (Alan Roper adds that a wide variety of conceptual meanings can attach to specific features of Arnoldian scenery in individual poems.)[2]

William A. Madden attempted a brief Bachelardian overview of the poet's work, but his conclusions do not accurately describe Arnold's poetry. Citing Tinker and Lowry's observations on Arnold's love of water, Madden says the Victorian poet may be "described as a poet of water." When fire, air, or earth enters Arnold's lyrics, these elements "frequently share some quality of water." But in Madden's descriptions, watery qualities taken on by other elements are always positive—lovely and comforting: moon and stars are felt as "quiet, cool, and pure"; air "fascinates in so far as it is light, cool, pure, and gentle"; earth is loved when "dewy and shaded, cool and flowery." By contrast, "Negative values are conveyed in the poems through images antipodal to those of water: the desert, the burning plain, the fever of passion, the volcano, the noise of cities, the furnace of the world, the noon-day heat."[3]

What I want to show in this chapter is that, although Madden's characterization of good waters and bad fires (an amplification of Culler's three-stage schema, where water is likewise positive, fire negative) correctly represents the metaphor guiding Arnold's *criticism*, this good-vs.-bad schema is belied by a subtler, more insidious pattern in Arnold's epiphanic *poetry*, where waters and fires are intermixed, interchangeable, and co-conspiratorial in their two-sidedness and duplicity.

Arnold's symbolic topography in "The Study of Poetry" fits Madden's portrayal perfectly; waters represent ideality, while fires signify the fall. Beginning to read "The Study of Poetry," we are struck by the metaphorical implications of Arnold's plan to "trace the *stream* of English poetry," or at least "to follow . . . one of the several *streams* that make the mighty *river* of poetry" (emphasis added). Arnold says that whichever of these two goals we choose to pursue (tracing a large and general "stream" of the history of poetry, or merely following a simpler and more limited "stream" that leads into a big "river"), our "governing thought should be the same"—namely, that poetry should "console" and "sustain" us.[4]

But evil fires soon appear. By the end of "The Study of Poetry" "We enter on *burning ground* as we approach the poetry of times so near to us—poetry like that of Byron, Shelley, and Wordsworth . . . " (emphasis added).[5] Maturation in literary history brings conflict with the classical "fathers" of Greece, and the conflict heats up. The consolations and sustenance of poetry, its refreshing and healing power, are things of an early age; later, fevers ensue as we traverse the painful terrain of the present time. Such a metaphorics of good waters (of the past) and hurtful fires (of the present) fits in well with the Arnoldian critical project of idealizing the freshness of the past and decrying the painfulness of more recent tendencies.

The epiphanies in Arnold's poetry, however, are much subtler, more paradoxical, and more unsteadying than the simple 'good water-vs.-bad fire' dichotomy in the criticism would suggest. A crucial feature of Arnold's recurrent epiphany patterns has gone unnoticed: the paradoxical interactions of contrasting element images—specifically, the surprising interconvertibility of water and fire.[6] To understand Arnold's epiphanic world, we need to explore deeply this unexpectedly protean behavior of elements, to follow through its implications. Two things must be kept in mind. (1) We will encounter at each stage of our investigation an ambivalent attitude toward water and an equally two-sided attitude toward fire. (2) There is an inseparable interfusion or interflux of water and fire at crucial moments of Arnoldian epiphanic experience.

Madden was perhaps on the verge of discovering this, but in drawing his sharp contrast between negative fire-values and positive water-values in Arnold, Madden inexplicably ignores half of his own earlier statement on Arnold's emotional attachment to water: "He attaches to water, which cools, purifies, and mirrors, *but also segregates, engulfs, and carries away*" (emphasis added).[7] And Madden never suggests the ambivalence or duplicity of Arnoldian fire. Yet in the shifting, elusive world of Arnold's lyrics (unlike the simpler world of his classicizing criticism), water and fire equally deceive. We can hardly tell which is which. Each of these seeming opposites is the other's double. Both are duplicitous, ambivalent, interimplicated. Phenomenological description of this duplicity is basic to the understanding of Arnoldian elemental epiphanies.

If conflict in Coleridgean epiphanies is dramatic, in those of Arnold it is subtle, insidious. We saw how Coleridgean elemental encounters express themselves in powerful physical motions that sharply contrast with the frail objects they unsettlingly animate. The resultant experiences produce an impression of awe, born of the disparity between powerful impulsions and their weak recipients. In Arnold, on the other hand, there is no specified natural object upon which the elemental forces expend their energy; the sensibility of the elegiac speaker or doomed protagonist is the only recipient of elemental influences. The focus is on the elements themselves—in Arnold's case, water and fire. Water and fire do not physically battle one another, as they might in Coleridge; instead, they seem to change into one another, to reveal thereby in symbolic fashion what they had duplicitously hidden: the inherently twofold nature of each element, the shared, coequal power of water and fire to attract *and betray*. The seeming opposition between water and fire as elemental opposites conceals, for Arnold, a subtler and more essential opposition *within* each element—its intermixture of attractiveness and hostility, pleasure and pain.

To suggest what this will mean in concrete terms, here are a few of the descriptive tactics that convey elemental interactions. Arnold often describes a fire with metaphors more suitable to water, or vice versa (a "sea of fire," or tidelike rolling waves of heated conflict in battle). He uses syntactical structures in which water and fire are joined and paralleled, and structures of image-doubling that encourage us to think of water and fire as duplicating each other. We find metaphoric mixtures of fiery and fluxile motions (flashing white arms compared with falling waters, sunlight described as raining down). Water and fire are not only co-present in intimate association but also gain in ambivalence from that connection, at all levels of experience. The epiphanies looked at here will highlight the profound ambivalence of Arnold's sensibility, for the undercurrent—or underfire[8]—of contrast at each level of being gives all the levels a rich, and troubling, equivocality of meaning. Water and fire are each both positive and negative. When they appear together, the bipolarity of each is intensified.

What emerges from Arnold's epiphanic pattern is the picture of a world where all values are radically compromised. The upper level in Culler's three-stage river schema no longer appears purely idyllic, for either at this level or at the sudden point of transition in the Gorge, a blended epiphany of water and fire speaks to Arnold not only of envisioned fulfillment but also of actual or immediately imminent loss. This water-fire exchange is mirrored and expanded in a more encompassing water-fire union on the lower level, where water and fire each appear strikingly as both good and bad. The water-fire ambivalences below intensify the ones above. For Arnold, water and fire are bright-shining, illuminating, revelatory, but also fluxile, transitory, death-directed.

One can view this Arnoldian experience as an ontological meditation on Becoming as a passing-out-of-being: the poet laments the fading of a promise. Once the bright mountain-cradle of the river's journey is abandoned, the remainder of the trip is as futile as it is predictable by the water-fire ambivalences on the early, upper level of life. Usually there is a maiden on the bank. When she vanishes—be her name Olivia or Marguerite or Rebekah or Pallas—the crucial turn is made, and our truest life is past. Once this figure of promise disappears like lightning from our sight, the river's descent is but a death-in-life. The initial epiphany of fulfillment, in its terrible brevity, prefigures its bittersweet results.

There is a psychological depth to Arnoldian epiphany. Not only is union impossible for the maiden and the male traveler, but the disappearance of the female figure of promise is so shockingly swift that the rapid onrush of the river is felt as a death. One feels strong implications of guilt here. An impulse of love on the upper stream, followed by a deadly guilt-feeling, quickly subjects the unfulfilled traveler to a reassuring and quietening but also mockingly parodic variant of the embrace he sought: a deep and fatal encompassing, by both water and fire, felt with fear and longing as a punishment-and-peace. The Arnoldian seeker acquiesces in this cosmic chastisement for his transcendent (excessive?) love-longings: his rapid descent and engulfment by the elements come to seem reassuringly right to him, and he tries to imagine this fatal engulfment as a new and deeper, if quieter, joy. This paradox, this fatal welcoming that is at once a tranquil embrace and an inescapable doom, extends the Keats-like joy-melancholy or ontological ambivalence (what we love does not last) into a psychological myth-type, the fatal fulfillment or punishment-and-peace of a love-death, a *Liebestod*. Since punishment or doom is the fated outcome of an initial impulse of love for a female and since the impulse arises early on the upper stream of life, one may also link both the impulse and its castigating results to the Oedipus story. What fascinates the phenomenologist is the way both ontological and psychological resonances arise from the structure of the water-fire vision itself.

We will explore Arnold's epiphanic pattern in poems ranging from short elegies like "Palladium" and "The Future" to the poet's major verse tragedies—the epic *Sohrab and Rustum* and the drama *Empedocles on Etna*, Arnold's two masterworks. The poem that best reveals the phenomenological pattern, the epiphanic paradigm that Arnold calls "A Dream," is yet another excellent but unstudied work in need of rescue from neglect—one of the poet's finest moments of concentrated intensity and pathos.[9]

In "A Dream" the poet presents his water-and-fire epiphany in rich detail. Because "A Dream" is key to the other, less explicit manifestations of the pattern, we will look at the poem's epiphany with some care. As the narrator-persona and his friend Martin[10] sail down an Alpine stream, blessings of all seasons combine in what appears an idyll. The morning sun colors the stream with vernal freshness, brings out the warm summery aromas of the pines, brightens the chestnut leaves and scarlet berries and golden gourds of autumn, and even changes to diamonds the mountains' wintry wall of snow.[11] But at the "rapid's top" of delight, troubling paradoxes begin.

The episode starts with an omen of death: the verb "shot" prefigures the "thundering" noise that will end the epiphany. The climax is a mere anticipation, lasting but "One moment":

> We shot beneath the cottage with the stream.
> On the brown, rude-carved balcony, two forms
> Came forth—Olivia's, Marguerite! and thine.
> Clad were they both in white, flowers in their breast;
> Straw hats bedeck'd their heads, with ribbons blue,
> Which danced, and on their shoulders, fluttering, play'd.
> They saw us, they conferred; their bosoms heaved,
> And more than mortal impulse fill'd their eyes.
> Their lips moved; their white arms, waved eagerly,
> Flashed once, like falling streams; we rose, we gazed.
> One moment, on the rapid's top, our boat
> Hung poised—
>
> ("A Dream," ll. 20–31)

Just as the erotic ambiance reaches its height—"we rose, we gazed"; "their bosoms heaved"—the sunbright flashing whiteness of the girls' arms, an echo of the glitter of the chalets and the diamond brightness of the mountain snows near the upper river, is likened to the falling stream that will force the travelers to leave the maidens forever. The ribbons that dance and play recall the "wild pastoral music" (l. 12) of the upper slopes; the flowers worn by the maidens recall the plants lovingly described above. But the welcoming white arms poignantly anticipate the estranging plunge of the river.

So this "more than mortal" epiphany of rising Eros is at the same time an epiphany of "falling streams," and to the precise extent that it may be read in sexual terms as a fantasy of fulfillment, it expresses a sharply contrasting premonitory conviction of imminent loss. Now the falling of the streams becomes the quicker "darting" of the relentless river as the scenario of mountain-skirts and maidens is replaced by "burning plains," aggressively "bristled with cities," and leading downward to the sea as terminus.

The theme of the concluding section is the interchange of the "burning" and fluxile elements, of water and fire as duplicitous welcomers, reassuring yet profoundly ominous:

> . . . —and then the darting river of Life
> (Such now, methought, it was), the river of Life,
> Loud thundering, bore us by; swift, swift it foamed,
> Black under cliffs it raced, round headlands shone.
> Soon the planked cottage by the sun-warmed pines
> Faded—the moss—the rocks; us burning plains,
> Bristled with cities, us the sea received.
>
> ("A Dream," ll. 31–37)

The "thundering" of the water sounds like a punishment, especially to readers aware, as Arnold surely was, of the celebrated biblical precedent for the "cities" on the "burning plains" to which the river leads: "And he looked toward Sodom and Gomorrah, and toward all the land of the plain, and beheld, and, lo, the smoke of the country went up as the smoke of a furnace" (Gen. 19:28).[12] The bleak prospect of these Sodom-like cities of the plain (recall that Proust's *Sodome et Gomorrhe* is known to readers of English as *Cities of the Plain*) symbolizes an unmistakable feeling of guilt; given the traditional sexual associations with "Sodom," we may hypothesize an unconscious fear of homosexuality.[13] But although the plains are burning and their cities are like bristles, both fiery plains and welcoming waters constitute a compound subject for the single, inclusive verb "received." Falling streams prevented the travelers from being received by the maidens, but the nether fire and the nether water are welcomers. They, at least, "received" the travelers, or would-be lovers, and the word is soothing. Yet the use of this word to describe the enclasping power of both an encompassing sea and a burning plain is also deeply disturbing.

Doubling in "A Dream" suggests ambivalence, two-sidedness, duplicity. There are two travelers, two maidens, and two lower elements to receive the travelers when the maidens cannot. The two forms of doubling—syntactical (double subject of a verb) and imaginal (two seers, two forms of what is seen)—are mutually reinforcing. We cannot think of the nether waters without the nether fires, nor can we separate the life-giving associations of each element from its deadly ones. And we cannot think of either the burning plains or the encompassing sea without recalling the shocking suddenness of the motion that transported us to both of them—"swift, swift," still another form of doubling.

Everything about the double, two-sided reception of the travelers in the final section of the poem is presaged in its central epiphany: the fire-water equivalence is anticipated in the fiery flashing of the maidens' arms "like falling streams," and the ambivalent feeling of fiery punishment and watery enclasping embrace is foreshadowed in the middle episode. It is not surprising that Arnold also wrote a play called *Tristram and Iseult*, for the paradoxes of his recurrent fire-water epiphany are those of a *Liebestod*.

The features of Arnold's epiphanies are not always as fully elaborated as they are here. But the most striking paradox of the paradigmatic "Dream" epiphany, clearly embodied in its water-fire fusion, recurs in the variants we will look at. The odd union of watery flux and fiery flash found on the upper level of being, or at the moment preceding a transition between levels of being, and then deepened and expanded in its mirror-image on the lower level, is crucial for Arnold. In the more discursive commentaries or interpretations he embeds in his works, the poet sometimes tries to enforce a separation of the symbolic values of water and fire. But the images themselves work against this, implying covertly their shared ambivalence. The fires of Troy, of Moses' burning bush, and of Empedocles' mountain are inseparable from epiphanies of water; Sohrab's river cannot be disjoined from an epiphany of fiery lightning. Thus, Arnoldian epiphanies of punishment-and-embrace are based on the interchange between water and fire.

In "The Future" Arnold's river has become "the river of Time" or human history. Though no one remembers any longer what life was like on the highest reaches of the stream—we cannot "see the green earth any more / As she was by the sources of Time" (ll. 27–28)—Moses and Rebekah appear in roles oddly akin to those of Arnold's (doubled) poet-persona and beloved maiden on the bank at the moment just before the great disjunction or (water)fall in "A Dream." The Rebekah-and-Moses section of "The Future" blends water and fire imagery in a way prelusive of the intertwined, ambivalent values of burning plain and sea below, just as in the transition passage of "A Dream." Arnold's epiphany of Rebekah and Moses is a puzzle. But if we view the fire-and-water epiphany as a partial embodiment of structures more richly elaborated in "A Dream," its importance within the poet's *Lebenswelt* becomes clear.

The Rebekah stanza and the Moses stanza of "The Future" are paralleled by juxtaposition and by analogous formal structures: each stanza consists of a double question, and both stanzas begin with a similar verbal formula—"What girl," "What bard." Such symmetries make us forget the time gap between the Rebekah and Moses stories in the Bible. Instead, we begin to see the two figures as mirroring each other, as counterparts or complements, like the traveler-poet(s) and maiden(s) in "A Dream":

> What girl
> Now reads in her bosom as clear
> As Rebekah read, when she sate
> At eve by the palm-shaded well?
> Who guards in her breast
> As deep, as pellucid a spring
> Of feeling, as tranquil, as sure?

> What bard,
> At the height of his vision, can deem
> Of God, of the world, of the soul,
> With a plainness as near,
> As flashing as Moses felt
> When he lay in the night by his flock
> On the starlit Arabian waste?
> Can rise and obey
> The beck of the Spirit like him?
>   ("The Future," ll. 34–49)

Rebekah "reads in her bosom" the depth of feeling she "guards in her breast"; we recall how, in "A Dream," the maidens "conferred; their bosoms heaved." And when, right after this, we see Moses "rise," at the "height of his vision," to a "flashing" that beckons, the next lines from "A Dream" come vividly to mind: "their white arms, waved eagerly, / *Flashed* once, like falling streams; we *rose*, we gazed" (emphases added). For Arnold, Moses' experience is but an intensified version of every traveler's feelings on the upper reaches of his life's river: "He spreads his arms to the light, / Rivets his gaze on the banks of the stream" (ll. 5–6).

Moreover, just as the climactic experience on the upper water level of "A Dream" begins with "We shot" and ends in parallel fashion with a "Loud thundering," so too the Rebekah-Moses epiphany immediately yields place to a vista of jostling cities filled with cries, so that our minds become chaotic, "Changing and *shot* as the sights which we see" ("The Future," l. 57, emphasis added): the word "shot" has changed its meaning, but subliminally it is violent. The loss of the vision of promise is felt as a deadly shock. Following the pattern of "A Dream," the sun becomes "Fiercer" on the burning "plain" below (ll. 64–65). The sea, always our terminus, "may strike / Peace to the soul of the man on its breast— / As the pale waste widens around him" (ll. 81–83), but the verb "strike" is as violent as the word "shot,"—nor does the "pale waste" promise much.[14] The paradoxical "Future" is insidiously comforting, peacefully bleak.

The apparent contrast between the fierce heat of the plain and the cooling solace of the sea is belied by an undercurrent of imagery that dissolves these distinctions. The burning plain always embraces or includes our pathway to the resolving sea; the reassuring sea, insidiously cruel, can be depended upon to "strike / Peace." Water and fire combine and interchange to convey a duplicitous resolution of punishment-and-peace. To "strike / Peace"—the contradiction implicit in the phrase sums up the insidious paradox of fiery plain and sea: water and fire are each both bad and good; each is as bad as it is good.

Kenneth Allott observes: "There is nothing in the [biblical] story to justify Arnold's praise of Rebekah except her instant obedience" to the request of Abraham's servant that she agree to marry Isaac. Allott adds that "Moses is hardly a more fortunate example for Arnold than Rebekah—he does not 'rise and obey / The beck of the Spirit' until he has exhausted all his arguments for delay, and God has become angry and worked two miracles."[15] But Rebekah's readiness for marriage does relate nicely to the "more than mortal impulse" that "filled" the "eyes" of the maidens on the bank in "A Dream" when they saw the male travelers. And Moses' rising and gazing in response to the brilliant "flashing" of divine insight granted to him not only corresponds to the travelers' response to the maidens' flashing white arms but also contributes to an epitome of the fire-water equivocality to be encountered on the lower level of the river journey. The fiery flashing to which Moses reacts is that of God's burning bush; it contrasts with, but also complements, Rebekah's "palm-shaded well." Once again, imagery of an impulse toward transcending love contains the seeds of its doom. The complementarity of the flashing, burning bush and the palm-shaded well anticipates the lower pairing of the burning plain and the sea that "strikes" peace. Water and fire thus interrelate at the all-too-brief climax of epiphanic fulfillment on the upper level of the river of history; down below, this blending of values expands into an ever more troubling ambivalence, a combination of destruction and embrace hinting at a *Liebestod*.

As we pass from an epiphany of Moses in "The Future" to a vision of Hector the Trojan in "Palladium," the sense of a tragic disjunction between the upper and lower waters becomes acute, yet the two levels are again covertly connected by fire-and-water ambivalences. Hector, fighting on the plain of Ilium (soon to be a burning plain; we know the fate of Troy), defends a hopeless cause. He fights heroically, but his heroism is effective only so long as the maiden on the bank, the Palladium or image of virginal Athena, remains in place beside the upper streams. Since Hector no longer sees her, he will remain undefended when she and her protective powers are taken away, even as her image had already faded from his sight when he reached the lower plain:

> Set where the upper streams of Simois flow
> Was the Palladium, high 'mid rock and wood;
> And Hector was in Ilium, far below,
> And fought, and saw it not—but there it stood!
>
> It stood, and sun and moonshine rained their light
> On the pure columns of its glen-built hall.
> Backward and forward rolled the waves of fight
> Round Troy—but while this stood, Troy could not fall.
>
> ("Palladium," ll. 1–8)

But again, as in "A Dream" and "The Future," all the paradoxes of the lower level of being ("far below") are epitomized and predicted amid the epiphanic joys of the upper stream. The "waves of fight" rolling "Backward and forward" in their ebb and flow "Round Troy," the burning city, present the familiar water-fire ironies of fallen conflict. (The burning of Troy would come to mind as quickly for Arnold's readers as would the Sodom and Gomorrah allusion implicit in the combination of "cities" and "burning plains" in "A Dream.") But we see this paradoxical unity foreshadowed in the revelatory illumination up above as "sun and moonshine rained their light / On the pure columns" of the Virgin's temple, a watery influx of fiery light. The surreal freshness of raining light prefigures, with deceptive innocence, one of the most deadly/intimate fire-water alliances in Arnold's poetry: a hot battlefield that behaves like a sea, with regular, tidelike motions of its rolling waves.

The logic of Hector's experience leads us to conclude that if the combat on the lower plain is futile, the upper image, too, ultimately fails. Arnold says that the Palladium is our soul:

> So, in its lovely moonlight, lives the soul.
> Mountains surround it, and sweet virgin air;
> Cold plashing, past it, crystal waters roll;
> We visit it by moments, ah, too rare!
>
> . . . .

> Still doth the soul, from its lone fastness high,
> Upon our life a ruling effluence send.
> And when it fails, fight as we will, we die;
> And while it lasts, we cannot wholly end.
>   ("Palladium," ll. 9–12, 21–24)

But Hector's protecting "soul" avails not: he cannot re-attain the upper stream with its virginal image and "virgin air," or the sacred temple with its raining light—blending the image-values of "white arms" that "Flash'd" and the "falling streams" juxtaposed in "A Dream." Our vision of virginal Pallas cannot save: its memory fades, its grace is gone. Not the preserving might of the pure Palladium, but the ironic glance of fatal Helen oversees Hector's struggle, which subtly becomes our own:

> We shall renew the battle in the plain
> To-morrow; red with blood will Xanthus be;
> Hector and Ajax will be there again,
> Helen will come upon the wall to see.
>   ("Palladium," ll. 13–16)

If the Trojan debacle, sparked by fickle Helen, varies the love-death motif, the defeat and death of the youthful Persian warrior in Arnold's tragic epic *Sohrab and Rustum* develops this theme even more poignantly: Sohrab dies because he obscurely knew his opponent in combat was his beloved father, whom love prevented him from killing. To some extent the father, Rustum, beloved yet inaccessible to lasting love, plays a role complementary to that of Sohrab in the way that Rebekah is the complement of Moses, or the Palladium of Hector. But in addition, Sohrab himself takes on the image associations of both the fallen poet-traveler and the virginal maiden on the bank, which we saw elaborated in "A Dream" and varied in "The Future" and "Palladium." Even more obviously in the central vision of this Oedipal poem than in the earlier epiphanies we have looked at, elemental forces on the lower level of being represent an embrace and a punishment, the peaceful reward and the cosmic chastisement of a doomed impulse toward transcending love.

Tragic hero-victim, Sohrab accepts this embrace/punishment so completely that, as he dies, his coursing, outflowing blood becomes the Arnoldian river at its moment of swift transition from an upper brightness to a watery-and-fiery welcome:

> . . . the blood
> Came welling from the open gash, and life
> Flowed with the stream;—all down his cold white side
> The crimson torrent ran, dim now and soiled,
> Like the soiled tissue of white violets
> Left, freshly gathered, on their native bank,
> By children whom their nurses call with haste
> Indoors from the sun's eye; his head dropped low,
> His limbs grew slack; motionless, white, he lay—
> White.
>
> *(Sohrab and Rustum,* ll. 840–49)

The repetition of "white" in describing Sohrab's skin and its likeness to "white violets" recalls the repetition of the same word "white" to characterize the clothes and arms of the flower-wearing maidens on the bank in "A Dream" (ll. 23, 28). Like those maidens, or the virginal Palladium, or Rebekah by her "pellucid" spring, Sohrab belongs to the world of pristine brightness. But like the desert-river Oxus, described as "forgetting the bright speed he had / In his high mountain-cradle" (ll. 886–87), Sohrab became a "foiled . . . wanderer" (l. 888) on a plain scorched by the "sun's eye."

Like the river that bears the poet-travelers downward in the paradigmatic vision of "A Dream" ("swift, swift it foamed"), the passing of Sohrab's life is described with a doubled use of "swift." The additional doubling of the ambiguous word "quick!" adds pathos and paradox to the life-death or love-death motif:

> Quick! quick! for numbered are my sands of life,
> And swift; for like the lightning to this field
> I came, and like the wind I go away—
> Sudden, and swift.
>
> *(Sohrab and Rustum,* ll. 721–24)

Sohrab, himself the death-life river, himself both poet-traveler and abandoned virgin, also combines—as so often in Arnoldian epiphanies—water and fire forces, the flowing river and the flash of "lightning." And if Sohrab is the river, he must enter the metaphoric sea.

His final, fatal sea welcome similarly blends star-fire with encompassing waters, for in the last words of the poem "new-bathed stars / Emerge, and shine upon the Aral Sea" (ll. 891–92), as if their flashing power had been latent in the watery depths.[16]

The story of Sohrab's death is a tragedy, but the *Liebestod* logic, the fatal fulfillment, of its fire-and-water ambivalences is implicit in all the poetic epiphanies we have studied. In "A Dream" the untimely cessation of happiness at the end of the brief mountain-cradle period of the river is made to seem less sad because the poet devotes more space to describing that early period of life. Still, the joyful flash of the maidens' arms was brief, and there is no remedy for its aborted promise along the lower stretches of the life-river, or in the all-too-final sea. Instead, we have seen how the paradox of punishment-and-peace, of the all-too-restful, fatal embrace that parodies the love first sought, repeatedly underlies, and undermines, any attempt at a convincing compensation in the long reaches below. Moses and Rebekah, too, saw their epiphanies for an instant, and "The Future" of the flow of their lives, of our lives under the fierce sun, is seen as a memory of what cannot return. Hector's war for Helen on the sea-like burning plain is a futile and absurd venture, almost a parody of a now unrecapturable brief unity with his own youthful soul or anima, his lost Palladium.

Sohrab, as we saw, is described with imagery Arnold elsewhere associates with the type of the virginal maiden (white flowers; white body; early shelter, on the upper reaches of the river, from the burning heat of noonday), as well as with imagery of the traveler-poet and of the suddenly falling river itself. So his early death is as fated as the untimely loss to sight of the virgin of promise from the upper reaches of the river in any of Arnold's other epiphanies: Olivia, Marguerite, Rebekah, Pallas. The loss of the vision is death to the seer: nothing new will arise after the river falls.

Empedocles, the semi-legendary pre-Socratic philosopher of *Empedocles on Etna*, is the ultimate Arnoldian tragic hero, for in his moment of dying he sees the Arnoldian epiphany of water-fire interchange. Empedocles pushes the logic of Arnold's epiphanic *Liebestod* imagery to its ultimate existential conclusion: he freely chooses the love-death that other Arnold personae have had inflicted on them by fate, the punishment/peace of a water-fire engulfment. Callicles the harper hymns Apollo as seen on Mt. Helicon, where the "white" forms of the Nine maidens embody the purity of the upper reaches of the river "at the cliff-top" (*Empedocles on Etna*, II. 438, 429), before the river's plunge. Callicles concludes Arnold's poem with an implicit plea for a total, inclusive, affirming view of the life-river: "The day in his hot-ness, / The strife with the palm; / The night in her silence, / The stars in their calm" (II. 465–68). But Empedocles rejects the lower reaches of the river of life. Rather than have "reality . . . / Knead" him in its "hot hand," rather than "sink in the impossible strife" of the journey of human existence (II. 385–86, 389) only to experience a needlessly postponed "calm" in the starry sea that ends it, Empedocles wants to experience the meaning of life, such as it is, with all its hopelessly intertwined paradoxes, in full intensity, this moment.

Bachelard, though he does not deal with water imagery in *Empedocles* and bases his view of the play largely on the work of Louis Bonnerot, says the text of this play is "in its essence the *poem of an Instant*, combining an Instant in a man's life with an Instant in the life of a World."[17] Individual-global epiphany: Empedocles' moment of death plus Etna's moment of eruption.

In "A Dream" Arnold's travelers did not have to wait long on the "darting river of Life" till consummation came: "us burning plains, / Bristled with cities, us the sea received." Empedocles seeks his comparable fire-and-water consuming/consummation on the instant. He wants a fiery "sea" to rush (before the mists rush) over his soul and welcomingly "receive" it:

> —Ah, boil up, ye vapours!
> Leap and roar, thou sea of fire!
> My soul glows to meet you.
> Ere it flag, ere the mists
> Of despondency and gloom
> Rush over it again,
> Receive me, save me!
> (*Empedocles on Etna*, II. 410–16)

Before jumping into the crater as he does here, Empedocles had cried out in despair to all the elements together: "Receive me, hide me, quench me, take me home!" (II.36). In this plea to be received, Empedocles had prayed to be quenched, as if he were a fire, seeking water. Predictably (if viewed as a compressed version of the epiphanic pattern of elemental two-sidedness), even the fire of Etna becomes for Empedocles a quenching force, a leaping, roaring "sea." In fiery surges he finds the "home" one might seek in the watery origin of life, *la mer/mère*.

But for Arnold water and fire are equally bound up in the inextricable oxymorons of life/death: it makes sense that the fiery upsurge of death should become, for Empedocles, both a sea-like, rushing, quenching savior and at the same time an incandescent, glowing rescue from the "mists / Of despondency and gloom" (II. 413–14).[18] This double metaphorical receiving, of water and of fire, is the fatally glorious intensification of the flashing-and-falling, the rain of light, the lightning and flowing, that create the Arnoldian seeker's ambivalent epiphany before the plunge from the upper river. Phenomenological scrutiny of the variants of the epiphanic pattern elaborated in the paradigm "A Dream" has shown that, for Matthew Arnold, water and fire remain—on every level of experience—interacting, duplicitous welcomers.

It does no good, then, for Arnold the classicizing critic (in "The Study of Poetry") to suggest metaphorically that the consoling and sustaining early "streams" of ancient Greek verse embody an ever-pure ideal while the "burning plain" of modern Romanticism represents a regrettable fall from the freshwater heights. For in Arnold's epiphanies the early stages of life and history are as thoroughly contaminated with ambivalence as the later ones. The pattern of Arnoldian epiphany indicates that Arnold the idealizing critic is trying to forget the subtler and more ambivalent lessons learned by Arnold the epiphanic poet.

Part Two:
Elemental Deaths
and Illuminations

FOUR

Love and Liminality in Tennyson

The Aweful Dawn-Rose and the Wheel

If our unit on "Elemental Diversity and Conflict" offered a general introduction to contrasts within and between epiphanic paradigms of Romantic and Victorian writers of poetry and prose, the present section on "Elemental Deaths and Illuminations" is the first of two more specialized groupings. The idea will now be to show how writers may be usefully and unexpectedly regrouped, and literary criticism correspondingly reconfigured, in ways based on neo-Bachelardian discoveries.

Juxtaposing Tennyson and Pater as envisioners of elemental deaths and illuminations—both conveyed in epiphanies of flowering fire— calls attention for the first time to a striking phenomenological linkage between these two writers. Too often our literary perspectives are conditioned by the limitations of genre categories; one expects, for example, to find Tennyson and Arnold paired as elegiac poets, or Pater and Wilde compared and contrasted as proponents of aestheticism in their essays.

Such customary groupings have their uses, but I suggest that new, phenomenological classifications will reinvigorate literary study. To perceive both Tennyson's verse and Pater's prose as focused on fiery poetic ecstasy intertwined with the theme of real or imagined death reveals a strong kinship worth our attention. The fact that Tennyson's epiphanic *fire flowers expand into the sky* while Pater's *fire flowers crumble into earth* brings the two men's visionary temperaments together even while it usefully distinguishes them: it gives us a phenomenological key to the two men's shared melancholy, while dramatizing the distinction between the philosophic outcomes or discursive mirrorings of their respective death-centered epiphanies—Tennyson's urgent intimations of post-mortal hope, as contrasted to Pater's tragic irony, the gorgeous but hectic luxuriance of Paterian flowers being intensified by the wounded or dying birds.

The two writers also belong together phenomenologically because of the extraordinary insistence of their fire-flower epiphanies. The epiphanies of Tennyson pervade the famous dramatic monologues (whether the speakers are men or women) as well as the epic-scale masterworks, *In Memoriam* and *Idylls of the King*. Pater's comparable epiphanies abound in his many "imaginary portraits" or visionary short stories as well as in his novels *Marius the Epicurean* and *Gaston de Latour*. Indeed, seeing in juxtaposition so many kindred exhibits of such concentrated power by two visionary creators who are not often viewed in a common context may stimulate us to revise accepted value judgments. I, for one, have been led by the analyses in this chapter and the next to a new appreciation of Tennyson and Pater—of Pater as unexpectedly equal in epiphanic brilliance and value to Tennyson. I now view these two writers as the most powerful British epiphanists of the Victorian era.

If this judgment is correct, or even if it is accepted in a modified form, phenomenological epiphany study will have consequences important for all critics of Victorian literature because this judgment initiates, and should help advance, a re-evaluation of the comparative stature of Tennyson and Pater. In addition, this Bachelardian approach will disclose literary data of major interest to psychoanalytic criticism, for the paradigmatic epiphanies of both Tennyson and Pater are kindred scenarios of traumatic guilt. For both these reasons I suggest that our findings in this unit on elemental deaths and illuminations will cast light on issues transcending the concerns of phenomenologists.

In the present chapter I will seek to define and survey Tennyson's epiphanic achievement. To do this I must describe not only the images his elemental visions share with those of Pater—glorious and death-allied blossoms of flame—but also the features that characterize Tennysonian epiphanies alone: the rolling, wheeling motions that accompany the fire-flowers' recurrent appearances and the elevating but foreboding sense of thresholdness or liminality that provides the spiritual frame for the heightened moment.

Tennysonian seers are most generally lovers, and they are watchers at the threshold. Whether the watchful quester is a lover of man, of woman, or of God, the appearance of the loved object is experienced as an epiphany granted to a humble suppliant from a higher being, and from a higher order of being. The characteristic Tennysonian epiphany is a "liminal" one—from *limen*, Latin for threshold, a word I am borrowing from the anthropologists van Gennep and Turner[1] to denote the stage of transition—from one state of being to another— that is central to every rite of passage. A Tennyson poem or visionary passage is a ceremony of initiation: the seeker is passive and may feel utterly dwarfed by the higher powers, the more exalted state of being, revealed by the supernal Beloved. The vision is an epiphany of glory, but the threshold where it appears is often death, or what seems like death.

Since "liminality" has been used in varied ways by some post-modern critics, it is best to clarify how I define it here: it signifies an experience of thresholdness, an intense moment felt to be on the borderline between the quotidian and the overpoweringly Other, between natural and awesomely supernal, or (most commonly in Tennyson's poems) between life and what seems to be death. As I employ it, the liminality concept seems a more useful way to describe Tennysonian intense moments than does Fredeman's related concept of penultimacy: Fredeman suggests that most of Tennyson's monologues present "not the end, but . . . the penultimate moment before the end."[2] W. David Shaw expands on this remark,[3] and Christopher Ricks even calls it "one of the most acute statements ever made about Tennyson."[4]

But I want to show that ultimacy, not penultimacy, is at stake in Tennyson's epiphanies. To Fredeman, penultimacy means that Tennyson's major dramatic monologues typically end "before any revelation is possible,"[5] before anything definitive can be shown. But explicit revelations of supposed theological truth are not the main point: Tennyson's epiphanies—his intense, mysteriously expansive moments—are themselves his imaginative ultimates. "St. Simeon Stylites," Fredeman's orienting example, is not typical: this oddly but intentionally hollow poem prepares us for an epiphany it then fails to deliver. Non-revelation is in fact the poem's subject, and that is why "St. Simeon Stylites" is one of the few major monologues lacking an aweful dawn-rose or a wheel, the unmistakable signs of Tennysonian epiphanic power.

"And on the glimmering limit far withdrawn / God made himself an awful rose of dawn." These lines conclude Tennyson's dream-poem ("I had a vision when the night was late"[6]) called "The Vision of Sin," a lyric of hallucinatory power that we shall use as paradigm for the study of Tennysonian epiphany. Immediately we note the "limit," the *limen* or threshold, which Tennyson also likes to call a "verge" or a "marge." When John Tyndall asked Tennyson what the dawn-rose meant, the poet replied that "the power of explaining such concentrated expressions of the imagination was very different from that of writing them."[7] "Concentrated" is the key word here: the dawn-rose, along with the wheeling motion that generally accompanies it, is the epitome, the essence, of Tennysonian elemental epiphany.

The epiphanic centrality I am claiming for this image in "The Vision of Sin" would seem to be corroborated by the remarkable testimonies quoted by Ricks (headnote to *Poems* 2:156): "In a letter (*Brotherton Collection*) T. described it ["The Vision of Sin"] as 'one of my poems, which I confess has always been a favourite with myself'. Allingham quotes Patmore, 18 August 1849: ' "Tennyson perhaps likes *The Vision of Sin* best of his own poems." ' " Though in this poem the (wheel-accompanied) aweful dawn-rose is called "God," elsewhere we will find the same epiphany in variant forms ranging from Eos, pagan goddess of dawn, to Rosalind, a formidable but mortal woman.

Here as always, epiphanic structures are our primary focus of interest, not the metaphysical or religious interpretations placed on them by either the poet or his commentators. Nichols argues that Tennyson's epiphanies are not mystical; Kincaid finds in the poet a lasting tension between the "novelistic" and "visionary" worlds; Culler thinks Tennyson doubted whether imagery could portray transcendence; Albright finds Tennyson trying to "dress up" the "sublime" in the "vestments" of the "commonplace."[8] My own thesis is that any consideration of supposed transcendent implications in Tennyson's verse must begin with detailed phenomenological scrutiny of the epiphanies that are deemed to have these implications. The epiphanic paradigm and its variants are the key to whatever Tennyson presents as intense, expansive, and mysterious.

Unlike Walter Pater, whose red-yellow blossoms (as we shall see) are a blend of fire and earth, Tennyson sees dawn-roses chiefly in the heavens. The giant sky flowers often expand apocalyptically to fill the heavenly dome with flame. But even when the skyblooms are less cosmically encompassing, they come from above: they are blends of flame and air, signifying what is higher. One may hope to merge with these fire flowers; sometimes they glow as with a mother's welcome. Or, more often, one may have to be searingly purged by them; Tennyson's sky-flames frequently bring to mind the prophecy of Malachi: "But who may abide the day of his coming? and who shall stand when he appeareth? For he is like a refiner's fire . . . " (3:2). Attempts to arrest the higher power, to force it to dwell with one on earth, may lead the importunate to violent death. Terror is never far from love in these sacred visions, for the beloved object, which may be a man or woman as well as God, is overpowering as it appears in, or appears to descend from, its supernal or superior realm, embodied in flowering flame. Whatever beloved object the vision is considered to embody—whether woman, or man, or Deity—the overpowering height and largeness of the idealized being brings with it major psychological difficulties. Love songs addressed to such a supernal embodiment of woman may reveal a strong misogyny; love yearnings for such a superior form of man may lead a woman to death or deadly despair. Relations with the immense and inaccessible fire-flower God may be consummated only after death. From love to hate, from despair to mystic ecstasy, the rose of dawn is aweful—awful and awesome—in the range of deep responses it calls forth from its too-distant heights.

Wheeling motions are the other crucial component of Tennysonian epiphanic experience (like the dawn-rose, these wheeling motions are best epitomized, as we shall see, in the paradigmatic "Vision of Sin"). Though occasionally (as in the madness of *Maud*) literal carriage wheels may roar with hallucinatory power, most often the wheels are semi-abstract: wheels of Being, orbs of circumstance, planetary spheres. It is the effect of the circular or spheric shape that matters, more than whatever may take on that epiphanic form. Indeed, the circle, sphere, orb, or parabola is primarily felt as the shape of a motion. To take one example we will look at more closely later, Sir Bedivere's body makes a powerful wheeling movement as he throws Excalibur into the lake before King Arthur dies, and the sword itself wheels through the air: like Ezekiel's prophecies (recall the wheels within wheels [Ezek. 1:16, 10:10]), the epiphany of Arthur's death must be introduced by wheel-like motions.

More typically, at least for Tennyson's male personae, the epiphanic seer is caught up in a *cosmically encompassing* circular motion, which—like the barely accessible transcendence and daunting supernal distance of the heavenly fire-flowers—makes the lover and quester a passive recipient of a greater cosmic or divine impulsion, of a life that is larger and fuller than one's own. Again, it is hardly possible for a Tennysonian lover to take the initiative: thus, his or her status is reduced. The lover waits, prays, and hopes. Yet the circular motion that bears the lover with it when the epiphanic moment is attained does have the feeling of a cycle; and since the cycles of nature are, after all, something immanent in our earthly life, something not wholly above us, the whirling motion felt in the heightened moment has the effect of joining, however briefly, two states of being ordinarily felt as separate, the higher and the lower realms. The Tennysonian liminal experience is paradoxical, like the very concept of a threshold of transition. It is a prospect of what is beyond the bourne, even beyond the threshold of death, yet it is revealed now and here, in liminal time and space.

Tennyson as prophet assumes the metaphoric role or guise of *poeta moriturus*. He assumes personae and portrays questers who think or imagine or fear they are about to die. But only at such a liminal, borderline moment between two realms of being can epiphanies of fire-flower dawnings and wheel-like motions happen.

We will divide our survey of Tennysonian dawn-rose-and-wheel epiphanies into five parts: (1) the paradigmatic "Vision of Sin," paired with its closely related companion piece, "The Palace of Art"; (2) the three major epiphanies of *In Memoriam*; (3) epiphanies experienced by various men in love with inaccessible, daunting, or supernal women; (4) more fragmentary epiphanies, experienced by melancholy women in love with unattainable men; and finally, (5) four brief but outstanding epiphanies from Tennyson's later epic-scale vision, *Idylls of the King*. In all these visions we will seek the epiphanic components most fully revealed in the initial paradigm: the fiery dawn-rose and the equally awe-inducing force of wheeling or whirling movement—both presented in a liminal situation, an area of contact between two distinct, often disjunct orders of being, a higher and a lower, which may nevertheless be magically or dauntingly united in the epiphanic moment. At this limit or threshold, in this border-area, the skyey rose of dawn-flame will reveal its aweful power, and the allied motions of circling, of cosmic orbs and spheres and wheels and cycles, will confirm that power—for better or for worse—in the epiphanic moment sought, often despairingly, by the Tennysonian quester or supplicant lover.

1

"The Vision of Sin," the Tennysonian paradigm-poem, dramatizes the inseparability of terror and delight in Tennyson's epiphanies of liminality. This lyric narrative features a guilt scenario, an allegorical palace of sinful self-absorption, but the "sin" and its purgation are as crucial to the liminal epiphany as is the eventual self-revealing of divinity. As the poem opens, a sin-laden youth, riding an earthy Pegasus that will not rise, approaches a palace, into which he is led by a "child of sin" (l. 5). Inside he finds a dreamy crowd waiting "for a fountain to arise" (such as Kubla Khan treasured in Coleridge's poem) in a dreamy atmosphere "Suffused" with sunset-light (ll. 8, 12). Right before, and then during, the fountain's awaited rising and spouting, a mysterious music generates a round dance of circles and orbs and whirls and wheels, into which the dreamers (now ecstatic dancers) are frenziedly drawn.

> Low voluptuous music winding trembled,
> Woven in *circles*, . . .
> Storm'd in *orbs* of song, a growing gale, . . .
> Ran into its giddiest *whirl* of sound,
> Caught the sparkles, and in *circles*, . . .
> Flung the torrent rainbow *round*.
> Then they started from their places, . . .
> *Wheeling* with precipitate paces
> To the melody, till they flew, . . .
> Dash'd together in blinding dew;
> Till, kill'd with some luxurious agony,
> The nerve-dissolving melody
> Fluttered headlong from the sky.
>   (ll. 17–18, 25, 29–30, 32–33, 36–37, 42–45,
>   emphases added)

These voluptuaries may be sinners, but they feel the whirling motion of the epiphanic wheels, and the music that embodies their frenzied spirit seems to die ("kill'd with some luxurious agony")—the death motif that so often indicates the epiphanic readiness of Tennysonian questers. It is as if, in the Tennysonian epiphanic world, we all are "sinners," all in need of some expiatory purging, some liminal ordeal, to make us worthy of the life that counts. Nevertheless, despite the strong emphasis on sin and guilt in this poem—an emphasis unmistakable, central, and psychoanalytically important—it seems appropriate to put the word "sinners" in quotation marks, for Tennyson has placed in his palace of "sin" a spouting, sparkling fountain (ll. 8, 21–22), conveying a welling-up of irrepressible life, a subliminally sexual and undeniably attractive presentation of exuberant vitality. (Fountain and dancing and sensual music blend in a "torrent rainbow" [l. 32].) Even when suffused with the sense of sin and death, the Tennysonian dreamer knows or intuits, at the deepest level of vision, that the never wholly extinguished life-force (with associations both sexual and spiritual) will return, that after the "death" will come a life-delivering liminal revelation of aweful power and beauty.

Indeed, as soon as the dance dies away, the dreamer or speaker-persona looks up "toward a mountain-tract" (from whence cometh his help—though in strangely fearsome guise), and there he observes that "every morning, far withdrawn, / God made himself an awful rose of dawn" (ll. 46, 49–50). From the sun-God sphere a stifling fog descends in the direction of a another sinister rider, "gray and gap-toothed" and "lean as death," but the poet cannot warn the strayed wanderer, for the poet's own "dream" is "broken" (ll. 60, 56). This second sinner duly enters a "ruin'd inn" (l. 63) and sings a song of epicurean cynicism, after which the poet sees a vision of human and animal corpses degenerating into lower forms of life, helped by a host of hungry worms. The fatality introduced by the rider "lean as death" has completely taken over the envisioned world. Oddly disembodied human voices speculate on the causes of moral degeneration. Yet after a final voice asks, "Is there any hope?" an answer "peal'd from that high land, / But in a tongue no man could understand; / And on the glimmering limit far withdrawn, / God made Himself an awful rose of dawn" (ll. 220–24).

Never can this awe-filled enigma be forgotten, so long as we seek Tennysonian epiphanic initiation. Let us sum up what is essential here, what features will continually recur in Tennyson's epiphanic moments. The "Vision" begins with a sleepy sunset; then the visionary and musical *whirl* of *seemingly endless circlings* catches *fiery "sparkles"* as the dancers *wheel*. Finally—both before and after a seeming *death* of the envisioned world of living things—*the fire-flower, the dawn-rose, blossoms forth as deity*, making the ostensibly sinful whirl part of a "liminal" experience and thus paradoxically a needed preparation. An initiatory ordeal has readied us for Tennysonian epiphany. "The Vision of Sin" is Tennyson's epiphanic paradigm, specifically labeled a vision or dream in the same explicit manner as the other paradigms whose variants we explored in previous chapters (Wordsworth's "Pilgrim's Dream," Coleridge's "dream" of Melancholy, Arnold's "A Dream"). The poem is our phenomenological key to the poet's pattern of liminal epiphany.

"The Palace of Art," a companion-piece to "The Vision of Sin," is almost as paradigmatic as that poem and deserves to be studied with it. In "The Palace" another self-absorbed epicurean (like the whirling dancers in "The Vision of Sin") builds another Kubla-Khanlike "pleasure house" for his hedonistic soul, and this time the pleasure house itself is powerfully imaged as a fire-flower. The entire palace is like a giant, sweet-smelling, multiple flower, for it is topped with four statues, each "tossing up / A cloud of incense all of odor steam'd / From out a golden cup" (ll. 38–40). The fragrant structure is also a flaming one; it almost blinds the eye, for while "that sweet incense rose and never failed, . . . The light aerial gallery, golden-rail'd, / Burnt like a fringe of fire" (ll. 45, 47–48). The windows aid the fire-flower effect by seeming to be "slow-flaming crimson fires . . . interlaced" like petals (ll. 50–51).

But this house is an inadequate fire-flower, for its builder has disregarded God's great rolling cosmic wheels. The builder has advised his royal soul to rule its pleasure-house oblivious of the larger rounding, whirling life: "Reign thou apart, a quiet king, / Still as, while Saturn whirls, his stedfast shade / Sleeps on his luminous ring" (ll. 14–16). Saturn's shadow on its ring seems stationary, but Saturn's wheelings or whirls are real—indeed, epiphanic, and ignored at the soul's peril.

God makes this clear by inflicting psychological death: He plagues the too-heedless soul with sudden and "sore despair," so that, like Herod, she feels "Struck thro' with pangs of hell" (ll. 224, 220), afflicted with the fires she had tried to arrogate to her own self-adoration. She must face the revelatory, the aweful, wheels and whirlings she had tried to remove from her awareness: "The hollow orb of moving Circumstance / Roll'd round by one fix'd law" (ll. 255–56). God's laws of motion seem hollow only because the Soul herself *feels dead*: "A spot of dull stagnation," "Shut up as in a crumbling tomb" (ll. 245, 273). She has herself become a parody-circle: "Back on herself her serpent pride had curl'd" (l. 257). She has reached, in a spiritual sense, the ultimate threshold: "I have found / A new land, but I die" (ll. 283–84). Feeling spiritually "on fire within"—not only because of her remorse but also as a sign of her liminal readiness—she resolves to leave the palace, to return only "When I have purged my guilt" (ll. 285, 296). God's rolling orbs and purging fires have replaced the soul's peaceful Saturnian ring-shadow and her self-adoring fire-flower palace. Good and evil, sin and salvation, use the same indissociable pair of images in a composite liminal experience of preparation and epiphany.

2

The three great moments of Tennyson's most expansive epiphanic achievement and best love poem, *In Memoriam*, are a prophecy, a memory, and a prayer—all phenomenologically interrelated in their shared vocabulary of cosmic wheels and awe-filled fiery roses of the dawn. The epiphany that I have called prophetic is itself quietly predicted by a phrasing in section 17, one of the earliest-written parts of the poem, where the poet says to Hallam's spirit, "For I in spirit saw thee *move / Thro' circles of the bounding sky*" (17.5–6, emphasis added). Then, in section 44 (beginning "How fares it with the happy dead?"), the speaker posits a possible intimation, amid the Lethe of adulthood, that childhood resources of vision are not wholly lost, and he advises, repeating the circle image, "O *turn thee round*, resolve the doubt" (44.14, emphasis added). True, maturation is a kind of fall: the baby, hardly distinguishing itself as a separate entity from "the circle of the breast," later "rounds . . . to a separate mind," a distinct and vulnerable personality (45.3, 9). But epiphanic images of circles and rounding show that unity is potentially present.

Unity is regainable in the dawn-bloom through imagined communion with the dead, enjoyed in prospect as something that will happen after one's own imagined death: "*In that deep dawn* behind the tomb . . . clear *from marge to marge shall bloom* / The eternal landscape of the past" (46.6–8). This is a dawn-rose unity not only of past and future but also of the loving foreseer and the loved one lost: "Look also, Love . . . *A rosy warmth from marge to marge*" (46.16). The poet is partly afraid of the possibility "That each, who seems a separate whole, / Should move his *rounds* and . . . should fall / Remerging in the general Soul" (47.1–4). He hopes to recognize Hallam, as a separate spirit, well enough at least to say, "Farewell! We lose ourselves in *light*" (47.16). In the meanwhile, the poet hopes that Hallam's spirit will be near him "When the *light is low* . . . And all the *wheels of Being* slow" (50.1, 4), and will be with him again at that moment when he faces "The twilight of eternal day" (50.16, emphases added). Hallam's spirit will brighten the rosy warmth that fills the sky and will quicken the circulation of the wheels of Being. Enjoyed in imaginative prospect is an eternal day's beginning, a twilight that is the rosy dawn of immortality: the light, no longer low, is rising, for the wheels of Being move the ascending spirit.

The second great epiphany is a triple memory: a mystic memory of spiritual reunion, a reported memory of Hallam's, and the poet-narrator's personal memory of loss. On a quiet night when "bats went round in fragrant skies / And *wheel'd* or lit the filmy shapes / That haunt the dusk, with ermine capes / And woolly breasts and beaded eyes" (95.9–12, emphasis added), the poet spiritually reenacts these wheelings and flashings of light. As he re-reads letters recalling his times with Hallam,

> The living soul was flash'd on mine,
> And mine on his was *wound, and whirl'd*
> About empyreal [literally, beyond the fire] heights
>   of thought,
> And came on that which is, and caught
> The deep pulsations of the world.
>
> (95.36–40, emphasis added)

Then, to add the rose and dawn to the whirlings and windings,

> A breeze began to . . .
> . . . fluctuate all the still perfume
> . . . and swung
> The *heavy-folded rose* . . .
> . . . and said
> '*The dawn, the dawn*,' and died away;
> And East and West, without a breath,
> Mixt their dim lights, like life and death,
> To broaden into boundless day.[9]
>   (95.54, 56, 58–64, emphases added)

After the epiphanic windings and whirlings, after the seeming death of the breeze, dawn-light fills the sky as east and west (like the poet-persona and the spirit of Hallam) merge their aery or spiritual flames or gleams in an atmosphere pervaded by the dawn-flower perfume of the heavy-folded rose.

Hallam had used the same epiphanic imagery in a lighter vein during one of his own reminiscences of travel, a memory of Vienna. The poet recalls how Hallam described the festivities where "wheels the circled dance, and breaks / The rocket molten into flakes / Of crimson" (98.30–32), a quite flowerlike shedding of petallike fires amid circles and wheels. But this memory of joy yields immediately to a memory of loss, of death: "Risest thou thus, dim dawn, again, . . . Day, when I lost the flower of men; / Who tremblest thro' thy darkling red . . . And Autumn laying here and there / A fiery finger on the leaves" (99.1, 4–5, 11–12). The fire touches the leaves, but the flower is lost, and dawn is dim and trembling: this is a time when the light is low, the fiery red is darkling, and the wheels of Being move slowly.

Beginning his third and last fire-flower-and-wheel epiphany with a memory of the first one, Tennyson ends it with a prayer for vision (paradoxically self-realizing). If Hallam was indeed "with me," the poet says, "While I . . . yearn'd to burst the folded gloom, / To bare the eternal Heavens again" (that is, to reach the fiery luminaries beyond the clouds that obscured them), "To feel once more, in placid awe, / The strong imagination *roll* / *A sphere* of stars about my soul, / In all her *motion* one with law," then, the poet implores Hallam's spirit, "be with me now, / And enter in at breast and brow, / Till *all my blood*, a fuller wave, / Be quicken'd" so that "The wizard lightnings *deeply glow*, / And every thought *breaks out a rose*" (122.1–8, 10–13, 19–20, emphases added). The roses of dawn are glowing blossoms of the blood, of enkindled thoughts quickened to wizard lightning-fire. Imagination feels itself to be at the glowing center of all the spheric motions of God's world of law, now blossoming into love.

3

Blending in imagination with the spirit of his friend Hallam, a guide who dwells in the upper world, Tennyson feels able to come upon "that which is," to catch the very pulse of Being: in a liminal moment, he can die into the dawn. But when the idealized spirit of a loved one takes the female form, problems are created for Tennyson's male singers, speakers, monodramatists. When the supernal woman descends or "stoops," her power is daunting, somehow felt as fatal ("Rosalind"). When she remains on high, she so dismays by her immortal plenitude that she induces in her faithful lover a death-in-life (Eos, in "Tithonus"). When society makes her unavailable, her lover's death into the dawn-bloom is more tragic than ecstatic (*Maud*). Even when she kindly comes down to earth to function as the poet's guardian and allegoric guide, she is profoundly unsettling (Freedom, in "The Poet"). Indeed, odyssean mariners pursue the visionary woman around the world, but it is as if they were chasing the sun, for she will never be possessed ("The Voyage"). Yet Tennyson depicts these larger-than-life women with the full resources of his epiphanic power. They are among his most complete elemental visions, and their complexity fascinates.

One of the delights of phenomenological criticism, as we have found several times in earlier chapters, is to come upon little-known epiphanies whose elemental force has been, mysteriously, neglected. "Rosalind" is one of these. Though her name (*rosa linda*, or "pretty rose") links her to earth, like all of Tennyson's idealized beloveds she is mainly a creature of the upper air, a "rose" of the sky. She is a "frolic falcon, with bright eyes, / Whose free delight, from any height of rapid flight, / Stoops at all game that wing the skies" (ll. 1–3). But "Stoops" is a problem; falcons stoop to conquer—and to kill.

You care not for another's pains
Because you are the soul of joy,
Bright metal all without alloy.
Life *shoots and glances* through your veins,
And *flashes* off a thousand ways,
Through lips and eyes in subtle *rays*.
Your hawk-eyes are keen and *bright*,
Keen with triumph, watching still
To *pierce* me through with *pointed light*.
. . . .
Come down, come home, my Rosalind,
. . . .
Too long you keep the upper skies;
Too long you roam and *wheel* at will;
But we must hood your random eyes
That care not whom they *kill*.
And your cheek, whose *brilliant hue*
Is so *sparkling*-fresh to view,
Some *red heath-flower* in the dew,
Touched with *sunrise*. . . .
. . . .
When we have lured you from above,
And that delight of frolic flight, by day or night,
From North to South,
We'll bind you fast in silken cords,
And kiss away the bitter words
From off your *rosy* mouth.
          (ll. 19–27, 33, 35–42, 46–51, emphases added)

Rosalind's transcendence is the poet's frustration. A Shelleyan "soul of joy," she cares not for the poet's pains. Everything about her is too lofty, elevated, inaccessible. She wheels about ("Too long you roam and wheel at will") in her own aery element. Yet she is a firebird, a pentecostal thousandfold fiery flashing. Falconlike, she pierces the poet with her stabs of light: *she is the awful dawn-rose* ("red heath-flower" touched with "sunrise"), seeming in her illimitable flight to encompass the heavens "From North to South" (like the divine illumination "from marge to marge" in *In Memoriam*), but her power is predatory, cruel, heedless of earthlings' pains. Her eyes "care not whom they kill" (l. 38). Her words are "seeming-bitter / From excess of swift delight" (ll. 30–31). The poet-persona resents his love for her, and he seems eager to take his own bitterness out on her, even to project it onto her and ascribe it to her. Feeling trapped by his love for the free creature, he himself becomes cruel, modulating from reverence to ugly sadistic fantasy. With his epiphanic vocabulary of fire and flowers and falcon-wheelings, Tennyson crafts a psychological study of extraordinary acuteness and dramatic force.

Tithonus' beloved is also an awful dawn-rose (Eos is Dawn herself) and a fiery epiphanic vision that consumes—with frustration if not quite with the warped bitterness of Rosalind's would-be captor. "Me only cruel immortality / Consumes," says Tithonus, "Here at the quiet limit of the world" (ll. 5–7), in the liminal space where a daunting transcendence shines forth beyond an uncrossable threshold. The vision once seemed a Tennysonian epiphanic paradise of radiant rings and flowery crimson dawn-glow, when Tithonus had watched

> The dim curls kindle into sunny *rings*;
> Changed with thy mystic change, and felt my *blood*
> Glow with the *glow that slowly crimson'd all*
> Thy presence and thy portals, while I lay,
> Mouth, forehead, eyelids, growing *dewy-warm*
> With kisses *balmier than half-opening buds*. . . .
>   (ll. 54–59, emphases added)

But now, having proven unequal to the demands of the higher life, Tithonus would like to die back to his former self, so he can "earth in earth forget these empty courts, / And thee returning on thy silver *wheels*" (ll. 75–76 emphasis added). The dawn-flower's golden rings and silver wheels move on without the abandoned, aged lover; the maternal, heaven-encompassing rosy glow of auroral Eos is no longer an ocean of balmy, fragrant warmth wherein to drown. The prospect of ecstatically dissolving into the dawn-rose was an illusion.

Yet for Tennyson the illusion of Tithonus is the essence of his own epiphanic art: memory, evoking what is no longer available, what has somehow died or become deadly, recreates and transfigures it in vision. The feeling of being threatened or encompassed by deadliness is inseparable from, is a spur to, an awful epiphany. Tithonus' disillusioned regret and the frustrated idealism of Rosalind's lover are alike unwilling homages to something (spatially and psychologically) higher. These would-be lovers' desires seem doomed; their inaccessible love-objects appear distant and emotionally death-dealing. Yet these same fatal beloveds are wheeling or wheel-borne skyey fireflowers, daunting apparitions of supernal power and grace. *Maud*, Tennyson's most ambitious testament of frustrated constancy to an ideal object, makes the idolized maiden Maud into a dawn-rose as heaven-encompassing as *In Memoriam*'s God: "Rosy is the West, / Rosy is the South, / Roses are her cheeks, / And a rose her mouth" (ll. 595–98). Her lover "bow'd to her on the moor," "Queen Maud in all her splendour" (ll. 749, 836). She was a "dawn of Eden," but "The fires of hell brake out of the rising sun, / The fires of hell and hate" (ll. 8–10). For Maud is as unattainable as Rosalind or Eos. Were she to visit the lover's imagined grave, his very dust (he feels sure), harboring no grudge, would faithfully imitate her dawn-rose nature and "blossom in purple and red" (l. 921).[10] Looking out at the city as he wastes the night in sighs, the lover hears "the roaring of the wheels," and when he imagines his wished-for grave, he seems to hear those same "wheels go over my head" (ll. 162, 242). The epiphanic Tennysonian wheels, as always, betoken transcendence, but the frustration of its inaccessibility to the fire-fevered, maddened lover has turned transcendence to a mocking nightmare.

Seeking to escape (by whatever means) from the nightmarish awareness that his beloved is, in society's eyes, unalterably above him in economic rank and stature (a superiority symbolized by the wheels that relentlessly roar "over my head"), Maud's lover finds he has real and active ways of dying into the aweful rose of dawn. He will fight in the Crimean War, where alongside the "deathful-grinning mouths of the fortress, *flames* / The *blood-red blossom* of war with a *heart of fire*. / Let it flame [as a fire] or fade [as a flower], and the war *roll* down like a wind [or a wheel], / We have proved we have hearts in a cause, we are noble still" (ll. 52–55, emphases added). The war, as it rolls on, adds a final wheel-like motion to the apocalyptic scene, with its blood-red fire-blooms recalling (even as they grimly parody) the glowing thoughts that break out as roses in *In Memoriam*. The investment of so much vitally Tennysonian epiphanic energy in this monologue of fiery love-hate makes it hard to separate the poet from his delirious, powerfully imaginative persona.

In "The Poet" Tennyson allows us to see the maternal, larger-than-life anima, here called "Freedom," as the poet's guarantor and aide, but even in this seemingly idealizing presentation, the supernal power of the utterly transcendent female is embodied in an epiphanic imagery that conveys alarm. The poet himself has arrowy thoughts "wing'd with flame"; each seed of his wit sprouts "A flower all gold" (ll. 12, 24). His flourishing example is so widely followed that "the world / Like *one great garden* show'd, / And thro' the wreaths of floating dark upcurl'd, / *Rare sunrise flow'd*" (ll. 34–36, emphases added). So even by himself the Poet blends a giant multiple flower with a vision of dawn, blooms with flames. To complete the elemental epiphany pattern, the redoubtable female personification of Freedom adds the indispensable circles, spheres, rounding fires: "round about the circles of the globes / Of her keen eyes / And in her raiment's hem was traced in flame / WISDOM" (ll. 43–46). The poem's final grand wheeling motion is Freedom's apocalyptic, wrathful whirling of the poet's wound-up scroll: "No sword / Of wrath her right arm whirl'd, / But one poor poet's scroll, and with *his* word / She shook the world" (ll. 53–56).

This aweful "Freedom" may well make one cower; "Freedom is mine," the powerful lady seems to say. Rather than make her the poet's towering (and terrifying) collaborator or partner, it is perhaps psychologically safer for Tennyson to present the supernal queen of the dawn-rose as the ever-ideal but inaccessible asymptote of a never-ending visionary progress, and that is what he does in "The Voyage." If, in "The Poet," the transcendent female threatens to displace the mere Poet with her apocalyptically world-shaking power, in "The Voyage" she is kept at a safe distance by being imaginatively equated with the unreachable orb of the sun itself. Hence, in "The Voyage": "We seemed to sail into the sun!" "Again we dashed into the dawn!" "For one fair Vision ever fled." "But each man murmured, 'O My Queen, / I follow till I make thee mine' " (ll. 16, 24, 57, 63–64). That will never happen, of course, since the Queen of the Dawn is unpossessible; but the hope of reaching her is a motive for the mariners to continue their perpetual wheeling motion, their endless rounding of the globe. Quixotic, perhaps, these mariners will at least not suffer disillusion in their ceaseless circlings: they can *seem* to dash into the dawn or sail into the sun without ever really having to die into the sky-fire.

(One may note in passing that the monologue "Ulysses" is like a more complicated version of "The Voyage," for Ulysses pictures "all experience" as "an arch wherethrough / Gleams that untraveled world, whose margin fades / Forever and forever when I move" (ll. 19–21). But the "arch" does not qualify as a Tennysonian epiphanic wheel, nor does the aweful dawn-rose make an appearance to Ulysses. To account for the poem's indisputable power it seems that we need to study the poet's assimilative transformation of epiphanic materials from other visionary sources—not just the oft-cited Ulysses episode in *Purgatorio* but also Byron's example and stimulus in his poem, "The Dream.")[11]

Aside from the moments when Tennyson imagines himself rejoined to the spirit of Hallam, epiphanies of fulfilled love are rare in the poet's work: when Tennyson tries to imagine such moments of complete fulfillment in love, the phenomenological pattern of elemental imagery is usually incomplete, and more often it is fragmentary, or its component parts are scattered.[12] In "Love and Duty" the epiphany of dawn-fires and wheels is very beautiful, but the rose is absent—and indeed, the privileged instant, ironically, is merely the moment of saying adieu:

> The lights of sunset and of sunrise mix'd
> In that brief night, the summer night, that paused
> Among her stars to hear us, stars that hung
> Love-charm'd to listen; all the wheels of Time
> Spun in station, but the end had come.
>
> (ll. 70–74)

The incompleteness of the image pattern, the absence of the epiphanic flower amid all the recognizably epiphanic "wheels" and sky-fires, indicates something missing in the meaning of the experience: hope is lacking. One may think of the "*dark* summer dawns" we see in "Tears, Idle Tears," a poem of loss in which the last sunbeam reddens over a sail "that sinks with all we love *below the verge*" of the spherical world (ll. 11, 9, emphases added), below the *limen* or limit from which some transcendence might have been hoped for. These are liminal epiphanies of loss.

4

The fragmentation or dispersion of the elemental pattern becomes especially clear in the narratives or soliloquies of melancholy women: "The Lady of Shalott," "Mariana," "Mariana in the South," "Oenone," "The Death of Oenone," "Demeter and Persephone." In "The Lady of Shalott" the high-born lady's walls and towers "Overlook a space of flowers" (l. 16), but the flower-space is separated forever from the dawn-god or sun deity, the (however unwisely) apotheosized Sir Lancelot, whose "broad clear brow in sunlight glow'd," whose helmet and helmet-feather "Burn'd like one burning flame together" (ll. 100, 94). (There is no epiphanic wheel here, but in "Sir Launcelot and Queen Guinevere," a companion piece to this poem with the same rhymes and rhythms, there is a "sparhawk" that "wheel'd along" [l. 12].) Paying the price of having looked out the window to see Apollonian Lancelot, the Lady dies, as it were, into the dawn of her sun-idol. They are not truly united, however, for Lancelot sees the Lady but an instant as her boat carries her to Camelot, and his indifferent-seeming words darken the grim moment of their funereal encounter. Mariana's vision is even darker: she sees a "rounding gray" (l. 44), no sphere of fire. For her, the wheels of Being stop, though she still hears the "slow clock ticking" (l. 74). "The day" is "sloping toward his western bower" (l. 80), but for her there is no union of sun-fire and rose.

"Mariana in the South" and the two Oenone monologues, three more poems about melancholy women that similarly offer only negative and fragmentary epiphanies, are revelations of fiery despair. For Mariana the sun is a "steady glare," a "furnace of the light," "flaming downward" until night rises, through "silent spheres," into what were "rosy-bright" spaces, now darkened after pointless pain (ll. 52, 55, 77, 91, 89): the epiphanic "spheres" remain, but the sunny, rosy fire-flowers are long vanished. Oenone, ignored by bright Paris, whose "sunny hair / Clustered about his temples like a God's," declares that in her powerless frustration, "wheresoe'er I am by night and day, / All earth and air seem only burning fire" (ll. 58–59, 263–64): it is the *In Memoriam* vision of apocalyptic fiery light filling the sky from marge to marge, but here seen wholly as the hell of the unattainable, no love-flower but a furnace. "The Death of Oenone" adds the epiphanic wheel, "The ring of faces redden'd by the flames" enfolding the corpse of Paris (l. 92). "The morning light" of her formerly happy marriage breaks through Oenone's "clouded years of widowhood" (ll. 102–3), and she leaps upon Paris's funeral pyre in a desperate attempt to regain the dawn-epiphany of her lost happiness. Oenone's search for epiphanic power is desperate indeed.

"Demeter and Persephone," by contrast, seems designed as a less ironic vision of eventual joy, but by splitting the epiphany pattern into disjunct fragments Tennyson actually counteracts or imaginatively undermines his own good tidings of prophetic hope. Persephone, bride of the Underworld, foresees the time when even the "dark lord" Pluto will "accept and love the Sun, / And all the Shadow die into the Light" (ll. 135–36). When that wonderful time arrives, Demeter and her daughter will reap the autumn harvest together, will reap the greater harvest of humanity's love, and will "see no more" the "Wheel" of Ixion and "all the hateful fires / Of torment, and the shadowy warrior glide / Along the silent field of Asphodel" (ll. 145–51). To "die into the Light" suggests a wonderfully Tennysonian epiphanic prospect, but if the experience of merger with sunlight is strictly cut off from the other crucial visionary requisites—"Wheel," "fires," and "asphodel" or immortal flower—the epiphany seems as incomplete as the fulfillment of the prophecy is unlikely.

5

Idylls of the King offers four excellent Tennysonian epiphanies to conclude with, liminal visions of dawn-fires and whirlings evenly distributed among male and female personae: Elaine, Sir Bors, Guinevere, King Arthur. In the course of this progression from Elaine to Arthur, the epiphanies grow in phenomenological completeness, elaboration, and power. The range of emotions is wide: desperate abandon, devout determination, perplexed visionary wonder, and (in the case of Arthur) an emotion combining acceptance of the law of things, faith in continuity, and a sense of life rounding to its appropriate close. I think the allegorical heaviness some have felt at various points in the epic[13] is significantly mitigated by Tennyson's epiphanic even-handedness. The chief epiphanies of *Idylls* are evenly divided between women and men, and the members of each gender group are of contrasting types: the betrayed woman and the betraying one; the questing seeker and the dying one. All have access to epiphanic power.

Here is Elaine, the lily maid of Astolat, abandoned by Sir Lancelot, whom she had loved and trusted:

> All in a *fiery dawning* wild with wind
> That shook her tower, the brothers heard, and thought
> With shuddering, 'Hark the Phantom of the house
> That ever shrieks before a death,' and called
> The father, and all three in hurry and fear
> Ran to her, and lo! the *blood-red light of dawn*
> *Flared on her face*, she shrilling, 'Let me *die*!'
> ("Lancelot and Elaine," ll. 1015–19, emphases added)

The merger with the crimson dawn-light recalls Tithonus, or the epiphanies of *In Memoriam*; the mixture of blood and fire with the dawnlight makes us think of Oenone ("All earth and air seem merely burning fire"). The wish to die takes us back to the deathward-tending liminal states of mind presented in the paradigmatic "Vision of Sin" and its companion-piece, "The Palace of Art." As for the flower-component of the epiphany, Elaine is herself the lily maid; there is a dawn-fire, but no dawn-rose. For this is an epiphany of loss, of incompletion.

In strong contrast, an epiphany of most gratifying completeness, of encompassing warmth and grace, is presented in the stirring utterance of Sir Bors, seeking the Holy Grail. Mocked by Druids, who tell him he follows a mocking fire, Sir Bors replies:" . . . 'what other fire than he / Whereby the blood beats, and the blossom blows, / And the sea rolls, and all the world is warmed?' " ("The Holy Grail," ll. 667–69).

Syntactical parallels equate the blood, the blossom, the sea, the world. All four are equated with the divine fire of life. The blood's circulation mirrors the sea's rolling or wheeling motion. The blooming blossom and the warmed world in combination recall the feeling of maternal solace and comfort that Tithonus had sought. Fire and rose and circling movement blend with the maternal sea and the warmly beating blood, making this powerfully condensed epiphany more welcoming than aweful, far closer to Tennyson's personal life-long visionary ideal than is Sir Galahad's seemingly grander evocation of the Grail. We have here Tennyson's pattern of epiphanic imagery—the aweful dawn-rose and the wheel—seen in its most loved and longed-for brightness.

Our third *Idylls* epiphany is re-created by a garrulous novice who tells of prophecies attending Guinevere's arrival:

> "Yea, but I know: the land was full of signs
> And wonders ere the coming of the Queen.
> So said my father. . . .
> He saw them—headland after headland *flame*
> *Far on into the rich heart of the west:*
>
> . . . .
> Himself beheld three spirits *mad with joy*
> Come dashing down on a tall wayside *flower*,
> That shook beneath them, as the thistle shakes
> When three gray linnets wrangle for the seed:
> And still at evening on before his horse
> The *flickering* fairy-*cycle wheeled* and broke
> Flying, and linked again, and *wheeled* and broke
> Flying, for all the land was full of life.[14]
>
> . . . .
> Yea, one, a bard . . .
> Had chanted on the smoky mountain-tops,
> When *round him* bent the spirits of the hills
> With all their dewy hair *blown back like flame*. . . . "
>> ("Guinevere," ll. 230–31, 240–41, 250–57, 275,
>> 280–82, emphases added)

The headlands' flames mix with the rich flaming heart of the western sun. Three spirits filled with ardent energy ("mad with joy") repeatedly wheel and wheel over a flower. Another moving circle ("cycle") is composed of the dewy-haired but also flame-haired spirits (dew suggesting flowers and thus working well in epiphanic combination with the "flame" by varying the theme of the dawn-rose) surrounding the chanting bard. This is the awesome dawning of Guinevere as presented to prophetic vision, a fiery dawn-flower amid many wheels.

In a moment, the bard's voice falters, "And pale he turned, and reeled" (l. 302); he too is subject to the epiphanic circling motions— but sadly so, for he weakens, reeling, as he foresees the Queen's "evil work" with Lancelot (l. 305). A reeling is a kind of circling, but it is also a kind of faint, an exhaustion or loss of power, a hint at the final climactic epiphany of Arthur's death into the dawn.

This fourth and final Arthurian epiphany is indeed the closing of a circle, for the section that presents it is identical to the early poem "Morte d'Arthur," the germ or original seed of the whole *Idylls* project. Sir Bedivere, after refusing twice to fulfill the king's command to throw the sword Excalibur into the lake, is finally scared into compliance

> And strongly *wheeled* and threw it. The great brand
> Made lightnings in the splendour of the moon,
> And *flashing round and round*, and *whirled* in an *arch*,
> Shot like a streamer of the northern morn . . .
> So *flashed* and fell the brand Excalibur;
>> ("The Passing of Arthur," ll. 304–6, 310, emphases
>> added)

Sir Bedivere makes a wheeling motion with his body, and the "brand" (which interestingly can mean "fire" as well as "sword"—here the sword behaves like fire, for it flashes and makes "lightnings") also "whirl[s] in an arch." Tennyson notes: "The extra syllable gives the rush of the sword as it is whirled in parabolic curve" (*Poems* 3:556n). Reporting to Arthur, Sir Bedivere says of his sword, "Then with both hands I flung him, wheeling him" (l. 325).

Arthur is placed in the funeral barge, his face white like the moon "Smote by the fresh beam of the springing east" (l. 385), adding the dawn-theme to the many epiphanic flashing wheels. More than that: "the light and lustrous curls" of the monarch "made his forehead like a rising sun" (ll. 384–85). Dying at dawn, Arthur is himself the dawn—perhaps even (with lustrous curls bordering the central rising sun in petallike arrangement) the sunflower or blossom of dawn. Though "now the whole Round Table is dissolved / Which was an image of the mighty world" (ll. 402–3), the parabola, the arch, the wheel of a completed rounding—these replace the circle that is broken. We last see Arthur's barge as "one black dot against the verge of dawn, / And on the mere the wailing die[s] away" (ll. 439–40). The vision, like Arthur himself, dissolves, blends, dies into the dawn. At the verge, the marge, the final limit, it offers a fitting picture with which to conclude our study of Tennyson's great liminal epiphanies.

FIVE

Beauty and Pain in Pater

The Red-Yellow Fire Flower,

The Dying White Bird

The literary legacy created by our second fire-flower epiphanist, Walter Pater, offers moments of elemental death and illumination that are fully as abundant and resonant as those of Tennyson. Moreover, the heightened aesthetic awareness that Pater made it his lifelong mission to advocate and to exemplify makes the understanding of his own rich treasury of original epiphanies central to a comprehension of his achievement as creator-and-appreciator of literary art at its most intense, expansive, and mysterious. Neo-Bachelardian analysis promises rewards from at least three points of view, in addition to the phenomenological one. It offers insights relating to psychology, to cultural history, and to the study of literary influence.

Psychologically oriented critics will be interested in the epiphanic paradigm that Pater varies throughout his *oeuvre*, an epiphany that—like Tennyson's equally paradigmatic "Vision of Sin"—presents a scenario of overwhelming though enigmatic guilt. Students of cultural history who want a clearer perspective on Pater's dual role as discursive advocate of aestheticism and original creator of epiphanies will be struck by the contrast between the alleged durability of aesthetic awareness—presented as a "hard, gem-like flame" in Pater's polemical writing[1]—and the perishability of fire flowers as presented in Pater's own most intense moments of aesthetic euphoria in his creative work. And students of literary mentorship may be surprised by the strength of Coleridgean influence on Paterian epiphany. One can find no more striking instance of the thesis that animates this book—that phenomenological epiphany analysis is important for critics of all persuasions.

Study of Paterian epiphany has been usefully initiated, but not from a Bachelardian perspective. Findlay's short essay on Pater's fires is celebratory but studies only two brief passages and no fire flowers or birds, while Jay Fellows' Pater book, though described by J. Hillis Miller as in part Bachelardian, in fact does not show such a methodology at all.[2] A common problem is that writers on Paterian epiphany, instead of looking at recurrences of an image-structure—that is, at real epiphanies—have focused instead on passages that *assert* that an epiphany is occurring. For example, F. C. McGrath cites a passage from *Marius*: "In this peculiar and privileged hour, [Marius'] bodily frame . . . was yet determined by a far-reaching system of material forces external to it, a thousand combining currents from earth and sky." Marius then reflects on the need for a "passive surrender, as of a leaf on the wind, to the motions of the great stream of physical energy without" (3:68).[3] Yet moments like this one do not reveal Pater's peculiar genius as a maker of epiphanies; too discursive to be intense, they quickly dissolve a minimum of concrete imagery (derived without much revision from Coleridge's "The Eolian Harp") into a vagueness of speculation.

Such passages "tell," but they do not really "show." A similar excerpt cited by Jay B. Losey illustrates the same problem:

> In the close neighbourhood of the greater Alps . . . one might yield one's self to the unalterable imaginative appeal of the elements in their highest force and simplicity—light, air, water, earth. On very early spring days a mantle was suddenly lifted; the Alps were an apex of natural glory, towards which, in broadening spaces of light, the whole of Europe sloped upwards. (4:146)[4]

This is the beginning of an attempted epiphany, but it soon—too soon—yields to allegorical abstraction about the "intellectual rising of the fatherland" (4:147). Genuine Paterian epiphanies do not run out of power so quickly, and they have more power to begin with.

Pater's strong epiphanies present the red-yellow fire flower, the dying white bird. These epiphanies are autumnal—in their coloring, their somberness, their flaming glory. Daniel T. O'Hara says Paterian aestheticism may be seen "reformulating all the cultural forms of the past within the once radiant circle of the work of art, for the expression of a vacant smile, a splendid torpor, pervading one's own separate world."[5] But the glorious fiery fullness of Pater's autumn colors—the sultry reds and yellows of the burning flowers and the sharp, ironic wintry whites of Icarian dying birds—works strongly, in Paterian epiphanies, against any sleepiness or smugness, effectively dismissing both "vacancy" and "torpor."

Though I have called Pater our second fire-flower epiphanist, he is not at all well known for this image but is associated in most people's minds with a very different kind of flame, a hard and gemlike one, symbolic of the aesthetic awareness he urges his reader to cultivate. As eloquently as anyone who ever wrote, Walter Pater presents the case for an aesthetic religion, a religion of artistic awareness, of heightened, refined sensation. "A counted number of pulses only is given to us of a variegated, dramatic life," says Pater. Our days are numbered. "How may we see in them all that is to be seen in them by the finest senses?" We must seize the day, *see* the day, feel it. "How shall we pass most swiftly from point to point, and be present always at the focus where the greatest number of vital forces unite in the purest energy?" In his way of phrasing the question, Pater answers it. Vital force at peak intensity, passing with maximum rapidity from point to point—what is this but fire? In sum, "To burn always with this hard, gem-like flame, to maintain this ecstasy, is success in life" (1:236).

But in Pater's own epiphanies, as noted above, the flames with which aesthetic questers burn are rarely gemlike. Durability and hardness—these we do not find in Pater's images of artists. Pater himself is a great artist: a masterly short story writer, a major novelist, an evocative historian of art who proceeds from the contemplation of poems and paintings to his own psychological portraiture of the sensibilities, the spirits, from which these works originated. Like Apuleius' story of Cupid and Psyche, which he calls a "gem" (2:61), Pater's works of literary art are lapidary marvels, jewellike in their precise and polished style. Yet the subjects of these real or imaginary life histories are usually artists whose sensibilities are not hard, not durable, but vulnerable and peculiarly imperiled—men whose joys are painful, whose intense but melancholy lives are brief. At once a martyr and a criminal, the characteristic Paterian artist is twice punished: through suffering and through guilt. His ecstasy requires his early death.[6]

These necessities are implied and embodied in Pater's recurrent elemental images of epiphany: the red-yellow fire flower, the dying white bird. Paterian fire is not Heraclitean fire. It is not a cosmic Logos, a divine principle of balance, of the conservation of energy, an ever-living universal flame, "kindled in measure and quenched in measure,"[7] rising up in one place the moment it is extinguished in another. Paterian fires do not last. They perish; they die into earth, into "mould" (a favorite word), into ashes. Pater's flowers, like his fires, are red and yellow; like his fires, they die into earth.

In Pater's epiphanies, then, we see none of Tennyson's sky-fires, his aweful roses of dawn: a Paterian lover of beauty, unlike a Tennysonian lover of God, or of man or woman, does not die into the dawn. However ardently Pater's fires may seek to rise into upper air, their unsought destination, or destiny, is always earth. Paterian poets with flower names—Florian, Jasmin, Hyacinthus, Rosenmold—predictably perish after a brief season, but even a more seemingly gemlike hero, Emerald Uthwart, shares this same doom of early death. There are no Tennysonian cosmic rolling or wheeling motions, no intimations of immortal, ruddy radiance on high, no liminal expectations. The fire flower falls.

Embodiments of the airy element, the abode of spirit, are no luckier. Like Noah's dove or the iconographic Holy Ghost, the white bird in Pater is a sign of hope, of aspiration toward a higher realm. But white birds die when the Paterian fire flowers are plucked; the occasional link between flowers and fruits in Pater's portraits works to strengthen the typology of Edenic temptings. With initiation into the suspect realm of aesthetic knowledge, of unsanctioned intensities of awareness, something in the spirit dies: innocence perishes, hope is deceived. What is more, the bird's death is usually linked to the death of a child; one feels that the bird is somehow coessential with the ill-starred child, with innocence doomed. But since the bird-deaths and child-deaths are associated with the red-yellow fire flowers, with maturation into aesthetic knowledge, the child himself (always a boy-child) often becomes a bird-killer, a murderer of his own innocence of spirit. He is both criminal and victim. The nature of the "crime," so to speak, is never spelled out, so the guilt is obscure. But it is so oppressive that expiation is usually required through sacrificial death.

Influences are important to the student of epiphany, and I would urge the likelihood of a mentor for Pater's characteristic epiphanies.

That probable mentor is Coleridge. Surely some of the imagery we have noted so far in Pater's imaginative world might seem even more Coleridgean than Coleridge himself. Pater's motif of guilt related to a bird's death—which is also a murder—will remind us of "The Rime of the Ancient Mariner." We know, however, that Coleridge only introduced the albatross's death into his poem at Wordsworth's suggestion;[8] it was not basic to the poet's obsessively recurrent patterns of poetic epiphany. For Pater, by contrast, the bird motif is crucial. Moreover, as used by Pater the theme of bird-death/human-death is greatly modified and expanded: red-yellow fire flowers have become part of the Paterian story along with guilt-inducing bird-deaths, and a wholly new commentary dealing with aesthetic initiation has replaced the Coleridgean scholia to "Mariner."

But the two men's deep kinship is worth noting and worth remembering. It is no accident that Pater attributes to Coleridge the "rich delicate dreaminess" and the "languidly soothing grace or cadence" so typical of his own writing (5:83). He links Coleridge with Paterian epiphanic flowers: "Coleridge is a true flower of the *ennuyé*, of the type of René" (5:104). As if wishing to repress or stifle awareness of his own possible subliminal conspiratorial alliance with Coleridgean mariners, Pater strikingly omits from his famous essay on Coleridge any quoted passage dealing with bird killing. Instead, he gives us birds of hope, like the implicit bird image he finds in these Coleridge lines:

> My cousin Suffolk,
> My soul shall thine keep company to heaven:
> Tarry, sweet soul, for mine, then fly abreast

—and in these:

> Amid the howl of more than wintry storms,
> The halcyon hears the voice of vernal hours
> Already on the wing.
>
> (5:88–89)

A bird of hope will appear for a moment in nearly all of Pater's visions, too. But the hope will be disabused, the innocent deflowered, the spirit grounded, the child interred.

As a final note on Pater's uses of Coleridge, we may derive grim amusement from one instance where Pater treats a Coleridgean source with cuttingly sardonic wit. In "Emerald Uthwart" Pater tragically parodies his own notion of the aesthetic perceiver as *gem*like fire; belying the gemlike nature of his name, Emerald is seen as "painfully recoiling from contact" with whatever seems "hard . . . and bright and cold" (8:203–4). Cruelly ironic Coleridgean echoes arise when we consider the early death and untimely burial of Emerald Uthwart in the context of phrasings from "Kubla Khan": "But oh! that deep romantic chasm which slanted / Down the *green* [= Emerald] hill, *athwart* [= Uthwart] a cedarn cover!" ("Kubla Khan," ll. 12–13). Pater continues his gloomy parody: instead of a green smaragdine gem, this cheerless tale offers a view of "green corpses," of "gan*gren*ed places, or the grass which soon covers them" (8:232, emphases added).

In "The Child in the House," paradigm tale for "Imaginary Portraits" and indeed for all Pater's masterworks of imaginary portraiture, the protagonist experiences two fire-flower epiphanies, two child-death epiphanies, and two imperiled-bird epiphanies (the last of these filled with the rhetoric of death, criminality, martyrdom, guilt). The entire story (really a long prose poem) is an extraordinarily rich composite epiphany, psychoanalytically the most fascinating work of Pater's. The persuasive verbal artifice makes the story feel like a waking dream of hallucinatory vibrancy—and it is indeed a literal "dream" of a remembered childhood home that motivates the adult protagonist to recreate in memory his early spiritual and poetic history (8:172). Explicitly based on and motivated by a "dream," Pater's "The Child in the House" is the central paradigm of his many varied epiphanies, the Paterian analogue to Tennyson's "The Vision of Sin" as Bachelardian phenomenological key to a recurrent elemental pattern.

In the first section of this chapter we will analyze "The Child in the House" as Pater's central composite paradigmatic epiphany of reds and yellows, fire flowers, and aggrieved or death-threatened white child-birds. Then, in sections 2, 3, and 4 we will use the phenomenological pattern manifested by "The Child in the House" to clarify its less explicit manifestations in other major works: first, in three of Pater's "imaginary portraits" or visionary short stories; next, in his celebrated novel *Marius the Epicurean*; and finally, in the unfinished but brilliant *Gaston de Latour*.

Pater's prose epiphanies suggest a question of definition that needs to be noted before we begin to analyze them. I have spoken of the Paterian paradigm, "The Child in the House," as a composite epiphany. This compact short story contains two visions of afflicted or dying birds, two of fire flowers, two of child deaths. The whole story is intense, hallucinatory, electrically charged, so I would rather call it a "composite epiphany" than a setting for several short ones. The label is not indispensable, but it is convenient: it makes the concept of "epiphany" more flexible. This flexibility fits Pater's "Child in the House," for his entire multifaceted epiphanic paradigm is intense, expansive, and mysterious.

1

As we might well expect after experiences of various writers' paradigmatic epiphanies, Pater's composite "Child in the House" epiphany begins with a "dream." Like "The Pilgrim's Dream" of Wordsworth, it is the dream of a wanderer—or at least of a walker—and, like "The Pilgrim's Dream," it has the mood of a legend. Walking "one hot afternoon," Florian Deleal overtakes "by the wayside a poor aged man" and "help[s] him on with the burden" he is carrying. In conversation the man names a manor house, which happens to be the one where Florian grew up, and "That night, like a reward for his pity, a dream of that place came to Florian, a dream which did for him the office of the finer sort of memory." As it turns out, "the accident of that dream" is "just the thing he needed" to help him in "noting . . . some things in the story of his spirit." Filled with the spirit of his dream, Florian can recreate in his memory all those crucial early childhood events that centered on his life within the "half-spiritualised house"—"the house and garden of his dream"—now freshly re-arisen in his imaginative memory (8:172–73).

The prototypical Paterian "child," *Florian Deleal*, whose name echoes the sound pattern of *fleur-de-ly*s (a white or golden flower), grows up in an appropriately aristocratic and elegant rural, courtly manor conformable to his own lineal descent from the artist Watteau. Reds, yellows, and whites (a suitable color scheme—the red and yellow of Paterian fire flowers, the white of Paterian birds) suffuse the setting for Florian's first epiphany: "those whites and reds" seen "through the smoke on very homely buildings" and "the gold of the dandelions at the road-side"; the "crimson lights" falling from the fog upon the chimneys and "the whites" glinting through openings in that fog upon tower or walk; "Golden-rod, and brown-and-golden Wall-flower" (8:175–76).

The first imperiled bird that deeply imprints on Florian's awareness forever the inseparability of "beauty and pain" (8:181) is a starling presented to him as a pet. But the newly caged-in mother bird and her abandoned nestlings (left outside near the manor) carry on such a plaintive and pain-wracked dialogue of deprivation throughout the night that even after he has opened the little prison to set the mother free, Florian still feels "remorse" for his part in the general conspiracy of things to generate grief, to "play pain-fugues on the delicate nerve-work of living creatures" (8:184). Pain is shared by bird and child in Florian's moving epiphany of *lacrimae rerum*.

The boy's first vivid fire-flower epiphany generates no explicit re-morse, yet it conveys an equally burdensome sense of imprisonment and regret. Florian sees *"a great red hawthorn in full flower*, embossing heavily the bleached [white here added to the fire-flower color scheme] and twisted trunk and branches, so aged that there were but few green leaves thereon—a plumage [bird theme] of tender, *crimson fire out of the heart of the dry wood"* (8:185, emphases added). Florian both enjoys and pays for this fiery aesthetic moment later, at night, as he dreams of entrancing but deeply disturbing fire-red flowers: "in dreams all night he loitered along a magic roadway of crimson flow-ers, which seemed to open ruddily in thick, fresh masses about his feet," indicating to Florian "a passionateness in his relation to fair out-ward objects, an inexplicable excitement in their presence, which dis-turbed him, and from which he half longed to be free," as indeed the mother bird, echoed by her nestlings, had painfully pleaded for liberty. "A touch of regret or desire mingled all night with the remem-bered presence of the red flowers," and "the longing for some undi-vined, entire possession of them" initiated a yearly increasing aware-ness, for Florian, of "a kind of tyranny of the senses over him" (8:185–86). Beauty and pain, pleasure and tyranny, are revealed in Florian's fiery flower dream of thick, fresh masses of crimson: the paradigmatic, unforgettable dream-intensity of the color insures that, in waking hours as well, "summer by summer," the "blossom of the red hawthorn" will always seem to Florian "absolutely the reddest of all things" (8:185), for better and for worse.

Fire-flower tyranny becomes far worse the moment Florian realizes, during his next epiphany, how intricately floral beauty and floral mortality are respectively joined, in his imagination, with children's loveliness and children's deaths. It is a "trick" that his "pity" plays on him, a troublesome epiphany of flower- and child-deaths, of intense yellows allying, in the Paterian yellow-red elemental color scheme, the amber skin and yellow hair of the flowerlike children to the intense crimson of the flowering hawthorn: "He would think of Julian, fallen into incurable sickness, as spoiled in the sweet *blossom* of his skin like pale *amber*, and his *honey*-like hair; of Cecil, early dead, as cut off from the *lilies*, from *golden* summer days," "of the turning of the child's flesh to [red-blue] *violets* in the turf above him" (8:187, emphases added). The "flame" in the hawthorn's "perishing petals" was "absolutely the reddest of all things" (8:185); the beauty of the dying child is linked with amber, honey, gold: the fiery red-yellow color scheme joins the earth-doomed mortal beings, flower and child. Child-beauty, like flower-beauty, is as intense as fire, and dies as soon. We may yearn for entire possession of flower-beauty, but it possesses us entire: *dying as the fire, we become the fiery flower.*

Florian's next red-yellow fire-flower trial (the word "trial" expresses the double implication of testing limits and of obscurely sensed judgment) is the richest in implications for an understanding of Florian/Pater as epiphanic artist. It is an epiphany not merely of intense perception but of creativity as well—a *fire-flower epiphany of artistic creation.* It begins with a variant of the temptation theme involving fruit rather than flowers: as Florian strolls along a *"red* gravel walk" looking for a "basket of *yellow* crab-apples," a "wasp on one bitten apple stung him, and he felt the passion of sudden, severe pain." The reflections on sensation to which this intense perception gives rise lead to the artist-episode: when an "older boy taught him to make *flowers* of sealing-wax," Florian remembers, he had "*burnt his hand badly at the lighted taper*, and been unable to sleep. He remembered that also afterwards, as a sort of typical thing—a white vision of heat about him, clinging closely" through the scent of the salve that had been applied (8:188–89, emphases added). (The "white vision" makes us anticipate an imperiled bird—but that will come later.) Now Florian has learned not only that aesthetic perception, fruit of a painful passion (or passion of a painful fruit), produces long-remembered hurt, but that aesthetic creation, the producing of one's own *burning flowers*, is even more dangerous (as fire is worse than wasps). Florian/Pater: maker of burning flowers.

The wax from which Florian made his flowers is itself an emblem of the impressionable Paterian fire-artist, as of his art: wax acquires its form from fire (painfully intense sensation), and fire consumes it (Paterian artists usually die young). Indeed, Florian's next epiphany begins when Pater tells us of the boy's fascination with the "waxen, resistless faces" that he sees on visits to the Paris morgue and to a Munich cemetery (8:190). The epiphany focuses on a memory of "an open grave for a child," the "black mould lying heaped up round it, weighing down the little jewelled branches of the dwarf rose-bushes in flower" (8:190–91), sad versions of the gemlike flame the artist wants to be. We see "waxen" faces powerless to resist the fire that would melt them away, gemmy roses weighted down by "mould."

The story's final epiphany completes its elegantly framed ABCBCA structure of epiphanies:

A) afflicted bird (pet bird suffering in cage)
B) fire flower (hawthorn of flaming redness)
C) child-death (Florian's young friends Julian and Cecil)
B) fire flower (of burning wax, made by Florian)
C) child-death (with open grave surrounded by dwarf roses)
A) dying bird (in the episode we are to look at now).

Florian is about to leave the house with his mother and his (recently sick) brother Lewis. On the morning of departure, "all things . . . seemed to have a white, pearl-like lustre in them." But this white pearliness, like the jeweled rose-branches around the child's open grave that Florian remembered, is a kind of tragic parody: innocence proves to have no gemlike permanence or durability but instead seems doomed to die. The tale's concluding sad epiphany must be quoted in full:

They had started and gone a little way when a *pet bird* was found to have been left behind, and must even now—so it presented it-

self to [Florian]—have already all the *appealing fierceness and wild
self-pity* at heart of one left by others to perish of hunger in a
closed house; and he returned to fetch it, himself in hardly less
stormy distress. But as he passed in search of it from room to
room, *lying so pale, with a look of meekness* in their *denudation*, and
at last through that *little, stripped white* room, the aspect of the
place touched him like *the face of one dead*; and a clinging back
towards it came over him, so intense that he knew it would last
long, and spoiling all his pleasure in the realisation of a thing so
eagerly anticipated. And so, with the bird found, but himself in
an *agony* of home-sickness thus capriciously sprung up within
him, he was driven quickly away, far into the rural distance, so
fondly speculated on, of that favourite country-road. (8:195–96,
emphases added)

This rhetoric plays a trick on our perceptions: as we read, it is hard
to avoid visualizing a *dead or dying bird*, accompanied by the more
startling image of a dead or victimized child. We hear the frantic ap-
peals of the victim (but *what* victim?) subliminally conveyed in the
phrase "appealing fierceness." (A hint of sadism[9] is conveyed too; one
would have expected "fierce appeal," not "appealing fierceness," for
the latter phrase suggests that the victim is somehow attractive in
being victimized.) We empathize with the victim's "self-pity." We see
something "lying pale," with a "look of meekness" in "denudation,"
something "little, stripped," and "white," with the "face of one dead."
It is hard, after such an experience, to keep in mind the fact that no
one has been killed; no one has been stripped naked; there are no
denuded or desecrated corpses to be seen. Florian and the bird are
both alive and more or less well, so far as the facts of the story's plot
are concerned. But Florian is in mental "agony," a misery caused by
his earlier imaginings of the abandoned bird. And we have shared
Florian's vision: a nightmare of vague but horrible metaphor, conveying a sense of unholy offenses against helpless innocence. Most of the
horror-inducing adjectives in fact describe neither Florian nor the
bird, but merely the rooms of a house. But they nevertheless convey
the sense of a violation or a death.

So Florian's, and Pater's, "agony" amounts to more than homesick-
ness if we believe the tale more than the teller, the epiphanic imagery

more than the facts of the plot. Florian is innocent, yet in some obscure way deeply guilty. Like the bird, Florian has been a sufferer throughout the story. Like other children, he has been a flowerlike victim of life's violence, its passionate fires. But in Pater's world flowers *are* fires, and the bird is also the bird's killer: Florian feels the bird's "self-pity" and "stormy distress," yet it is Florian who has abandoned the bird to the scene of victimization that he now guiltily fills with imagined metaphors of denudation and death. We are all guilty. The artist is he who feels it most. And the dreadful guilt is obscurely sexual. Like Tennyson's paradigmatic "Vision of Sin," Pater's epiphanic paradigm, "The Child in the House," is a haunting—and haunted—aesthetic "vision of sin."

Each of Pater's elemental motifs (fire, flower, bird) implies all the others; they are richly interwoven. We may take one final miniature epiphany as our last example from this paradigmatic story. Florian's first pet was a "white angora" cat with a "face like a flower." Afflicted by fatal illness, the cat "became quite delicately human in its valetudinarianism, and it came to have a hundred different expressions of voice," until finally "its little soul flickered away" (8:183–84). The familiar themes combine. Cats are bird *killers*. But Florian's cat also has the whiteness of the metaphoric *victim* in the story's concluding *bird*-passage. This distinctively gifted cat is like the Paterian artist of refined sensations in its hundred delicate vocal expressions. Its *face is a flower*, and its *departing spirit flickers like a fire*. Florian, saddened, asks for another pet to *replace the cat*. He gets a caged *bird*—and guilt, and the obscurely sexual remorse that goes with it (recall that the wish to liberate the bird from the tyranny of the cage was like Florian's equally powerful desire to free himself from the burden of longing for some barely understood "entire possession" of the fiery hawthorn blossoms). Every image is overdetermined with the symbolic implications of all the others in the cluster. *Birds are flowers are fires are pain.*

2

Among the remaining seven of the eight "Imaginary Portraits" or visionary short stories, "Apollo in Picardy" and "Sebastian van Storck" that most fully embody the "Child in the House" epiphanic paradigm of red-yellow fire flowers and dying white birds and of evident victims who are obscurely killers as well, or vice versa. "Apollo" gives us two clearly delineated epiphanies, and in "Sebastian" we find another sharply outlined epiphanic moment. In the remaining tales, the epiphanic fragments are scattered. But "Duke Carl of Rosenmold" will claim our attention as offering at least a fire-flower epiphany (though a birdless one) of considerable persuasiveness and power.

Of the two epiphanies offered by "Apollo in Picardy" the first is a revelation of fires, flowers, and birds; the second deals with birds alone. Apollyon is Pater's most Coleridgean creation, an Ancient Mariner in medieval guise, foredoomed to kill birds and humans and to suffer unabsolved; yet, to conform to Pater's own epiphanic requirements, this radiant and baleful being, the aerial killer of birds, must be equally a fire, and linked with flowers. Called "Brother Apollyon" by his fellow monks (who cannot rightly make out his mumbled foreign name), the spellbinding harpist is Pater's presentation of the reincarnate sun god, Apollo *redivivus*: under his epiphanic heliacal influence, Prior Jean experiences a revelation whose overwhelming power threatens to produce insanity. The prior feels "flashes of the eternal and unorbed light," but these heavenly "lightning flashes" are "flashes of blindness," which induce a mad delirium. The reverend prior finds himself drawing grotesque illuminations in his manuscript: "winged flowers, or stars with human limbs and faces" (8:164–65)—the phrasing artfully conveys a combined Paterian epiphany of bird-wings, flowers, and star-fire. Apollyon's more-than-earthly sunlight is worse than ominous, it is deadly: the prior feels as if he "lay faint and drowning in it" (8:164). Brother Apollyon seems to bring to the monastery heat-filled, blazing "flowers from a summer more radiant far than that of France"; they make the half-crazed prior feel "that he had never really seen flowers before" (8:161). Apollyon himself is a sort of embodied fiery star, an incarnate sun, and the winged or birdlike flowers he reveals to the half-delirious prior indicate the role of this force of fire and flowers as related with equal intimacy to the fate of birds.

Indeed, after this insanity-inducing, delirious epiphany of birds, flowers, and heliacal star-fire, we are also given a threefold epiphany of Apollyon as simultaneously birdlike, bird-beloved, and fatal to birds. Apollyon has the whiteness associated with Pater's epiphanic birds—"rich, warm, white limbs" (8:149)—and he is both a bird hunter and paradoxically the beloved of birds: they flee to him "caressingly" after he wounds them (8:157) when he takes the boy Hyacinth hunting with him. More, this bird-loved bird-killer, a "man or demon" (8:158) rumored to have committed murder, seems somehow responsible for an unprecedented bird massacre that befalls the monastic pigeon-house. Yet one can see Apollyon's own "silver harp surely, lying broken likewise on the sanded floor, soaking in the pale milky blood and torn plumage" (8:160).

This is the most intense, most tragic aspect of the bird-epiphany of Apollyon, for the sun god himself is now revealed as the birdlike, childlike ("milky") victim of an uncontrollable fatality irremovable from his own nature. When he enjoys nude sports with *flower*-named Hyacinthus, Apollyon—tragically—has no way of predicting that his *fiery* discus (a sun shape of more than gemlike hardness) will slice through his fellow athlete's skull. Mariner-like, Apollyon finds that his bird killings are necessarily followed by murder. But perhaps he obscurely foresaw this on an unconscious level, for after the dovecote fatalities he had "seemed to desire absolution from some guilt of blood heavier than the slaughter of beast or bird" (8:160; cf. "He prayeth best, who loveth best / Both man and bird and beast"). We have here an exemplary Paterian epiphany: when *blinding fire and overwhelmingly lovely flowers* appear on earth in an embodied epiphany of superhuman brightness and peril, the consequent deaths are shared alike *by birds and by flowerlike young men*. There are no victors: milky blood soils the harp strings of the remorseful, white-skinned, starry, aerial killer.

"Sebastian van Storck" offers a splendid epiphany of bird, fire, and flower; indeed, Sebastian himself is both bird and *pater* (the stork that brings babies), and like Apollyon he is both life force and death dealer. In vivid contrast to fire-flower Apollyon, Sebastian is repelled by anything red or yellow, but—in a bizarre variation on the Paterian epiphanic theme—this very repulsion, the fear of an intimate contact with yellow-and-ruddy passion rather than the actuality of such a contact, leads to the usual fatal consequences of Paterian epiphany. A red and yellow revelation of fire, flower, and bird—an epiphany delightful to the reader but baleful to Sebastian—is an elemental illumination for us, an elemental death for van Storck's female admirer.

The summer that gleams "russet and yellow" for such cheerful souls as the painter Albert Cuyp ominously seems "wellnigh to suffocate

Sebastian van Storck" (4:81–82). For when the sun falls "red on the old trees of the avenue" and seems to be engaged in a combat of colors with the yellow "candle-light" (more fiery reds and yellows), a certain Mademoiselle van Westrheene arrives, "ruddy and fresh in her white satin, trimmed with glossy crimson swans-down" (4:90–92). This combined epiphany of yellow, white, and red, this apparition of passion enclosed in birdlike purity (indeed, she basically comes to court Sebastian, but it is all very proper) holds no charms for van Storck but exercises nonetheless a predictable, baleful power.

What may be "Centre of heat and light" for others repels Sebastian, for what he wants is nothing red-colored, neither the "ruddy beauty" of the young lady nor the "ruddy colouring of the . . . house these people lived in," but rather a birdlike blankness with no fiery crimson in it, a "white, unruffled consciousness" (4:108, 101, 109), a sense of oneness with a vaguely Spinozistic deity who is loved but loves not. When van Storck writes Mademoiselle van Westrheene that he will not consider marriage, she dies in despair: "the cruel letter had killed her" (4:103). Evidently her ruddy health was intimidating; Sebastian's weak manuscript verses are described as "barely potential gold" (4:99)—and if the gold here is anything like the kind that Jupiter expended on Danaë, Sebastian may well have felt that it, or he, was no manly match for the challenge of his potential partner's healthy physical ruddiness. The meeting of his "barely potential" *gold* and her vital, fully actual *ruddy* beauty could result in Sebastian's mortal loss of self-esteem. So he unintentionally kills the metaphoric bird, the girl in the swansdown-trimmed white dress: his "cruel letter had killed her."

The red-yellow-white epiphany of Mademoiselle van Westrheene is the only clearly outlined, fully developed epiphany in "Sebastian van Storck." The remaining imaginary portraits in Pater's story-series embody the Paterian phenomenological pattern less completely. But "Duke Carl of Rosenmold," though it lacks birds, offers one fine epiphany of fires and flowers, reds and yellows, in a tale of aesthetic delight and criminal guilt and expiatory sacrifice and untimely death.

The few paragraphs in which Pater portrays the young Carl constitute an effective if slightly diffuse epiphany of flowers and fires, of wax and light, of yellow and red. Glorious-fateful reds and yellows abound in Carl's appearance, his character, his *Bildung*. Carl is "sanguine, floridly handsome" ("sanguine" of course is etymologically related to blood, while "florid" means "ruddy"); he soothes the irascible temper of the old Duke "like the quiet physical warmth of a [red] fire or the [yellow] sun" (4:125). Newly discovered verses by the old poet Conrad Celtes bring "a beam of effectual daylight to a whole magazine of observation, fancy, desire" (4:124) in young Carl, an ominous metaphor of aesthetic initiation as a fiery explosion in a gunpowder storeroom. Carl presides in a theater "lined with pale yellow satin" and boasting a portrait of Apollo in "red and blue"; the "innumerable wax lights" bring in the wax theme from "Child in the House," the theme of perishable and painful art-awareness (4:125). Carl loves "the carnation and yellow of roses or tulips" in the paintings of Rubens; the young Duke invites all to share the aesthetic "honey" in the "florid" treasures about him (4:127, 129). With Carl, we revel in the reds and yellows, wax-fires and flowers, of life-as-art.

But Carl also plays with death, as he plays with aesthetic fire; indeed, in Pater's epiphanic language the two kinds of play are inseparable and imply each other. So, unsurprisingly, Carl's double offense against morality—(1) his inconsiderate prank of pretending to be dead so he can enjoy the aesthetic pleasures of his own funeral, and (2) the elaborate, aesthetically enjoyable, but irresponsible fantasy-test he imposes on his lady love—result in Carl's death as well as that of poor, innocent Gretchen. Duke Carl of Rosenmold's flower of youth, his "rose," is destined early for the "mold," the rich, black soil, for it is inseparable from the flourishing or flowering of an aesthetic temperament, always a combustible hazard—a ruddy and seemingly cheerful fire, but a powder magazine as well.

3

Marius the Epicurean, the *Bildungsroman* or novel-length imaginary portrait of a pre-Paterian aesthete in ancient Rome, offers vivid and fully-developed Paterian epiphanies that, like the "spots of time" in Wordsworth's *Prelude*, are the true subject and focus of the fundamentally autobiographical work. Part 1 (Marius' boyhood and youth) culminates with the epiphany accompanying the death of Marius' best friend and mentor, Flavian. Part 2 (Marius as a young man) builds up to two epiphanies, related to the public speech of Emperor Marcus Aurelius and to the gladiatorial show whose sadistic barbarity the wise ruler oddly ignores. Part 3, a ruminative transition, is the shortest of the book's four sections, with only five chapters (the first two parts have seven each, and the last has nine). This short section contains no epiphany properly speaking, though in the tawdry funeral of the emperor's cynical brother we may see a brief parody of such a privileged moment. Part 4, by contrast, is a fourfold triumph, beginning with two epiphanic episodes and ending with two more. Each of these pairs of revelatory prose-poems contains one pagan epiphany and one that is Christian. Pater's imagination, like that of Marius, declines to choose among religions or myths—or rather, it has always already chosen, or been chosen. The recurrent epiphanic pattern alone—the red-yellow fire flower, the dying white bird—is essential and necessary; all cultural context is contingent. In other words, Pater is a strong epiphanist, and when in touch with the source of his obsessive epiphanic imagery he will succeed brilliantly, whatever theological construction he puts upon that source.

Brought up in a manor house of "red and yellow marble" featuring a "white pigeon-house" (an introductory color scheme that certainly prepares us for the Paterian epiphanies shortly to ensue), Marius nevertheless learns from his mother, who dismantles all his bird traps, that his own soul is like a bird and requires freedom (2:18, 20, 22). Marius' schoolfriend Flavian (a name that recalls "Florian" in "The Child in the House") reveals to him the refined delights of Apuleius' tale of Cupid and Psyche, the story of a winged, birdlike god-youth and an enamored female who inadvertently burns Cupid with candle-wax while disobeying the gods' prohibition to look upon his beauty (as Florian burns himself while making wax flowers).

These familiar themes of red and yellow, of the bird-child, and of beauty-as-pain lead up to the elemental epiphany of Flavian's inevitable death. From a plundered "golden coffer" of the sun god Apollo (so it is rumored) a plague comes to afflict the boy with "burning fever." Amid "rich-scented" rare Paestum roses the dying Flavian dictates to Marius a mystical cosmic "nuptial hymn" of his own composition (2:112–13). Marius feels *"guilty"* as Flavian looks at him with "misty eyes": has Marius somehow failed in friendship, in love? In his cowed humility, Flavian resembles a "smitten child or animal." Though Marius lies down beside him to lend him warmth, Flavian's soul—that "strange fluttering [birdlike] creature"—is nevertheless extinguished "as utterly as the fire" (2:118, 119, 124, 123). A tragic alter ego for Marius, Flavian is fire and bird and child, fluttering and fevered and flower-surrounded, a mystic lover of the pestilential sun-force that consumes him, bequeathing to his surviving friend an obscure legacy of "self-reproach" (2:118).

Having completed his aristocratic schooling, Marius becomes the amanuensis of the Emperor, and we find that Marcus Aurelius' stoical speech at a public pageant presents the occasion for another epiphany of equal sadness and equal power to stir. Carrying over the theme of Flavian's "strange fluttering" birdlike soul, Aurelius stoically reminds his hearers that "the soul of him who is aflutter upon renown after death" forgets that the remaining bearers of his memory are "themselves on the wing but for a while" (2:202). As the death-speech of Aurelius ends, a procession of torches, "a long stream of moving [fiery] lights across the white Forum," conducts the philosophic monarch up the stairs to his palace. A severe winter, "the hardest that had been known for a lifetime," is beginning: wolves descend from the mountains to devour ill-buried victims of the plague; eagles drive "flocks of smaller birds across the dusky sky"; and "at no time had the winter roses from Carthage seemed more lustrously yellow and red" (2:211). Birdlike souls (to borrow Aurelius' metaphor) are pursued westward to their untimely deaths with the inevitability of the gradually ascending line of fiery torches leading the emperor home. From Carthage, a place famously linked with lusts and fires, come roses with riotous colors of "yellow and red," rioting amid the combined dangers of feverish plague and wintry ice. The chapter (called "The Divinity That Doth Hedge a King") actually ends with the words "yellow and red," always the Paterian epiphanic fire-flag of beauty's ashy fate.

But the chapter "Manly Amusement," with which Part 2 as a whole concludes, offers an even sadder epiphany of dying birds and devouring fires: though the gladiatorial show presented is the sort that the admirable young Flavian would have watched with a "light heart" (2:235), what it reveals is a tendency toward thoughtless cruelty at the heart of human nature—inseparable in this respect from the pain-inflicting reds and yellows of Nature's own beautiful and cruel whimsy, as Pater depicts it. There are "great red patches" of blood on the yellow sand of the amphitheater, lit with "sunshine, filtered into

soft gold" and adorned by a "trellis-work of silver-gilt and amber" and
by a "rain of flowers and perfume" (2:235). The pageant that Marius
sees is in honor of Diana, protectress as well as huntress, so the festival
planners have made sure to select as many pregnant animals as possible in order to allow for the "dexterously contrived escape of the
young" from their mothers' "torn bosoms." The spectacle reminds the
viewer of "similar practical joking upon human beings" during occa-
sions like the one when a criminal "was compelled to present *the part
of* [birdlike] *Icarus*; and, *the wings failing* him in due course, had fallen
into a pack of hungry bears" (2:238–39, emphases added). Though
this appalling revelation allows Marius "to mark Aurelius as his infe-
rior now and for ever on the question of righteousness" (2:241), its
conformity to the Paterian typology of epiphany makes the distinction less clear. The blood-reds, sand- and amber-yellows, fires, flowers, and the doomed avian Icarus (bird-death motif) combine to in-
tegrate humanity's cruelty with that of Nature or of the supernatural
(the plagues from Apollo). There are indeed tears at the torn heart of
things; there is also death at the heart of the search for "spectacle."

Part 3 is like a brief intermission in which we are treated to a lighter
kind of experience, a diverting pseudo-epiphany designed to show us
Rome's decline. As Marius ruminates, in Part 3, over his apparent
philosophical options, he notes somewhat reassuringly (Marius is a
syncretist at heart) that stoicism at court blends rather well with the
epicureanism (or "new Cyrenaicism") he had previously favored (3:4,
19–20). But Marius remains deeply troubled by the emperor's "toler-
ance of evil" (3:51). The falseness infecting the monarch's idealism,
the discomfiture of Marius as baffled quester, are well embodied in a
parodic pseudo-epiphany, the funeral of Aurelius' dissolute brother,
Lucius Verus. Instead of the requisite typological doomed bird we
note the "tawdry artifice, by which an eagle—not a very noble or
youthful specimen of its kind—was caused to take flight amid the
real or affected awe of the spectators," a court chamberlain sub-
sequently reporting to the Senate that the "imperial 'genius' had been
seen in this way, escaping from the fire." The corpse of Lucius lies on
a "flame-shaped structure," and above the dead body itself towers a
pretentious "waxen effigy of great size." Though Lucius had evidently
died on the way "to some amorous appointment," he is "duly"
awarded the spiritual "privilege of divine rank" (3:30–32), a most

meretricious apotheosis. Bird, wax, and flame—a nice trio of Paterian epiphanic motifs—are all present, but all parodied. The unconvincing enskyment of Lucius leaves a widening spiritual gap that Marius quickly tries to fill with a sketched-out synthesis of Plato and Aristotle, but even this supposed moment of insight remains unenlivened by epiphanic imagery and lacks conviction.

Part 4, which will conclude the novel, makes up for these deficiencies at the outset with two superbly realized epiphanic events in "Two Curious Houses": a dinner in honor of the great writer Apuleius (of "Cupid and Psyche" fame), with Marius in attendance, at a mutual friend's home in Tusculum; and Marius' later visit to a mortuary chapel within the home of a Christian named Cecilia. At the party for Marius' former literary idol, epiphanic reds and yellows and birds and fires all quickly appear. Apuleius himself is wearing a golden-folded garment with "harmoniously tinted flowers"; the atmosphere is warmed by the "dusky fires of the rare twelve-petaled roses"; one hears music plaintive as a bird's; and one even sees a "favorite animal, white as snow" (a cat, perhaps? like Florian's?). *The Death of Paris* is danced, and—best of all—a supposed "Socratic dialogue" is read (3:78–81). Halcyon, the dialogue tells us, once a woman, was changed to a bird in order to lament the more plaintively for her lost love Ceyx. Socrates praises myths, for (he contends) each of us is like a little child, loving transformations and making imaginative wax figurines as naturally as a bee makes honey. The speaker recites the dialogue with florid eloquence (a collection of his sayings will later be entitled " 'Florida' or Flowers"). In the distance the hearers detect a disturbing conflagration (3:83–86).

One of the very richest of all Paterian epiphanies, this experience—combining birds and flowers and wax and fire—subtly links beauty's intense pleasures and its grievous pains. If Halcyon does not die, in her embodiment as victimized bird she mourns her lover for all eternity, and the death-and-deprivation theme is fortified by the *Death of Paris* dance. Pater's Socrates depicts each and every one of us as a Florian-like artist, modeling things out of wax and loving the poetic power of myths about bird-victims like Halcyon. The epiphany begins with the sensuous, "dusky fires" of "roses" (their gorgeous redness and forbidden-fruit symbolism deepened by the nearby "mulberries, pomegranates, and grapes" [3:78]), and it ends with the literal flames of a conflagration visible beyond the villa, with palpable threats of spreading ravage, of massive, fiery death.

Christian ritual, similarly, presents itself to Marius as "esthetically, very seductive," and epiphanically rich. An old flower garden, a "picture in pensive shade and fiery blossom," leads the worshiper into a "hollow cavern or crypt," originally a simple family tomb but now growing to a "vast *necropolis*" of "venerable beauty." Marius sees "lights, flowers, their flame or their freshness being relieved to the utmost by contrast with the coal-like blackness of the soil itself, a volcanic sandstone, cinder of burnt-out fires. Would they ever kindle again?" The deceased children are compared with "dead violets"; yet the "little red phial of blood" and the "red flowers" Marius sees are held to be emblems of the departed souls' "heavenly 'birthday' " (3:96–102). Only the white birds are missing from this moving epiphany of fires and flowers, of mortality and hope.

Birds reappear during the deeply moving epiphany that Marius experiences while visiting his family's burial ground, "the spot that was to him like no other." The very leaves of the old poplars are "like golden fruit, the birds floating around it." Amid "the faded flowers, the burnt-out lamps," Marius sees, through a gap in a "minute coffin of stone," a "protruding baby hand"; he then notices, next to his mother's urn, the urn of a boy who had died at about the age Marius himself had been at his mother's death, a servant-boy who had, as it were, taken Marius' place with her. With a "blinding rush of kindness," he feels a wholly new understanding and empathy for his scarcely-known father as well. Marius flings down his "flowers, one by one, to mingle with the dark mould" (3:204–7). It is a complete Paterian epiphany: *birds, flowers, spent fires, and rosen-mold*; the death of a child, a spot of time, a scene of mortuary beauty, and a surge of love that sears and blinds like Apollo's fires.

Marius' own death by plague follows soon after, also a powerfully epiphanic moment. Emperor Aurelius has abandoned the "minor peace of the Church," so the earth has been "stained afresh with the blood of the martyrs Felix and Faustinus—*Flores apparuerunt in terra nostra!*" (3:211–12). Marius is sure no such *flores* or "miraculous poetic flowers" will spring from his red blood (3:214). Yet his Christian friends are applying to his hands and feet "a medicinable oil," such as soothed the wax-fire wounds of Florian; and Marius, "like a child thinking over the toys it loves," finds that "the bare sense of having loved" is medicine for the spirit (3:222–24). This epiphany of Marius' death blends with that of his visit to the family burial ground and is an extension of it, a meditative commentary on the love it aroused, on the reconciliation that the "blinding" love made possible for the newly sorrowing "child."

4

And there is more. The novel-length imaginary portrait called *Gaston de Latour*, though left unfinished and unpublished at the author's death, is a rich lode for the phenomenological connoisseur of Paterian epiphanic moments. Indeed, if we put aside most of the last chapter, which (apart from its first few pages) is predominantly an essay on the pantheist philosopher Giordano Bruno and offers no epiphanies,[10] we may even describe the brief novel as a remarkably well-integrated and organically complete work, framed by two of Pater's most elaborate and yet forceful epiphanic achievements. The book begins with bird carnage inflicted by King Charles IX, a barbarous hunter but also an esthete and poet, with whom the poetic-minded Gaston identifies. And the early passages of the Bruno chapter show us King Charles' death, shortly after Gaston has been indirectly responsible for the death of Gaston's lovely wife, Colombe (a name meaning "dove," iconographically equivalent to "white bird"). Typologically, the book is neatly rounded off (or it would be, if Pater had not gone on with the Bruno chapter): it begins with multiple bird-victims, and it ends with the boundlessly guilt-inducing death of yet another symbolic white bird—both episodes complete with all the requisite flowers, fires, yellows, reds, in ever new and ingenious variations. In between, there is a double epiphany evoked by two more poets: Gaston's friend Jasmin and his literary idol Ronsard.

The introductory epiphany of King Charles is forceful and prophetic. As Charles comes riding through the yellow "corn," his half-blasphemous oaths are like red "flashes of hell-fire." In the "daintiest" of apartments, appointed with "*flambeaux*" or torches, the monarch washes off the blood "with which not his hands only were covered; for he hunted also with the eagerness of a madman—*steeped* in blood." Then the king sups "very familiarly on his own birds"; there is no mistaking the sadistic relish Pater shows in his descriptions of the royal bird-slaughter. The dainty ruler uses a rose-water dish (the red flower theme); his fine white skin is "pale" as "wax"—even the Paterian wax-theme is not omitted from this epiphany of birds, flowers, fires, yellows, and reds. On a window, finally, the poetic monarch scratches, with a diamond, some lines of verse, his mad ardors becoming, for a moment (we may say), seemingly hard and gemlike. Pater concludes this epiphany of death-and-beauty on a somber note: "The life of Gaston de Latour," we learn, "was almost to coincide with the duration of the Religious Wars" (9:14–15). So King Charles' headstrong, deadly follies will continue to shadow the protagonist. Indeed, Gaston admires the king; he later makes a point of sleeping in the same bed the king had occupied—in the same room where Gaston's relative, Gabrielle de Latour, had long ago "died of joy" after her husband's unexpected return (9:20–22). In Pater's world, every sort of ardor (for hunting, for husband, for religion, for poetic art) is, as in its root meaning, a "burning"—destructive, brief. Joy kills.

Of Gaston's three school chums, it is Jasmin, the aspiring poet, whose floral name indicates the beauty, delicacy, and flowerlike perishability (9:49–50) we know to be epiphanic requisites. In "Peach-Blossom and Wine" Jasmin, Amadée, and Camille experience the Paterian epiphanic moment. Finding themselves "ready to trifle with death," the threesome engage in a risky adventure from which they are lucky to return, later in the "bloomy night, with blood upon their boyish flowers." Looking for ghosts, spirits, or whatever lively phantom images happen to be abroad, the boys do at last meet their apparent ghostly doubles,

> their very selves, visible in the light of the lantern carried by Camille; they might have felt the breath upon their cheeks: real, close, definite, cap for cap, plume for plume [bird-motif], flower for flower, a light like their own flashed up counter-wise [fire-theme], but with blood, all three of them, fresh upon the bosom, or in the mouth. (9:75)

The boys may seem to dispel the threefold bloody vampire by drawing a sword, hoping to make the devils take "flight at its white [birdlike] glitter through the air" (9:76). But none of the three young seekers will live long; their "threads" will "be cut short, one by one," before

Gaston's eyes (9:49–50). Bird, flower, and fire motifs combine in a prophetic epiphany of Paterian fate.

Next, we have the powerful Ronsard epiphany. Jasmin has given Gaston some Ronsard to read, and in this vivid poetry he learns of "field-flowers," "birds," the "flush and re-fledging of the black earth"—a fascinating image cluster combining redness and bird-flowers and rosen-mold. Whether Ronsard writes of the skylark, of the red rose, or of the yellow "jonquil," his poetic music has always "something of the sickliness of all spring flowers since the days of Proserpine," that ancient bride of Death (9:50–51). The verse of Ronsard, Gaston felt, was poetry that "bled," poetry that could "absorb him"—"him, and the earth, with its deeds, its blossoms, and faces" (9:52–53). In this extraordinary phraseology, Pater shows us a true poetry of the underworld, a dark poetry of earth (soil, mold) that is blood-rich but devouring still, welcoming all blossoms and faces and flowerlike children. Ronsard's poetry lends to the red rose "something more" than "its own natural blush"; it deals with seemingly ordinary objects—"wine, fruit, the plume in the cap," "flower or bird"—but "The juice in the flowers, when Ronsard named them, was like wine or blood" (9:54). Nothing in this image group is "ordinary": the plume and bird, the extra-red rose, the flower's richly winelike but morbidly bloodlike (red) juice are crucial elements in the making of a Paterian epiphany.

The Ronsard epiphany concludes on a less sanguineal (or sanguinary) note with "the clangorous passage of the birds at night foretokening rain, the moan of the wind at the door, the wind's self made visible over the yielding corn" (9:54–55). But the mood of foreboding prevails. The black earth calls; speaking through the poet of Proserpine, it is ready to "absorb" both "blossoms" and "faces." A powerful coda to the epiphany is furnished by Ronsard's memory of the "special apples" he liked to give to the king: *mille fleurs* [thousand-flower] pippins, painted with a thousand tiny streaks of red, yellow, and green." It is ominous that "A dish of them came to table now . . . from the darkest corner of the cellar" (9:68), earth's tenebrific summons bodied forth in *red-yellow fiery flower-fruits*.

Gaston's mad ardors blend with those of his bird-killing poet-monarch in the final tragic epiphany of Pater's novel. "Delirium was in the air" of the "hotly coloured world of Paris," and it "laid hold on

Gaston too" (9:124). Pater explains that, at this point, the St. Bartholomew's Day massacres precipitated by Charles have bloodied the city, and when Gaston is summoned home to attend his dying grandfather, Gaston's Huguenot wife, terrified by the carnage brought on in the spirit of the king's militant Catholicism, imagines she has been betrayed. Running off to seek Gaston, Colombe dies, and her child, too, has likely perished. Colombe (named for a white bird) is also compared to a "child" in her sense of abandonment—a "cruel picture driven as with fire" into Gaston's guilty soul (9:130–31).

A little later, when Pentecost arrives, the fire-flower nightmare-epiphany of the dead innocence of child and dove bursts out with feverish, world-inflaming brightness. The Pentecostal fire, the descent of the Spirit—amid whatever "corruption in flower (pleasantly enough to the eye), those influences never failed him. At times it was as if a legion of spirits besieged his door: '*Open unto me! Open unto me! My sister, my love, my dove,* [note the white bird motif—Pater's emphases] *my undefiled!*' " (9:135). Yet it is on Pentecost that King Charles' death is announced, so that

> streams of blood blent themselves in Gaston's memory of the event with the gaudy colours of the season—the *crazy red trees in blossom upon the heated sky* above the old grey walls; like a fiery sunset, it might seem, as he looked back over the *ashen* intervening years. (9:135, emphases added)

The words of love from Solomon's song, addressed to the metaphoric white dove of undefilement, give voice to a despair that transcends irony. Gaston's apocalyptic epiphany of *blood and blossoms of fire* makes the mad barbarism of the ruthless aesthete Charles inseparable from Gaston's own Mariner-like guilt for the *death of his own "dove,"* his golden-haired white Colombe, wife-as-abandoned-child, as well as for the probable death of their offspring. Few artists have written such moving epiphanies of bewilderment and loss and abiding guilt.

The analyses of epiphanies we have undertaken in this chapter may well change the way we read Pater generally. For example, even Pater's *The Renaissance: Studies in Art and Poetry*, a work of evocative criticism and thus, to a considerable degree, different in aim and in genre from the stories and novels we have scrutinized for epiphanic structures, will look somewhat different now, at the close of our

Bachelardian phenomenological survey of several Paterian books. Indeed, in the last full-length essay of *The Renaissance*, the portrait of Winckelmann that comes right before the brief gemlike "Conclusion," we find our last example of Paterian epiphanic technique.

Winckelmann seeks the "buried fire of ancient art"; his "enthusiasm burns like lava," and in sensing this pre-Paterian fiery ardor we feel "the beating of the soul against its bars," the caged bird (1:184, 185, 189). Winckelmann's early death was one which, "for its swiftness and its opportunity, he might well have desired" of the gods (1:196). We note Winckelmann's "fiery friendships" (1:197). "He makes gods in his own image, gods smiling and flower-crowned, or bleeding"; "the earth is golden and the grape fiery for him" (1:201)— again the familiar red and yellow, flowers and blood and sun and flame. Winckelmann admired the Greek "power of the wing—an element of refinement, of [birdlike] ascension" (1:202–3). The ideal classic sculpture Winckelmann loved is as an image seen in "white light" (1:218), with a "moral sexlessness," a childlike purity, an "absence of any sense of want, or corruption, or shame"; "Greek sensuousness" is "childlike" (1:221–22). Indeed, the "colourless abstraction of these divine forms . . . has already a touch of the corpse in it" (1:224): what is childlike is moribund. Little can be done by the power of the wing: the white bird-child is destined for death, even as the bleeding, flower-crowned flower gods.

The buried fire of ancient art, as of Pater's own, has descended into the dark mold, which is yet repeatedly refledged—to die once more— with each imagined, epiphanic portrait. If Pater's fire-flower bird-children, unlike the dawn-bloom conflagrations of Tennyson, cannot hope to ascend into a skyey immortality, Pater's deep-rooted attachment to chthonic myths of fertility gods, along with his own impressively prolific re-creation, in endlessly new embodiments, of the same earthbound but ever reborn spirit of flowering flame, insures for his portrait-epiphanies a regenerative immortality. It is an elemental immortality not of air but of earth. Tennyson's and Pater's contrasting kinds of epiphanic immortality suit their differing types of "Elemental Deaths and Illuminations."

Part Three:
Elements, Heroism,
and History

SIX

Epiphanies from
Odin to Teufelsdröckh
Carlylean Heroism and
the Gospel of Fire

In the final unit of this book, "Elements, Heroism, and History" (Chapters 6 through 8), we will take a Bachelardian look at epiphanies of historical process. The works that contain these recurrent patterns of elements, motions, and shapes—now seen by their authors as embodiments of an imaginative approach to the meaning of human history—are of various indeterminate or exploratory genres. Carlyle's *On Heroes, Hero-Worship, and the Heroic in History*, presented as a series of lectures, might better be called a sequence of extended prose poems. His *Sartor Resartus*, a seriocomic, semi-autobiographical conversion narrative supposedly pieced together from bags of disorganized documents bequeathed by a German Professor of Things in General, similarly challenges generic classification. Tolstoy's *War and Peace*, the focus of the next chapter, defies novelistic norms: here not only are major characters allowed to experience epiphanic moments but the author-persona himself intrudes to present elemental revelations on his own behalf, epiphanies embedded in long lectures on historical theory that sound like attempted rebuttals of Carlyle. Barrett Browning's *Aurora Leigh*, investigated in the final chapter, is a visionary epic that could just as well be called a verse novel. Taken together, these three concluding chapters will allow us to show how phenomenological scrutiny clarifies the epiphanic shaping of historical vision in works not commonly regarded as history books.

It is precisely the unconventional nature of the literary forms these three writers use that will allow us to achieve a rewarding analytical clarity. History books, explicitly so called, are often less likely to reveal their central informing epiphanies than are the avowedly imaginative, cross-generic writings of Carlyle, Tolstoy, and Barrett Browning. True, in the nineteenth century history texts themselves were sometimes more fluidly defined than in most of the twentieth century, so that the historian Jules Michelet, for example, whom Roland Barthes has brilliantly studied from a thoroughly Bachelardian point of view,[1] felt free to reveal his determining epiphanies almost as explicitly as might a novelist or verse writer. The present-day ("post-modern") tendency for historians to admit candidly and self-consciously the nature of the poetic shaping that is inseparable from any recounting of an historic event—a self-consciousness exemplified, for instance, in Simon Schama's *Dead Certainties (Unwarranted Speculations)*—may eventually bring us back to greater explicitness of epiphanic presentation in historical works. Already in Michel Foucault's massive *Folie et déraison* it is clear that the crucial founding metaphor or "guiding image" of this pathbreaking history of changing conceptions of madness—the "Ship of Fools"—derives much of its power from Foucault's encounter with Bachelard's imaginative world: "Some of Foucault's most beautiful pages in *Madness and Civilization*, on the aquatic world plied by the medieval 'Ship of Fools,' owe a very large debt to the way Bachelard analyzed the reverie of water."[2] So works of history can sometimes respond very profitably to the Bachelardian approach.

But mixed-genre writers, like the three I have chosen for the final unit of this book, make their founding epiphanies of historical process exceptionally clear. So they offer a particularly rewarding opportunity for us to study epiphanies of history by using the revised, systematized form of Bachelardian method that has already proved fruitful in our earlier chapters. As with Tennyson or Pater, we will first seek out, in the case of each historical seer, a particularly intense, complete, fully elaborated paradigm, which we can then trace through its more fragmentary or attenuated manifestations.

Juxtaposing the three historical seers in the three chapters that constitute this final unit of our book will allow the respective writers to provide implicit mutual critiques: each epiphanist points up what the others have chosen to omit in their respective visions of history. I do not mean to imply that we can, or should, revise our relative aesthetic ranking of the three writers' literary works as totalities; Carlyle's *Heroes*, for example, is most certainly not commensurate with Tolstoy's *War and Peace* in overall literary greatness—and no comparative study of epiphanies is going to alter that judgment. What *can* be usefully learned from the juxtaposition of the two men's epiphanic patterns is the scope and limits of each *epiphanic pattern*.

Carlyle and Tolstoy are monists, epiphanists of immanence, of unity: Carlylean history is fiery and eruptive; Tolstoyan, oceanic, with currents and tides. Barrett Browning's vision is dual: spirit tries to transform dead matter, to transfigure it out of existence, or out of its unspiritual nonexistence, its rocky deadness, into fiery life: her imagination is engaged in a constant attempt to transcend history, to spiritualize it and lift it onto a higher plane of possibility. Epiphanies of historical process (and—with Barrett Browning—suprahistorical transcendence) show dramatically how the elemental imagination both enlivens and limits perspectives in all three writers.

Abstractly summed up, the historical thinking of Carlyle, Tolstoy, or Barrett Browning—along with their respective corollary ideas on historical heroism or its absence—may well fail to convince. There is no more reason to affirm, with Carlyle, "The History of the World is but the Biography of great men"[3] than there is to agree with Tolstoy: "In historic events the so-called great men are but the labels giving names to events, and like labels they have only the slightest connection with the event itself."[4] Juxtaposed, the doctrines of Carlyle and Tolstoy neatly nullify each other: Carlylean faith in the all-importance of heroes in history is no more tenable than Tolstoyan belief in the impossibility of historical heroes. Barrett Browning, though closer to Carlyle, would disagree with both men: she thinks that heroism is possible, if only for seers with a transformative type of vision, but she maintains that heroism is hardly confined to great "men." Yet without its accompanying elemental epiphanies, Barrett Browning's own gospel of spiritualizing the inert might seem just as improbable as Carlyle's or Tolstoy's doctrines, stated in the abstract.

The elemental epiphanies of the three seers are effective *as visions*. Every vision has limits. Yet without some unifying vision, at least as a starting point—no matter how tentatively suggested, even "under erasure," with the limits of the proposed pattern admitted in advance—it would seem impossible to write history at all. And if this is granted, then it is likely that most grand views of historical process evolve from some founding image pattern. Scrutiny of the epiphanic patterns that form the imaginative basis for visions of history and for theories of heroism (or its opposite) in Carlyle, Tolstoy, and Barrett Browning may also make us more discerning analysts of other theories, or imaginative presentations, of history and of historical figures.

In the lectures *On Heroes, Hero-Worship, and the Heroic in History*, a "prophetic" work in the Romantic tradition, Carlyle tries to re-create for us the moments of poetic-religious illumination experienced by a variety of visionary questers, men who see history's deepest meanings and who are spiritually enlarged—to become world-historical personages themselves—by what they see. Carlyle's epiphanic pattern appears in its most powerful, elaborate form in his introductory vision of Odin, then gradually decreases in both intensity and elaboration as the book proceeds. So, from the perspective of its organizing imagery, Carlyle's myth of history is a vision of a Norse paradise gradually lost. Odin's fiery glory reappears ceaselessly among us, but in ever-dimming, diminishing forms. Odin is the primal visionary, as well as the primal vision, but both seer and seen are becoming ever less real. Carlyle does not say this, for to do so would counteract the book's ostensible thesis that heroism is not only an always-available option but is the only thing that gives meaning to human history. Yet Carlyle's epiphanic imagery embodies a tale of decline.

But in *Sartor Resartus*, an earlier work, Carlyle had tried to counteract history's entropy, to revive, as it were, the fiery vision that in his later book, *Heroes*, he would associate with Odin. My analysis will reverse chronology for the sake of greater clarity: the *Heroes* lectures are more systematic as an exposition of epiphanic structures, and if we study them carefully to start with, *Sartor*'s fire-structures will make more sense when we look at them later.

As promised in the introduction, each of our final three phenomenological analyses in this "Elements, Heroism, and History" unit will indicate a need to alter our customary perspectives on the given writer's work. In both *Heroes* and *Sartor* our Bachelardian focus on the problematics of epiphanic fire will disclose an inner contradiction with a clarity not attainable by any other analytic technique. *Heroes*, on the surface an inspirational work designed to revive faith in heroism, undermines its own evangel by showing how the fire that signifies both heroic perception and heroic action gradually gutters out in the course of history. Sermonizing about heroics gradually yields before the logic of the elemental epiphanies themselves, as Carlyle the epiphanist of failing fires undermines the cheerful and heated zeal of Carlyle the fire-gospeler.

In *Sartor*, despite the vivid fire epiphanies that erupt quite gloriously into the text, the problem of inner contradiction is even more severe, for here the true epiphanies of the book, the fiery flashes, counteract all too well the surface metaphor that is supposed to govern the book, namely the idea of clothes, of tailoring. Put simply and bluntly, fire consumes fabric. Carlyle—or his seriocomic spokesman, Professor Teufelsdröckh (Devil's-dung)—wants to tell us, in his surface rhetoric, that the world spirit constantly dresses itself in new costumes to fit the changing times; that what truly matters will always remain; that spirit endures despite cultural crises—which are only changes of clothing. But in the fiery epiphanies that are the poetically effective (that is, imaginatively convincing, even overpowering) center of *Sartor*, it becomes clear that Spirit is Fire. Spirit-Fire does not wear or change or tailor clothes. It burns them up. It's no wonder, therefore, that the Professor of Tailoring leads a life that has little to do with his own clothes-philosophy; Carlyle the fire epiphanist does not really believe in it.

I have never found the inner contradictions in Carlyle's writing concretized in this way in non-phenomenological treatments of his work. Just as we used Bachelardian method to clarify the conflict between Coleridge as critic and Coleridge as epiphanist, between Arnold as critic and Arnold as epiphanist, so too the same method brings out for the first time an elemental basis for the split between Carlyle the discursive teacher of heroism or of cultural tailoring and Carlyle the epiphanist of fire (for there are no Carlylean epiphanies of clothing—instead of tailoring-epiphanies what we get is half-jocular sartorial satire). Phenomenological method, here as elsewhere, offers a new focus of analysis that should interest critics generally.

1

The components of Carlyle's recurrent epiphanic pattern in *Heroes* are an element, a focal point, a surrounding contrast, and a type of motion. The element is fire. The focal point is a center, usually of an implied sphere, or else the center may itself be a sort of sphere: a heart or an eye. Or the central focal point may enlarge into a section of a sphere: a vortex, a cone, or a pillar. The surrounding, contrasting mi-

lieu is generally darkness or something initially resistant to fire: hardened wrappings or coldness. The type of motion in Carlylean epiphanies is swiftly penetrative, eruptive, or aggressive. Most typically,
when all component parts are present, we get an image of a violent
fire flashing or erupting outwards from a vital center into a surrounding darkness (though sometimes, much less often, the fiery light
"glares in" on a darkness in the mind). The critical literature contains
no discussion of this fourfold Carlylean epiphanic pattern (fire, center,
darkness, flash) in *Heroes,* except for Chris R. Vanden Bossche's remarks expressing agreement with my exposition of it in an earlier
article.[5] Robert W. Kusch, who finds fire significant only in Carlyle's
French Revolution, claims that the Igdrasil tree is the controlling metaphor for *Heroes*—an image mentioned only three times in the book.[6]
G. B. Tennyson notes Carlyle's light-dark contrasts and the allegedly
"subordinate use of fire" but devotes more attention to water, a surprising choice in view of its far lesser frequency in the *Heroes* text.[7]

Taken as a whole, the Carlylean epiphanic pattern recalls Byron's
definition of poetry as "the lava of the imagination whose eruption
prevents an earth-quake,"[8] or Childe Harold's quintessentially Byronic wish to express himself in a word that would be "Lightning"
(*Childe Harold's Pilgrimage,* 3.97.7). But for Carlyle the eruptions and
lightnings tend to peter out at the end, as indeed they usually do with
Byron also.

Carlyle's history lectures are really an extended exercise in nostalgia for prehistory. The portrait of Odin, which is the book's most fully
developed literary epiphany, depicts a man of whom history has left
no record: he is a fire-epiphany of Carlyle's. Both Torfaeus and Saxo
Grammaticus supposed that Odin had been an actual Norseman, and
Snorri assigned him the role of inventor of poetry, a bard later deified
by an admiring people (23). Carlyle adopts the euhemerism of these
early writers, but he goes further: Carlyle makes Odin the single mortal incarnation of the Norse spirit, the single subject of all Norse myth:
"is not that Scandinavian Mythology in some sort the Portraiture of
this man Odin?" (29). In instinctive communion with the "wild deep
heart" of this "Type Norseman," the "heart" of the Norse people
"burst-up [a warm-hearted flame motion] into boundless admiration
round him" (28). But Carlyle admires Odin more boundlessly still,
for all of Carlyle's historical heroes are but variations on the Odin

theme, bearers of the Odin imagery, though in gradually diminishing intensity.[9] Carlyle admits with surprising candor: "Of Odin there exists no history; no document of it; no guess about it worth repeating" (23). Yet he then goes on to create a purely imaginative Odin-guess of his own to serve as archetypical model for everything he cares about. All of Carlyle's historical heroes try to imitate Carlyle's unhistorical Odin.

For Odin is not simply a Carlylean fire-vision; he is the exemplary, paradigmatic fire-epiphany, the essential phenomenological key to all of Carlyle's fiery prose poetry about heroes and heroism and history. As "The Vision of Sin" was the paradigm of the aweful dawn-roses and wheeling motions in Tennysonian epiphanies, as "The Child in the House" was key to the Paterian pattern of fire flowers and white birds, so Carlyle's Odin presentation is the fullest elaboration of his epiphanic, world-historical eruptive fires. Carlylean epiphanic flames contrast with those of Tennyson and Pater in not being explicitly linked with death. Yet the volcanolike eruptiveness of Carlylean fire—its suddenness, impulsiveness, explosive volatility—lends a markedly unstable quality to Carlylean heroic epiphanies. They are forceful but soon ended.

Carlyle's Odin paradigm is a triple epiphany, or an epiphany presented from three complementary perspectives. Carlyle portrays three distinct but related kinds of upbursting fiery light: the poetic or mythopoetic, the natural, and the supernatural. All are coessential with the spirit of the man-god Odin, and all combine to produce a threefold epiphany of Odin's power, paradigmatic for the power of every Carlylean historical hero. First there is the spark or gleam of insight in the primal Norse consciousness as the myth of Odin-as-god is created:

> This light, kindled in the great dark vortex of the Norse mind, dark but living, waiting only for light; this is to me the centre of the whole. How such light will then shine out, and with wondrous thousandfold expansion spread itself, in forms and colours, depends not on it, so much as on the National Mind recipient of it. (26)

Instead of the Jobean voice from the whirlwind, we have a primal light kindled in a whirlpool or vortex, a central light expanding thousandfold, much as it does in Carlyle's own developing myth. Next, there are the upbursts of nature's own fires from a hidden central depth, as in "that strange island Iceland," birthplace of many Norse poets, which Carlyle describes as

> burst-up . . . by fire from the bottom of the sea; a wild land of barrenness and lava; swallowed many months of every year in black tempests, yet with a wild gleaming beauty in summertime. . . . (16)

Finally, there is the sudden awareness on the part of the man Odin that both his own fiery power of imagination and nature's expansive energies are participants in the power of a still greater Prime Mover. Odin may have felt, Carlyle speculates,

> that perhaps he was divine; that he was some effluence of the "Wuotan," "*Movement*," Supreme Power and Divinity, of whom to his rapt vision all Nature was the awful Flame-image; that some effluence of *Wuotan* dwelt here in him! (25)

Even in this state of insight, to be sure, Odin does not feel the light radiating through the entire sphere (so to speak) of his consciousness. Along with this "glorious new light" he also experiences the "whirlwind chaotic darkness" of mystery and struggle (25). Light is always in conflict with darkness; illumination is attained amidst troubled chaos, as a violent breakthrough, against the background of a terrifying unknown. But Carlyle in his own statements tries to identify as completely as he can with the central Divinity, with Wuotan as movement: "Force, Force, everywhere Force; we ourselves a mysterious Force in the centre of that" (8). (Force, for Carlyle, is truly everywhere; all it needs to do is activate its fiery energy to the fullest, making overt what has been partly latent. The only real antagonist of fire is darkness, which is simply an emptiness waiting to be filled with light. Carlyle is a monist.) For Carlyle, the revival of Odin's primal outrush of light is the ideal—to dispel the dark by becoming aware of the underlying coessentiality of human, natural, and divine fires or powers.

This threefold outburst of illuminating flame, which is the essence of Odin's apotheosis, is the Carlylean paradigm for the epiphanic description of every great man:

The great man, with his free force direct out of God's own hand,
is the lightning. His word is the wise healing word which all can
believe in. All blazes round him now, when he has once struck
on it, into fire like his own. (13)

It is also the paradigm for most Norse myths, which thus prove to be
variations on the Odin or great-man theme.

The power of *Fire*, or *Flame*, . . . is with these old Northmen,
Loke [*sic*], a most swift subtle *Demon*, of the brood of the Jötuns.
. . . Hymir's Cows are *Icebergs*: this Hymir 'looks at the rocks'
with his devil-eye, and they *split* in the glance of it. (17–18)

Loki is embodied swift flame; Hymir's fireglance is an apocalyptic
upburst like Odin's apotheosis.

Ragnarök, the Norse twilight of the gods, is a phoenixlike fire-
epiphany summarizing Carlyle's own conception of cultural development as a series of baptisms by fire:

though all dies, and even gods die, yet all death is but a phoenix[10] fire-death, and new-birth into the Greater and the Better!
It is the fundamental Law of Being for a creature made of Time,
living in this Place of Hope. All earnest men have seen into it;
may still see into it. (39)

Dying Norse kings were sent out to sea in ships made to "blaze-up
in flame" (32); one imagines Carlyle himself might have wished for
such a send-off. Certainly Lecture 1, "The Hero as Divinity," summa-
rizes for Carlyle the testament of Norse prehistory, its legacy to future
ages whose heroes are challenged to transcend themselves by emu-
lating the flashing epiphanic upsurge of fiery Odin.

The next stage down from the divine is "The Hero as Prophet." Here
too nature, God, and man join their fiery eruptive energies in a combined epiphany, closely akin in spirit to the Odin paradigm. Mahomet
is a "fiery mass of Life cast-up from the great bosom of Nature herself.
To *kindle* the world; the world's Maker had ordered it so" (46). The
result was a "bastard kind of Christianity, but a living kind; with a
heart-life in it," since Mahomet, "with his wild sincere heart, earnest
as death and life, with his great flashing natural eyesight, had seen
into the kernel of the matter" (63). The prophet's fiery central heart

and eye flash into the coessential heart of reality. But "bastard" (a word indicative of the cultural biases that painfully mar Carlyle's supposedly laudatory lecture) is certainly a problem. The Koran, Carlyle avers with ethnocentric arrogance, "is as toilsome reading as I ever undertook. A wearisome confused jumble, crude, incondite; endless iterations, long-windedness, entanglement; . . . insupportable stupidity, in short" (64–65). Mahomet still has the epiphanic Odin-vision, but his powers of expression are, in Carlyle's view, inadequate to their subject. Nevertheless, it is clear from the conclusion of Lecture 2 that Carlyle deeply admires Mahomet's "great fiery heart, seething, simmering like a great furnace of thoughts" (67):

> These Arabs, the man Mahomet, and that one century,—is it not as if a spark had fallen, one spark, on a world of what seemed black unnoticeable sand; but lo, the sand proves explosive powder, blazes heaven-high from Delhi to Gr[a]nada! I said, the Great Man was always as lightning out of Heaven; the rest of men waited for him like fuel, and then they too would flame. (77)

The Islamic Ragnarök epiphany is impressive: the hero as prophet is a worthy incarnation, if only a stammering spokesman, of the fiery God-nature at the heart of things.

Stage three, "The Hero as Poet," continues to show a high intensity of epiphanic power, though Dante proves more amenable than Shakespeare to description in Carlylean chiaroscuro. Carlyle's image of Dante is an artful blending of all the familiar Odin-epiphany components with something of Dante's own *Inferno* vision:

> His greatness has, in all senses, concentered itself into fiery emphasis and depth. . . . Through all objects he pierces as it were down into the heart of Being. I know nothing so intense as Dante. . . . You remember that first view he gets of the Hall of Dite: red pinnacle, redhot cone of iron glowing through the dim immensity of gloom;—so vivid, so distinct, visible at once and for ever! It is as an emblem of the whole genius of Dante. (92)

Fiery center, conic section of a sphere, piercing movement, and surrounding darkness are all vividly presented. And since Dante is in touch with the "heart of Being," his primal fire is almost as clearly coessential with that of God and of nature as was Odin's or Mahomet's. It matters little that Carlyle claims to consider it a vulgar "Byronism of taste" (95) to prefer the *Inferno* to the other two books of Dante's *Commedia*, for we see how readily Carlyle's own vision of the central prophetic fire merges with Dante's picture of the infernal city of Dis. Carlyle himself is a very Byronic prose-poet, and his own preference for the fiery *Inferno* is unmistakable: he simply transvaluates Dante's flaming vision of Dis and adapts it to his own purposes. His Inferno-vision of Dante's genius is the closest thing to the original Carlylean Odin ideal in the entire lecture on "The Hero as Poet."

To contrast Dante with Shakespeare, and at the same time to create a way of including both poets under his basic fire-epiphany rubric, Carlyle works out a dichotomy of wild and serene fires. "Two fit men: Dante, deep, fierce as the central fire of the world; Shakespeare, wide, placid, far-seeing, as the Sun, the upper light of the world" (101). But this sun too is not merely placid; it makes things "dissolve" before it, as would a wilder fire, and it penetratingly "discloses" those essential powers that are "wrapped-up" in obscurity. So Shakespeare, too, becomes a sort of fiery Prometheus, though more "blessed" than that rebel Titan:

> It is unexampled, I think, that calm creative perspicacity of
> Shakespeare. The thing he looks at reveals not this or that face
> of it, but its inmost heart, and generic secret: it dissolves itself as
> in light before him. . . .
>   The seeing eye! It is this that discloses the inner harmony of
> things; what Nature meant, what musical idea Nature has
> wrapped-up in these often rough embodiments. (104–5)
> Is he not an eye to us all; a blessed heaven-sent Bringer of Light?
> (111–12)

To be sure, Shakespeare was "conscious of no Heavenly message" (112). But Mahomet, too, was at his best when he was least self-conscious. "The truly great in him too was the unconscious. . . . whatsoever is truly great . . . springs-up from the *in*articulate deeps" (112). By calling Shakespeare a *"Prophet"* (111), and by ending his section on Shakespeare as Prophet with a comparative reference to Mahomet, Carlyle deftly manages to leave us with a Shakespeare who seems to have absorbed something of Mahomet's Carlylean wildness:

the "placid" Shakespearean sunlight becomes more exciting, its fieriness more striking.

In Lecture 4, misleadingly titled "The Hero as Priest," Carlyle says at the outset that he will consider his two representative figures, Luther and Knox, "rather as Reformers than Priests" (116): his need to make this distinction is bound up with the central epiphany pattern that shapes his thinking. In terms of Carlylean epiphany, priests are placid fires, while only reformers have the fully Carlylean appeal of wild fires, volcanically erupting through accumulated layers of hardened obstruction:

> [The Priest] is the Prophet shorn of his more awful splendour; burning with mild equable radiance, as the enlightener of daily life. (115)
> The mild shining of the Poet's light has to give place to the fierce lightning of the Reformer. . . . (117)
> Offences accumulate till they become insupportable; and are then violently burst through, cleared off as by explosion. Dante's sublime Catholicism, incredible now in theory, and defaced still worse by faithless, doubting and dishonest practice, has to be torn asunder by a Luther; Shakespeare's noble Feudalism, as beautiful as it once looked and was, has to end in a French Revolution. The accumulation of offences is, as we say, too literally exploded, blasted asunder volcanically. . . . (119)

Stimulated by Luther, Carlyle can generate one of his most characteristic epiphanies of central fiery heat, smiting flash, and sudden, cosmic illumination:

> There was born here, once more, a Mighty Man; whose light was to flame as the beacon over long centuries and epochs of the world. . . . (128)
> He flashes-out illumination from him; his smiting idiomatic phrases seem to cleave into the very secret of the matter. (139)
> It is a noble valour which is roused in a heart like this, once stirred-up into defiance, all kindled into a heavenly blaze. (140)

But John Knox, a "narrow, inconsiderable man, as compared with Luther" (148), cannot kindle Carlyle: despite his "heartfelt instinctive adherence to truth" (148), Knox generates no fiery Carlylean Odin-epiphanies. Only the cause Knox serves—"the noblest of causes," Carlyle asserts—"kindles itself, like a beacon set on high; high as Heaven, yet attainable from Earth . . . " (145). This is the closest the Scottish Presbyterians can come to the bravery of "their old Scandinavian Sea-king ancestors" (144): with no poetic epiphany forthcoming from Knox, Carlyle sees his Odin-vision in trouble, so he prudently edges some Norse "ancestors" into his portrait of Knox's followers, as if to help keep the Odin spirit alive. But the result lacks conviction. Indeed, the Reformation era as a whole gives Carlylean fire-epiphany special difficulties, for Carlyle remembers how fire was used to silence that staunch pre-Protestant John Huss: the Council of Constance "*burnt* the true voice of him out of this world; choked it in smoke and fire. That was *not* well done!" (133). Here Carlyle's way of partly rescuing his epiphany pattern is to imply a contrast between the pure fire of inspiration and the smoky fire of suppression.

Carlyle's problems as would-be epiphanist of fiery heroism increase with "The Hero as Man of Letters." Though theoretically this kind of hero can serve as a "light of the world," guiding humanity as by a "sacred Pillar of Fire" (157), the three men of letters Carlyle discusses—Johnson, Rousseau, and Burns—"were not heroic bringers of the light, but heroic seekers of it" (158). The Odin-vision is nearly gone, and these three men spend their lives longing to recapture it—a sad comedown from the prehistoric glory of Lecture 1. Of course, Carlyle could have made his presentation of the literary hero more optimistic by selecting as his prime example Goethe, who gives us a world "Illuminated all, not in fierce impure fire-splendour as of Mahomet, but in mild celestial radiance;—really a Prophecy in these most unprophetic times . . . " (157). Carlyle says the public would find information about Goethe unexciting since Goethe is so largely unread. But the study of Carlylean epiphany patterns suggests an alternative explanation for the avoidance of Goethe in this lecture: Carlyle prefers an imperfect, fiercely flashing blaze to even the most flawless of "mild," placid lights (odd appraisal of Goethe!).

So the three men Carlyle selects for presentation as heroic men of letters are imperfect strugglers, imperfect fire-dreamers and less-than-adequate fire-heroes, seeking in somewhat bewildered fashion the intermittent coruscation of the fearful blaze. Samuel Johnson, after all, spoke "still in some sort from the heart of Nature," so he too

was a "Prophet": "Very curious how, in that poor Paper-age, so bar-
ren, artificial, thick-quilted with Pedantries, Hearsays, the great Fact
of this Universe glared in, for ever wonderful, indubitable, unspeakable, divine-infernal, upon this man too!" (180). Rousseau, on the
other hand, was superficial and wordy: "The suffering man ought really 'to consume his own smoke'; there is no good in emitting *smoke*
till you have made it into *fire* . . . " (184). Rousseau is affectedly sensual: his sensuality is "Not white sunlight: something operatic; a kind
of rosepink, artificial bedizenment" (187). Yet "there is in the inmost
heart of poor Rousseau a spark of real heavenly fire" (186); indeed,
with his political theories, he "could not be hindered from setting the
world on fire" (188). Robert Burns's story, however, is pathetic.
Burns's "noble rough genuineness . . . with its lightning-fire, with its
soft dewy pity;—like the old Norse Thor, the Peasant-god" (190), his
"highest fire of passionate speech," his Mirabeau-like gift for "a flash
of insight" (191)—all are reduced, through his fatal susceptibility to
social lionizing, to the tiny light of a firefly stuck upon a spit:

> Richter says, in the Island of Sumatra there is a kind of
> "Lightchafers," large Fire-flies, which people stick upon spits,
> and illuminate the ways with at night. Persons of condition can
> thus travel with a pleasant radiance, which they much admire.
> Great honour to the Fire-flies! But—!— (195)

Carlyle reminds us that "Odin's *Runes* were the first form of the
work of a Hero; Books, written words, are still miraculous *Runes*, the
latest form" (160). Yet Lecture 5, on modern literary Odins, ends with
comic frustration. Carlyle gasps at the pitiable fate of the hero as lightning bug, a tragicomic travesty of the paradigmatic Odin-epiphany of
eruptive flame.

Carlyle feels the pathos of Burns's plight as diminutive firefly, for
Carlyle too is a man of letters in the modern age: chronologically, the
lectures should actually end at this point, for Carlyle must backtrack
historically if he is to include both Cromwell and Napoleon as repre-
sentatives of his final category of heroism, "The Hero as King." But
Carlyle does not want to write a "Paradise Lost," he wants to end on
a note of triumphant affirmation. And the "Hero as King" seems to
him the "summary for us of all the various figures of Heroism," a
man who can "furnish us with constant practical teaching, to tell us

for the day and hour what we are to do" (196). (One may ask: if the king succeeds in this, how will a society of heroes—whether as divinities, prophets, poets, priests, or men of letters—ever arise? No hero wants to be told what to do every hour.[11] Luckily, Carlyle's kings are no great successes.)

Carlyle's Cromwell epiphany preserves the element of inner fire but surrounds it with a chaotic darkness:

> An outer hull of chaotic confusion, visions of the Devil, nervous dreams, almost semi-madness; and yet such a clear determinate man's-energy working in the heart of that. A kind of chaotic man. The ray as of pure starlight and fire, working in such an element of boundless hypochondria, *un*formed black of darkness! And yet withal this hypochondria, what was it but the very greatness of the man? . . . Samuel Johnson too is that kind of man. Sorrow-stricken, half-distracted; the wild element of mournful *black* enveloping him,—wide as the world. It is the character of a prophetic man; a man with his whole soul seeing, and struggling to see. (217–18)

One senses more visionary groping here than epiphanic clarity, both in Cromwell and in Johnson. But of the two, Johnson is the less hypochondriacal. Indeed, at one point Carlyle seems, very oddly, to be suggesting that Johnson would have made a far better Cromwell than Cromwell did:

> Fancy, for example, you had revealed to the brave old Samuel Johnson, in his shrouded-up existence, that it was possible for him to do priceless divine work for his country and the whole world. . . . Would not the whole soul of the man have flamed-up into a divine clearness, into noble utterance and determination to act; casting all sorrows and misgivings under his feet, counting all affliction and contradiction small,—the whole dark element of his existence blazing into articulate radiance of light and lightning? (225–26)

Johnson's hypothetical moment of epiphanic illumination gets a far better epiphanic treatment than anything experienced by the "historical" Cromwell, who by contrast is treated nervously, protectively, with a rhetoric of anxious defensiveness:

> The Sun flings-forth impurities, gets balefully incrusted with spots; but it does not quench itself, and become no Sun at all, but a mass of Darkness! I will venture to say that such never befell a great deep Cromwell; I think, never. . . . The Sun was dimmed many a time; but the Sun had not himself grown a Dimness. . . . I for one, will not call the man a Hypocrite! (228)

As for Napoleon, he falls far short even of Cromwell's distinctly maculate attainments as epiphanic fire-hero:

> I find in him no such *sincerity* as in Cromwell; only a far inferior sort. No silent walking, through long years, with the Awful Unnamable of this Universe; . . . latent thought and valour, content to lie latent, then burst out as in blaze of Heaven's lightning! Napoleon lived in an age when God was no longer believed; the meaning of all Silence, Latency, was thought to be Nonentity. (237–38)
>
> Napoleon's working, accordingly, what was it with all the noise it made? A flash as of gunpowder wide-spread; a blazing-up as of dry heath. For an hour the whole Universe seems wrapt in smoke and flame; but only for an hour. It goes out: the Universe with its old mountains and streams, its stars above and kind soil beneath, is still there. (242)

An impure blaze, Napoleon quickly goes out in futile smoke. The universe only "seems" transfigured, and only for an hour. The union of divine, natural, and human spiritual powers for which Odin set the initial standard is, in its fullest sense, a thing of the prehistorical past. The fires that powered the myth have gradually weakened through history and have nearly fizzled out. Like the myths of history in Hesiod, Ovid, and Nebuchadnezzar's dream, Carlyle's myth of history leads downward, though his boisterous rhetoric often tries to belie his pessimism.

Fire, center, darkness, flash—phenomenological method has revealed the components of the pervasive Carlylean epiphanic pattern in *On Heroes, Hero-Worship, and the Heroic in History*. But, as we have noted, only Odin truly fulfills the pattern: in him, seer and seen are one. The man sees the god in himself and in the world. And so the world sees him as world-god, as unifying the poetic-human, the natural, and the supernatural in one immanent-and-transcendent flame.

2

Sartor Resartus, more properly *Ignis Reignitus*, kindles this threefold epiphanic flame. But here the seer is not wholly one with what is seen. Teufelsdröckh, the philosophical "tailor," like Adam with his fig-leaf apron, has experienced a fall. Reversing the story of Satan, we may say that Teufelsdröckh has fallen, not into fire, but away from fire.

Yet the fall is far from complete: a man of fiery vision, Professor Diogenes Teufelsdröckh (God-born Devil's-dung), Professor of Things in General at the University of Weissnichtwo (Know-not-where), has retained a Carlylean skill at conjuring up epiphanies of Things Generalized into a fiery unity of the natural, the human, and the super-human. For Teufelsdröckh-Carlyle, the world—of nature, of humanity, of divinity—remains a revelation only insofar as we can still see in it the chaos that was before creation and that must remain undiminished so long as creation retains energy and remains process, not mere osseous crust, mere product. Process means Becoming, and fiery Becoming means imperfection: the world as fire is not more sane than mad, not more heavenly than hellish, not more product than impulse, even—Carlyle frequently and startlingly admits—not more God than Devil. We recall how, for Samuel Johnson, nature flashed forth "divine-infernal" (180). *Sartor* presents such all-inclusive epiphanies of Fiery Becoming in each of the book's three parts.

As for Odin (as human seer) volcanic Iceland was the very flame-image of Wuotan, so for Professor Teufelsdröckh a fiery smithy in the Black Forest is an altar of sacrifice that images the Sun, divine incarnation of the Mystery of Fiery Force:

"As I rode through the Schwarzwald, I said to myself; That little fire which glows star-like across the dark-growing (*nachtende*) moor, where the sooty smith bends over his anvil, and thou hopest to replace thy lost horse-shoe,—is it a detached, separated speck, cut off from the whole universe; or indissolubly joined to the whole? Thou fool, that smithy-fire was (primarily) kindled at the Sun; is fed by air that circulates from before Noah's Deluge, from beyond the Dogstar; therein, with Iron Force, and Coal Force, and the far stronger Force of Man, are cunning affinities and battles and victories of Force brought about: it is a little ganglion, or nervous centre, in the great vital system of Immensity. Call it, if thou wilt, an unconscious Altar, kindled on the bosom of the All; whose Dingy Priest, not by word, yet by brain and sinew, preaches forth the mystery of Force; nay preaches forth (exoterically enough) one little textlet from the gospel of Freedom, the Gospel of Man's Force, commanding, and one day to be all-commanding."[12]

The gospels of freedom and force are the evangels of flux and fire. This epiphany of the smithy, of Hephaestus Pantocrator, which comes nearly at the end of Part 1 of *Sartor*, is that section's visionary climax. Nature is divine-infernal Fire: Odin's volcanic Iceland is Teufelsdröckh's sacrificial smithy.

The whole of "Natural Supernaturalism," coming near the close of Part 3, is one immense fiery epiphany, but two of its most exhilarating moments offer epiphanies of individual mental creativity and of historical upsurges of power. The first of these transcendent moments shows Madness (mental chaos) as the necessary underlying lava-layer of our created cerebral planet; the second epiphany displays the flaming procession of historical humanity from the inane to the inane, or (what is the same thing) from God to God. That chaos is inseparable from creation itself, insofar as creation remains act rather than result, is the most powerfully convincing message of the epiphanies constituting the Carlylean Gospel of Fire. "What is madness?" asks Teufelsdröckh:

"Ever, as before, does Madness remain a mysterious-terrific, altogether *infernal* boiling up of the Nether Chaotic Deep, through this fair-painted Vision of Creation, which swims thereon, which we name the Real. Was Luther's picture of the Devil less a Reality, whether it were formed within the bodily eye, or without it? In every the wisest Soul, lies a whole world of internal *Madness*, an authentic *Demon-Empire*; out of which, indeed, his world of

Wisdom has been creatively built together, and now rests there, as on its dark foundations does a habitable flowery Earth-rind." (207, emphases added)

Humanity takes on, as it were, the name of its philosophic seer Diogenes Teufelsdröckh, the name of God- and devil-born, as does the planet earth itself. The Gospel of divine-infernal Fire-Force is a psychological vision of energy as eternal delight. "Internal madness" is mental energy felt as a welling up of lavalike fire.[13] Impulses and insights erupt in the manner of the volcanic action that (as we learned from the Odin vision in *Heroes*) first formed Iceland.

The chapter concludes with an epiphany of the human race flaming across the sky from one volcanic abyss to the other: here the madness of mental energy is generalized into a panorama of human history as a spectacle of "stormful" fire:

"So has it been from the beginning, so will it be to the end. Generation after generation takes to itself the form of a Body; and forth-issuing from Cimmerian Night, on Heaven's mission, APPEARS. What Force and Fire is in each he expends: one grinding in the mill of Industry; one hunter-like climbing the giddy Alpine heights of Science; one madly dashed in pieces on the rocks of Strife, in war with his fellow:—and then the Heaven-sent is recalled; his earthly Vesture falls away, and soon even to Sense becomes as vanished Shadow. Thus, like some wild-flaming, wild-thundering train of Heaven's Artillery does this mysterious MANKIND thunder and flame, in long-drawn, quick-succeeding grandeur, through the unknown Deep. Thus, like a God-created, fire-breathing Spirit-host, we emerge from the Inane; haste stormfully across the astonished Earth; then plunge again into the Inane. Earth's mountains are levelled, and her seas filled up, in our passage: can the Earth, which is but dead and a vision, resist spirits which have reality and are alive? On the hardest adamant some foot-print of us is stamped in; the last Rear of the host will read traces of the earliest Van. But whence?—O Heaven, whither? Sense knows not; Faith knows not; only that it is through Mystery to Mystery, from God and to God." (212)

The source of all eruptive, flaming energies, metaphysically called God, physically styled Emptiness or the Void ("the Inane"), psychologically denominated Madness, is the "natural supernatural," the epiphany of fire force in its progress from genesis to apocalypse in each life, in the history of humanity, and in the All.

The book's epiphanic center, also the spiritual center of the life of Teufelsdröckh, is of course the famous "fire-Baptism" (135). Consumed in a slow-wasting fever of delusion, of determinism and materialism, his heart "smouldering in sulphurous, slow-consuming fire" (for Carlyle is such a monist that, for him, evil is distinguishable from good chiefly by being a different kind of fire, a suppressed and suppressing rather than eruptive fire), Teufelsdröckh suddenly feels saved from the heat of fever by the stronger stream of life-giving flame-energy:

> " 'What *art* thou afraid of? . . . what is the sum-total of the worst that lies before thee? Death? Well, death; and say the pangs of Tophet too, and all that the Devil and Man may, will or can do against thee! . . . Let it come then; I will meet it and defy it!'
> And as I so thought, there rushed like a stream of fire[14] over my whole soul; and I shook base Fear away from me for ever. I was strong, of unknown strength; a spirit, almost a god. Ever from that time, the temper of my misery was changed: not Fear or whining Sorrow was it, but Indignation and grim fire-eyed Defiance." (134–35)

For a moment Teufelsdröckh is Odin, almost a god. He has been baptized into the praxis of the Gospel of Fire, the assertion of one's freedom against Fear. Can Teufelsdröckh himself become a Carlylean embodiment of the "heroic in history"?

Teufelsdröckh's problems should be over, epiphanically speaking. But though he has seen the light and felt the fire of Force, has experienced in revelatory fashion the will to live and to radiate life everywhere and always, Teufelsdröckh unfortunately cannot be said to measure up fully to the high requirements of his elemental vision, his recurrent fiery epiphany. The good Professor falls away from fire, as it were, in three ways: in his abruptly truncated love life, in his emphatically *un*fiery ethics of sorrow and self-denial, and finally in his problematic preoccupation with cloth—something that's bound to go up in flames when there's a fire.

In his sad experience of unrequited passion, the Professor's fires are early quenched. "Alas, witness also your Diogenes, flame-clad, scaling the upper Heaven, and verging towards Insanity, for prize of a 'high-souled Brunette,' as if the Earth held but one, and not several of these!" (116). It is indeed pathetic. "Suffice it to know that Teufelsdröckh rose into the highest regions of the Empyrean, by a natural parabolic track, and returned thence in a quick perpendicular one" (118), all because of his hyperbolical overestimation of the trivial Blumine (Flora). This formerly aspiring Luciferian lover, unable to scale the heights (for Blumine has "resigned herself to wed some richer" [117]), is last seen, in the chapter "Romance," "falling, falling, towards the Abyss" (118). "Sorrows of Teufelsdröckh" are soon to follow. Love is important in the fiery world of Carlylean epiphany: "thus, in the conducting medium of Fantasy, flames forth that *fire*-development of the universal Spiritual Electricity, which, as unfolded between man and woman, we first emphatically denominate LOVE" (108). But in the sacred realm of passion, Teufelsdröckh is the fire that failed.

Alas, the phrase "sorrows of Teufelsdröckh" continues to ring unhappily in our ears as, surprised and incredulous, we hear the foiled Professor tell us that the *"Worship of Sorrow"* is "of God" (155). Admittedly, the gospel of self-renunciation is wittily presented. Assume that Happiness equals the ratio of what you get to what you expect ($H = G / E$). To reduce your desires and expectations to near-zero, to the infinitesimally small, to the fraction one over infinity, will mean that anything you get in life (call it "x") will be multiplied by one over infinity and will thus equal—Infinity. The algebra (see *Sartor* 152–53) is clever,[15] and the psychology of reducing one's expectations to almost nothing is a tactic that many people may find appealing when in a stoical mood. But the requisite *epiphanic imagery* is lacking—is simply left behind and forgotten. Reducing your hopes to an asymptote of zero is not the same as flaming stormily across the sky. Self-derogating renunciation is not flamingly apocalyptic, not elementally epiphanic, and so—in Carlyle's own epiphanic terms—not persuasive, not bespeaking the "grim fire-eyed Defiance" of Teufelsdröckh's "fire-Baptism." On the contrary, the self-renouncing Teu-felsdröckhian *"Worship of Sorrow"* recalls and reaffirms precisely the "sorrow" which that moment of truly heroic defiance was supposed to eradicate with its empowering baptismal stream of godly or divine-infernal flame.[16]

In the chapter of *Sartor* called "Incident in Modern History" Carlyle tries to anticipate criticism of the metaphorical inconsistency of his book by posing the question whether Teufelsdröckh, the theorist of history as fiery revelation, has fully considered the implications of his own epiphanic fiery teaching. Teufelsdröckh, as *sartor*, as philosopher of clothes, has taught us to see all of human history as a succession of changing garments for the essential fiery body of spirit; indeed, bodies themselves are but clothes for Spirit, and cultures add but one more (constantly changing) set of costumes. But how does the meta-phor of clothing fit together with the metaphor of fire? Earth, one may say, is metaphorically clothed—with plants, with snows, with ever-altering seasonal outfits; it is dressed in motley guises. But fire, by contrast, is the eternal enemy of clothing: *fire consumes fabric.* Has Teufelsdröckh considered that his problematically paired metaphors, his combination of flames and clothes, may have started an unin-tended metaphoric war between the fiery spirit and its historical, cul-tural garments—reducing all of culture and history to combustible costumes destined to be incinerated as soon as Spirit tries to put them on? According to the logic of Teufelsdröckh's own epiphanic imagery, it would be wasted effort for Flaming Spirit to attempt getting dressed at all:

> Striking it was, amid all his perverse cloudiness, with what force of vision and of heart he pierced into the mystery of the World; recognising in the highest sensible phenomena, so far as Sense went, only fresh or faded Raiment; yet ever, under this, a celes-tial Essence thereby rendered visible; and while, on the one hand, he *trod the old rags of matter,* with their tinsels, *into the mire,* he on the other every where exalted Spirit above all earthly principalities and powers, and worshipped it, though un-der the meanest shapes, with a true Platonic Mysticism. What the man ultimately purposed by this *casting his Greek-fire into the general Wardrobe of the Universe;* what such more or less complete

rending and *burning of Garments* throughout the whole compass of civilised Life and Speculation, should lead to; the rather as he was no Adamite, in any sense, and could not, like Rousseau, recommend either bodily or intellectual Nudity, and a return to the savage state; all this our readers are now bent to discover; this is, in fact, properly the gist and purport of Professor Teufelsdröckh's Philosophy of Clothes.

Be it remembered, however, that such purport is here not so much evolved as detected to lie ready for evolving. (165–66, emphases added)

The last evasive sentence shows Carlyle's grave doubts about his own capacity to "evolve" the "purport," to resolve the inconsistency between the metaphor of fabric and the epiphanies of fire. For Teufelsdröckh offers no epiphany of fabric despite Carlyle's large ideological and rhetorical investment in this motif (signaled most obviously in the book's title): the chapter that follows Carlyle's initial query (about the connection between clothes and Teufelsdröckhian fire) suggests that the Quaker George Fox's leather suit was superior to the nudity of the Cynic Diogenes insofar as Fox taught a superior doctrine of love. But the logic of the equation between leather suits and love is obscure. The chapter "Adamitism" early in the book is Carlyle's lecture to Teufelsdröckh on the perils of clotheslessness ("Consider, thou foolish Teufelsdröckh, what benefits unspeakable all ages and sexes derive from Clothes" [45]). But the chapter's tone is satirical; clothes appear as comic formulae for, and creators of, an authority that is made to look foolishly arbitrary, whimsically authoritarian—a cartoon.

In sum, as lover, as moralist, as clothes-philosopher, Teufelsdröckh is not up to the level of his epiphanies of fire—fire as the primal energy that makes every smithy a Zoroastrian altar to the sun, and to its parent suns; fire as the lava of madness that seethes at the center of our skull-planet; fire as the flaming procession of historical personages in a cultural pageant from genesis to apocalypse that mirrors the life of each historical actor from birth to death; fire as a stream of uprising energy that affirms each person's will to live as forceful, fluxile, free. The seer is no longer identical in essence and power with what is seen; Teufelsdröckh is not Odin.

But Carlyle, endlessly ingenious in deploying his epiphanic resources strategically in unexpected ways, defensively rescues the situation by presenting *Sartor Resartus*, with all its inconsistencies and imperfections, as one more epiphanic embodiment of the chaotic turbulence that is fire itself:

> It were a piece of vain flattery to pretend that this Work on Clothes entirely contents us; that it is not, like all works of Genius, like the very Sun, which, though the highest published Creation, or work of Genius, has nevertheless black spots and troubled nebulosities amid its effulgence,—a mixture of insight, inspiration, with dulness, double-vision, and even utter blindness. (21)

Sartor, like Teufelsdröckh, is imperfect, chaotic. But so is the Sun, and so are sunlike Genius, the fiery history of humanity, and the upbursting volcanic energy that—in epiphanic terms—is Carlyle's God.

A clever stratagem—but the conflict between fire and clothes is a deeper problem than the mere imperfections of fire itself as symbolized by sunspots. Phenomenological scrutiny has disclosed a contradiction that puts *Sartor* into a sharp new focus, clarifying current debates that center largely on the book's degree and mode of irony. Paul Jay sees *Sartor* as self-deconstructing, trapped in the "web of ironies it has spun," the chief irony being the book's supposed status as a conscious "hoax."[17] By contrast, Peter Allan Dale sees the book's humor as "friendly," "sympathetic rather than satiric," with an aim that is clearly "not Denial but Affirmation."[18] Anne Mellor finds Carlyle directing ironic "skepticism" only at "man's inevitably doomed attempts fully to perceive, comprehend, or express" the "life-force carrying men onward and upward,"[19] a life-force that Carlyle affirms and celebrates. As readers, we are obliged to decide: is *Sartor* intentionally self-deconstructing? fundamentally affirmative? or intended to celebrate the life-force but to express doubts about humanity?

I suggest that none of these thoughtful formulations is fully satisfactory. *Sartor*, as I have tried to show, is a book that embodies in its very imagery an inherent contradiction between its alleged governing metaphor (clothes) and its actual epiphanic successes (eruptive fires). Because of this inner contradiction we cannot characterize the book adequately in terms of a single intention or effective aim; it would not be accurate to call *Sartor* either consciously self-deconstructing or consciously affirmative or even consciously modest about humanity's limitations.

Rather, *Sartor*, like *Heroes*, is a conflicted work, with its discursive "medium" of presentation contradicting its epiphanic implications or "message." The work leaves the reader confused because Carlyle himself seems to waver, unclear whether he should give credence to his philosophy of culture as changing sartorial fashion or to his epiphanies of Spirit as eruptive-destructive apocalyptic fire that threatens all outward forms and consumes all cultural fabric.

SEVEN

Water, Movement, Roundness

Epiphanies and History in Tolstoy's War and Peace

War and Peace is incomparably more than merely an attempted refutation of Carlyle's *Heroes* in a contest of rival epiphanies of history. Yet it provocatively plays that role among the other things it does. The extensive authorial disquisitions on history that are inserted into (or appended at the conclusion of) Tolstoy's massive narration could be collectively entitled *On the Nullity of Heroes and the Vanity of Hero-Worship*. These authorial essays contain counter-Carlylean epiphanies. (Indeed, no epiphanies could possibly be more counter-Carlylean, even though Tolstoy does not explicitly invoke the name of Carlyle as representative of the theoretical position he is attacking.) To Carlyle's clamant historical hero-fires upbursting from a central heart into a surrounding darkness Tolstoy replies, as it were, with visions of historical tides and currents into which individuals willy-nilly merge or blend—the wiser ones gladly. If Carlyle's Napoleon is at least a flash of gunpowder, Tolstoy's is nothing but an arrogant drop in an historic wave. In staging a phenomenological debate of epiphanists of history by juxtaposing *War and Peace* and *Heroes*, we will have to neglect many of the features that make the former work one of the world's best novels. But we will be doing something interesting and useful nonetheless, for in highlighting the epiphanic pattern of *War and Peace* we will find its imaginative center.

War and Peace is an uncommonly rich phenomenological lode for the Bachelardian seeker of epiphanic patterns, particularly as these relate to the envisioning of a model of historical meaning. For in *War and Peace* Tolstoy achieves (among other goals) an ambitious threefold purpose. First, he vividly evokes the epiphanies—the intense, expansive, mysterious moments—experienced by five very different but (in their contrasting ways) appealing and sensitive seekers or seers:

Pierre, Platon Karatayev, Prince Andrei, Petya, Nikolai Rostov. Second, Tolstoy expounds his own (that is, the narrator-persona's) comprehensive theory of history. Finally, he conveys to the reader the pervasive sense of an intimate connection between the seers' visions and the historical destiny of which, according to Tolstoy's theory, these people's lives are a part. The way Tolstoy makes this connection imaginatively powerful is by presenting an epiphanic vision through his own authorial persona in his remarks on history, an authorial epiphany of historical process that shows the same basic element-motion-shape pattern as do the epiphanies of the five seers. The Tolstoy persona becomes, as it were, the sixth seer, the sixth envisioner[1] of the recurrent epiphanic pattern, which we are now given to understand is nothing less than the pattern of history itself.

Gary Saul Morson's *Hidden in Plain View* is the best presentation we have of Tolstoy's many strategies for endowing *War and Peace* with its extraordinarily lifelike open-endedness in character creation and plot structure. For Tolstoy, as Morson shows, individual selves are in some ways really aggregates, multiplicities; incidents and entire characters may fail to realize their potential in the overall "plot" of *War and Peace*, yet such failed potentials are themselves intended to be an important part of the novel, for they are part of human life.[2] In these and other respects the openness of the book's structure is indeed unprecedented.

But Morson goes too far when he calls *War and Peace* a "book with an absent center."[3] Emphasizing the polyphonies, the dialogic interchanges, the pluralism and relativism of the novel, Morson runs into difficulty in dealing with the emphatic pronouncements of the narrator-persona regarding the theory of history. Tolstoy's attempt to make absolute "statements that are completely non-novelistic, that is, both nonfictive and nondialogized" is an attempt that, in Morson's view, "ultimately fails" because the reader is conditioned by the book itself—a "book with an absent center"—to see events as open-ended and open to multiple perspectives.[4]

But *War and Peace* is not, in fact, centerless, and in demonstrating this fact we will be obliged to argue against Morson's influential presentation. For there is a central link between Tolstoy's lectures on the theory of history and the complex lives of seekers within the Tolstoyan tale. That link is a *shared pattern of epiphanic vision*. Tolstoy is a seer; even in the midst of his abstract-sounding declarations of alleged historical principle, he uses metaphors with vivid imagery—elemental, epiphanic imagery that acquires a life of its own. Tolstoy—or his narrative persona—actually presents an epiphany as the basis for his (and the novel's) vision of history. And Tolstoyan characters are seers too; they, too, experience epiphanies, whose powerful oneiric imagery varies that of the narrator-persona himself. Each Tolstoyan quester is multifarious, many-sided, but the pattern of the questers' epiphanies, taken together, turns out to be surprisingly unitary.

War and Peace, then, *does have a center*: it is the shared pattern that links all the Tolstoyan questers' epiphanies and connects each of them with the narrator-persona's own epiphany of history. Neo-Bachelardian phenomenological analysis will enable us to discover the genuine imaginative center of Tolstoy's massive work. And in doing so it will aid our understanding of Tolstoy's problems as polemical novelist in two additional ways. (1) We will see how the vision of history that Tolstoy derives from his epiphanic material contradicts troublingly the ethical doctrines that he also wants to teach. (2) Since Tolstoy's epiphanic pattern unites his own vision of history as author-persona with the several epiphanies of his fictional questers, this overall pattern reveals a strong totalizing tendency quite at variance with any Bakhtinian dialogism that *War and Peace* may otherwise exhibit. We shall thus be shedding light both on the book's unacknowledged inner contradictoriness and on its unsuspectedly powerful—even willful—tendency to offer an epiphanic viewpoint that will see all individual lives and visions as part of a vast historical unifying scheme.

To isolate the epiphanic image-pattern of *War and Peace* seems at first a tricky undertaking. The distinctive material element, form of motion, and type of shape in the Tolstoyan seekers' visions and in the interpolated essays on history's meaning usually occur only individually or in partial combinations. Indeed, they all appear simultaneously only once (though that single appearance is decidedly the central epiphany of the book: Pierre Bezukhov's dream about Platon Karatayev). But the component images[5] of Tolstoy's element-motion-shape pattern, even when they occur only singly or two together, never serve simply to illustrate an idea. Because they take on a life of their own and attain a surreal emotional strength, they lend unity to the mixture of poetry and polemic, of individual experience and speculative exploring, that animates the book.

To analyze *War and Peace* from this point of view, the following method will be used. First, element, motion, and shape will be studied together in Pierre's central dream-vision, an explicitly labeled "vision" or "dream" to serve as paradigm, in intensity and completeness, for more fragmentary versions of the epiphanic pattern. Pierre's dream plays the same paradigmatic role in *War and Peace* that Carlyle's vision or epiphany of Odin played in *Heroes*.

Once the paradigmatic epiphany offered by Pierre's dream has been analyzed, other epiphanic passages will be examined in which the three components of Pierre's paradigm appear only one or two at a time. The first group of passages describes the personally experienced epiphanies of individual seers or questers; the second group conveys Tolstoy's (that is, the narrator-persona's) own epiphany of history. Both sets of epiphanies, the personal and the historical, express the same fundamental mood or experience as does Pierre's dream of Platon Karatayev: the sense of living in a harmonious, rhythmic unity with an encompassing cosmic totality. Element, motion, and shape—water, rhythmic motion, and sphere—will be seen as the vehicles of this vision, the components of the recurrent epiphanic pattern, throughout the whole of Tolstoy's masterpiece.

Because he is the chief quester in *War and Peace*, Pierre Bezukhov's dream-epiphany is crucial. Platon Karatayev, peasant sage, is Pierre's spiritual mentor. After Platon's death Pierre has a dream in which the meaning of Platon's life and death becomes clear and by implication the meaning of Pierre's own destiny is revealed. As Pierre sinks into slumber, he hears a voice—his own or someone else's, he cannot tell—saying,

"Life is everything, Life is God. Everything changes and moves, and that movement is God. And while there is life there is joy in the consciousness of the divine. To love life is to love God. Harder and more blessed than all else is to love this life in one's sufferings, in undeserved sufferings."

"Karatayev!" came to Pierre's mind.

And suddenly there rose before him, as though alive, a long-forgotten, gentle old man who had given him geography lessons in Switzerland. "Wait," said the little old man. And he showed Pierre a globe. The globe was an animate, vibrating ball with no fixed dimensions. Its whole surface consisted of drops closely pressed together. These drops moved, changed, several merging into one, or one splitting into many. Each drop tended to expand, to occupy as much space as possible, but others, with a like tendency, compressed it, sometimes destroying it, sometimes merging with it.

"That is life," said the teacher.

"How simple and clear it is," thought Pierre. "How is it that I did not know this before?"

"In the center is God, and each drop strives to expand so as to reflect Him to the greatest extent. And it grows, merges, disappears from the surface, sinks to the depths, and again emerges. That's how it was with Karatayev: he expanded and disappeared. Do you understand, my child?" said the teacher.[6]

Emerging at birth from total unity with God, Platon Karatayev had gradually risen to the surface of the sphere of life as he advanced toward the self-consciousness and discrete individuality of adulthood. Even as he strove to perfect his own powers, however, Platon only reflected the central power of God. A water drop reflecting the round ocean that is God, Platon Karatayev had no qualms about dying: for Platon dying simply meant regaining the center so as to merge completely with the sphere of which he had always been, consciously or unconsciously, a part. Such is the dream-lesson taught to Pierre.

It is worth pausing here to note the likely presence of an intertextual determinant in Pierre's dream: the *sphaera cuius centrum ubique* or divine sphere whose center is everywhere, an epiphanic component we earlier found adapted in Wordsworth's "Pilgrim's Dream" narrative. Like Wordsworth, Tolstoy as epiphanist participates in a tradition that allows certain intertextual constants to recur in new visionary variants.

All components of the fundamental Tolstoyan epiphanic element-motion-shape pattern come together in Pierre's paradigmatic experience. The element is water. The shape is the sphere. And the type of movement is regular, gradual, rhythmic. Each "drop strives to expand" and "grows, merges, disappears from the surface, sinks to the depths, and again emerges." The sphere is womblike in its liquidity, heartlike in its systolic-diastolic motion: movements from center to surface and back again are as rhythmically regular as breathing. In this passage the motions are chiefly up and down; elsewhere in *War and Peace* they may also be horizontal, like ocean currents; or else regularly repeated mergers and separations, like those of the drops on the sphere's surface, are simply rhythmic in a general way, without any specified direction ("These drops moved, changed, several merging into one, or one splitting into many"). But all Tolstoyan visionary motion is instantly recognizable because these diverse sorts of movement always share one basic quality: regular, unforced, natural rhythm, steady and constant.

Element, motion, and shape—water, gradual rhythmic motion, and sphere—are almost equally distributed among the epiphanies of all the major male questers in the book. Sphericity marks Pierre's early impressions of Platon. Harmonious, unforced rhythmic motion characterizes the central epiphanies of Prince Andrei and Petya Rostov (indeed, the rhythm in both cases is even combined with a sort of "music"). Water appears in the "sea" metaphor with which Tolstoy describes the ecstatic transport of Petya's brother Nikolai. We shall treat each of these visions in turn, showing their links to Pierre's water-sphere dream of the motion of souls. This analysis will demonstrate the kinship of all Tolstoyan epiphanies, their underlying similarity to the illuminating experience of Pierre, and the meaning they all share with Pierre's dream. This meaning is always the same: the harmonious, unforced unity of the individual with the rhythms of the greater cosmic totality.

Pierre's early impressions of Platon introduce the theme of roundness, and this theme constitutes their chief link with the later dream-epiphany of the water-sphere. The roundness of Platon, as Pierre first describes him, troubles most readers of *War and Peace*. We are reluctant to imagine Pierre's spiritual guide as a Dickensian roly-poly caricature; such grotesqueness is unexpected. As Pierre later recalls his fellow prisoners,

> they were all dim figures to him, all except Platon Karatayev,
> who always remained in his heart as a vivid, precious memory,
> the personification of everything Russian, kindly, and round.
> When at dawn the next morning Pierre looked at his neighbor,
> his first impression of him as something round was fully
> confirmed: Platon's whole figure in his French military coat

belted with a piece of rope, his cap, and bast shoes, was round; his head was perfectly round; his back, chest, shoulders, and even his arms, which he always held as if about to embrace something, were round; and his friendly smile and large, tender brown eyes were round. (*WP* 1161; *SS* 7:58)

The impression is grotesque because Tolstoy is trying to transpose onto the plane of naturalistic description an epiphanic intuition mystical or pantheistic like Platon's, or like the one expressed in Pierre's later water-sphere dream. Other passages make it clear that Platon's roundness, here expressed rather naïvely as a physical quality, is really a metaphysical one, like the roundness of Being according to Parmenides, or the metaphorical roundness of God in the traditional image of the sphere whose center is everywhere. The reason why, in Pierre's mind, Platon "always remained what he had seemed that first night; an unfathomable, round everlasting personification of the spirit of simplicity and truth" (*WP* 1163; *SS* 7:60), is that Platon's rounded simplicity is absolute, it is Truth. Indeed, it stems from the Absolute, from something "unfathomable" and "everlasting," from a larger whole of which, like Pierre's water droplets in the dream, Platon is always a part:

Every utterance, every action of his, was the manifestation of a force unknown to him, which was his life. But his life, as he saw it, had no meaning as a separate entity. It had meaning only as a part of a whole of which he was at all times conscious. His words and actions flowed from him as smoothly, spontaneously, and inevitably as fragrance emanates from a flower. He could not understand the value or significance of any word or deed taken separately. (*WP* 1163; *SS* 7:60)

Pierre's dream-sphere and Platon's roundness mean the same thing: the sense of an individual life as intuitively conscious of the larger unknown life it reflects. Kindred shape, kindred insight.

By contrast, Prince Andrei's epiphany shares with Pierre's water-sphere dream not a shape but a pattern of motion: an up-and-down rhythm, a sequence of harmonious, regular rises and falls. Note also the motion of "expanding and spreading out," like that of the water drops on the surface of Pierre's sphere:

Prince Andrei heard (without knowing whether it was delusion or reality) a soft, whispering voice repeating over and over again in a steady rhythm: "piti-piti-piti,"[7] and then "ti-ti," and again "piti-piti-piti" and "ti-ti." And to the sound of this whispering music Prince Andrei felt that over his face, from the very center of it, a strange ethereal structure of delicate needles or splinters was being erected. He felt that he must carefully maintain his balance (though this was exceedingly difficult) so that the rising edifice should not collapse; nevertheless it kept falling to pieces and slowly rising again to the sound of the rhythmical, whispered music. "It is growing, extending! It keeps expanding and spreading out!" said Prince Andrei to himself. While he listened to the whispered sounds and felt the sensation of the edifice of needles rising and expanding, every now and then the red halo of the light around the candle caught his eyes, and he heard the rustle of cockroaches and the buzzing of the fly that plopped against his pillow and his face. (*WP* 1101–2; *SS* 6:431–32)

While keeping track of the regular rising and falling movements of this melodious, rhythmic structure, Prince Andrei at the same time notes a white sphinxlike shape by the door. For a while the whole mélange of perceptions seems too much to take in, but just as Prince Andrei is about to give up exhaustedly, "all at once feeling and thought floated to the surface of his mind with extraordinary power and clarity" (*WP* 1102; *SS* 6:432)—just like an ascending drop within Pierre's water-sphere. While in this elevated state, Prince Andrei experiences "that feeling of love which is the very essence of the soul and which requires no object"; he knows the "bliss" of loving "God and all his manifestations" (*WP* 1102; *SS* 6:432). Filled also with new love for Natasha, Prince Andrei feels the need to forgive her for her earlier attempted betrayal. And now, to the earlier white sphinx (just a shirt transformed by Prince Andrei's semidelirium) is suddenly added a "new white sphinx," as Natasha herself approaches the sickbed. At this point, "like a man plunged into water," Prince Andrei loses consciousness (*WP* 1103; *SS* 6:433).

The ascent-descent pattern of the epiphany is complete, as in Pierre's water-sphere paradigm; water is even mentioned to reinforce the parallel. The love-death of Prince Andrei, after his rise to unusual clarity of consciousness, precisely parallels Platon's descent as a water drop, his regaining of the center after initially rising to the surface of Pierre's liquid globe. Prince Andrei has learned from his epiphany the power of "divine love" to help him see another creature as God's manifestation: "for the first time he imagined her soul" (*WP* 1102; *SS* 6:432). Rhythmic risings and fallings, symbolizing an intimate, harmonious bond between an ascent to conscious clarity and a descent to unconscious communion, ally Prince Andrei's elemental epiphany of love and transcendent unity with the epiphanies of Platon and Pierre. All three seers make us recall the Heraclitean maxim (epigraph to Eliot's "Burnt Norton") that "The way up and the way down are one and the same."[8]

Like Prince Andrei's vision, young Petya Rostov's epiphany of the musical fugue carries over the pattern of motion from Pierre's water-sphere dream. We see the same successive, regular, harmonious blendings and separations as in Pierre's globe of droplets, together with the "rhythmical, whispered music" from Andrei's experience of the rising and falling structure of needles. This harmony-epiphany of Petya's begins as the sky clears after a storm. The heavens seem to participate in an up-and-down rhythmic motion: "At . . . times the sky seemed to rise high overhead, then to sink so low that one could have reached out and touched it. Petya's eyes began to close and he swayed slightly" (*WP* 1260; *SS* 7:168–69). The up-and-down rhythm helps set a mood quite reminiscent of Pierre's dream.

> The trees were dripping. There was a low hum of talk. The horses neighed and jostled one another. Someone snored. *Ozheeg-zheeg, ozheeg-zheeg* . . . hissed the saber on the whetstone, and all at once Petya heard a melodious orchestra playing some unfamiliar, sweetly solemn hymn. . . . The music swelled, the melody developing and passing from one instrument to another. What was playing was a fugue—though Petya had not the slightest idea what a fugue was. Each instrument . . . played its own part, and before it had finished the motif, merged with another instrument that began almost the same air, then with a third, and a fourth; and they all blended into one, and again separated, and again blended, now into solemn church music, now into some resplendent and triumphal air.[9]

"Oh, but I must have been dreaming," Petya said to himself as he lurched forward. "It's only in my ears. Perhaps it's music of my own making. Well, go on, my music. Now! . . . "

He closed his eyes. And on all sides, as from a distance, the notes vibrated, swelling into harmonies, dispersing and mingling again. (*WP* 1260; *SS* 7:169)

Petya wonders if it is he or someone else who is making the music, just as Pierre was unable to tell whose voice was saying, "Everything changes and moves, and that movement is God" ("someone, he or another, articulated his thoughts" [*WP* 1272; *SS* 7:181]). Indeed, Petya's and Pierre's epiphanies are separated by barely a dozen pages in the novel, and their strong typological similarity makes it clear why Tolstoy felt no need to provide any additional interpretive commentary for Petya's. Both epiphanies also share with Prince Andrei's dream the connection of a rising with a contrasting but interfused sense of depth:

And from unknown depths rose the swelling, exultant sound. "Now, voices join in!" Petya commanded. At first, from afar, he heard men's, then women's voices steadily mounting in a rhapsodic crescendo. Awed and elated, Petya listened to their wondrous beauty.

The voices blended with the triumphal victory march, the dripping of the trees, the *ozheeg-zheeg-zheeg* of hissing saber . . . and again the horses jostled and neighed, not disturbing the harmony, but becoming part of it [literally, "entering into it," "vkhodia v nego"]. (*WP* 1261; *SS* 7:169–70)

All three epiphanies—Pierre's, Andrei's, Petya's—affirm a serene consciousness of, and a blending with, a harmonious cosmic totality. The three visions achieve this through rhythmic motions of rising and of "mingling again," "entering into it."

The final epiphany of a Tolstoyan quester to be looked at here—the reaction of Petya's brother Nikolai to an imperial review of troops—is patriotic rather than cosmic. Merger with a nation is a far different thing from merger with the cosmos. For this reason, Nikolai's experience cannot be regarded as quite analogous with the visions of Pierre, Platon, Andrei, and Petya. Yet it too is an experience of love and a reverie of merger in a mysterious larger unity. As such, it shares with Pierre's water-sphere dream-epiphany the metaphoric use of the element water: "Every general and soldier felt his own insignificance, was conscious of being a grain of sand in that sea of men, and at the same time felt his own might, being conscious of himself as part of that great whole"; Nikolai's own feeling is one of "tenderness and ecstasy such as he had never before known" (*WP* 301, 303; *SS* 4:331, 332–33). Nikolai is even ready to cry at his inability to express his exultant surge of love for the czar, and he thinks that if the latter should speak to him, "I should die of happiness" (*WP* 303; *SS* 4:333)—a striking modification of the love-death motif from Andrei's and Pierre's dreams.

The element of water is just as important as round shapes and rhythmical, regular motions to Tolstoy's vision of unity in multiplicity. Only the nonentities in *War and Peace*, the petty egotists Boris Drubetskoy and Julie Karagina, deeming themselves a "breed apart," cannot identify with the great metaphoric sea of the one life within us and abroad: "Meeting at large gatherings Julie and Boris gazed at each other like kindred souls in a sea of prosaic people" (*WP* 665; *SS* 5:346). Unlike even the relatively limited Nikolai, they can never become conscious of themselves as "part of that great whole"; unlike Andrei (and Platon and Pierre), they can never understand that "Love is God, and to die means that I, a particle of love, shall return to the universal and eternal source" (*WP* 1175; *SS* 7:74).

Study of the epiphanic element-motion-shape pattern of *War and Peace* has revealed the unity of the Tolstoyan questers' individual intuitions of themselves as partakers of a love that passes understanding. But this same image pattern is equally basic to Tolstoy's own meditations on the nature and meaning of human history as a whole. For Tolstoy, the age-long process of human activity that constitutes history could take on the same resonant unity, the same symbolic cohesiveness and visionary immediacy as the epiphanies of a Pierre, a Petya, or a Prince Andrei. Moreover, Tolstoy as historian and Platon Karatayev as spiritual master teach the same lessons, which may be grasped through the same visionary, epiphanic expressions: water, regular rhythmic motion, and spheres.

Tolstoy's incorporation of this element-motion-shape pattern into his own epiphany of history begins with a strong emphasis on the

"motion" part of the pattern. After listing, for more than four paragraphs, the "myriads of causes" that have been adduced by one historian or another, or that might hypothetically be adduced, to account
for Napoleon's invasion of Russia, and after making sure these causes
have been enumerated in as dull a style as possible in order to show
how monotonously alike are their insubstantial claims to our attention, Tolstoy offers the following conclusion, which merits study:

> There was no single cause for the war, but it happened simply be-
> cause it had to happen. Millions of men, renouncing human feel-
> ings and reason, had to move from west to east to slay their fel-
> lows, just as some centuries earlier hordes of men had moved
> from east to west slaying their fellows. (*WP* 731; *SS* 6:9)

In other words, no single factor caused the war except some principle of reciprocal motion, of pendular rhythmic movement—an
epiphanic pattern exemplified by vast surges or sweeping movements
of large masses of men. The rhythm of movement pattern is introduced seemingly quite casually and briefly, as if the second sentence
quoted above were simply a more or less obvious implication of the
first. Tolstoy is saying: (1) the war happened because it had to happen,
and (2) this means that it was part of an eastward movement that
had to happen in order to counterbalance an earlier westward movement that had to happen. But the second statement implies a principle
that Tolstoy never proves, though it undeniably held a strong grip on
his epiphanic imagination—namely, the principle that mutually
counterbalancing large-scale movements of people somehow "have to
happen." Tolstoy never offers any proof of his conviction that the Na-
poleonic eastward onrush was a necessary counterpart to the westward sweep of the Golden Horde in the thirteenth century. But he
does very tellingly refer, at one point, to Attila's invasion and to the
Crusades, which are clearly to be construed as another pair of westward and eastward counterbalancing movements. The "movement of
the peoples at the time of the Crusades," described as a "movement
of peoples from west to east," is juxtaposed to the "migration" in the
reverse direction led earlier by Attila (*WP* 1427, 1445; *SS* 7:349, 370).

Tolstoy does not elaborate, however, on this solitary additional example, so the rhythmic principle that westward and eastward pendular movements are the essential stuff of history (i.e., that they are

what simply "has to happen") remains the unproved axiom of Tolstoy's theory of history. Its grounding or support is an imaginative one. And once it is assumed, the inevitability of all else follows. If we admit

> that the purpose of the upheavals of European nations is unknown to us, that we know only the facts—the murders, first in France, then in Italy, in Africa, in Prussia, in Austria, in Spain, and in Russia—and that *the movements from west to east and from east to west comprise the essence and end of these events,* . . . [then] it will be clear that all those minor events were inevitable. (*WP* 1355; *SS* 7:269, emphasis added)

Compared with these massive, reciprocal, rhythmic motions, which constitute the *essence* of historical reality (note Tolstoy's word "essence," "sushchnost' ") and which provide history's underlying pattern, various political murders in seven countries are merely minor events. Tolstoy insists upon the *absolute formal symmetry, the rhythmic regularity, of eastward and westward movements*:

> The fundamental and essential significance of the European events at the beginning of the nineteenth century lies in the bellicose movement of the mass of European peoples from west to east and then from east to west. This was instigated by the movement from west to east. (*WP* 1356; *SS* 7:269)

For Tolstoy's epiphanic imagination, this principle or pattern of rhythmic movement is vividly compelling. But the imaginative appeal of such movements for Tolstoy cannot be fully understood apart from the "element" and "shape" constituents of his pattern of historical epiphany. Rhythmic motion, water, and spheres mean as much to Tolstoy the epiphanic historian as they did to Pierre the epiphanic dreamer.

First, the element: water. History is like a sea and behaves as a sea does:

> Seven years had passed since the war of 1812. The storm-tossed sea of European history had subsided within its shores and seemed to be calm; but the mysterious forces that move hu-

manity (mysterious because the laws determining their actions
are unknown to us) continued to operate.

Though the surface of the sea of history appeared to be mo-
tionless, the movement of humanity went on as unceasingly as
the flow of time. Various groups of people formed and dissolved;
the causes that would bring about the formation and dissolution
of kingdoms and the displacement of peoples were in the course
of preparation.

The sea of history was not driven by gales from one shore to
another as before: it seethed in its depths. Historical figures were
not borne by the waves from one shore to another as before.
(*WP* 1351; *SS* 7:264)

The "sea of history" in this Tolstoyan epiphany is driven by gales
from one shore to another, with lulls (such as the period of "reaction"
after the victory of the Holy Alliance) when it seethes in its depths.
The horizontal wave motions of large-scale invasions and migrations
bring about the "formation and dissolution of kingdoms and the displacement of peoples." Napoleon, according to Tolstoy, was a bad philosopher precisely because he failed to realize this. Like King Canute,
Napoleon thought he could direct the sea, whereas he was but "the
figurehead on the prow of a ship," and even his startling return from
exile was but the "last backwash" of an eastward wave (*WP* 1203,
1360; *SS* 7:107, 274).

But horizontal currents are not the only indicators of changing
movement in the historical sea: vertical motions are also crucial, as
in Pierre's paradigmatic epiphany, his water-sphere dream. During
the lulls between major horizontal sweeps, upward surges from below, mysterious seethings of the sea from its "depths," cause diverse
groups of people to be successively "formed and dissolved." Each new
horizontal movement, westward or eastward, is initiated by a prepara-
tory stage of vertical surgings from below. These seethings from the
depths provide the crucial link between Tolstoy's ocean-epiphany
of history and Pierre's water-sphere epiphany of "life." "Groups of
people" form and dissolve as a result of seethings originating in the
depths of the historical sea, just as individuals rise to the surface and
dissolve back to the center of Pierre's water-sphere. (Recall also the

description of drops that "moved, changed, several merging into one, or one splitting into many," on the surface of the sphere.) Moreover, just as Pierre learns that "in the center is God," so likewise Tolstoy learns from his vision of history that "*only the Deity*, prompted by no temporal agency, can *by His sole will* determine the direction of mankind's movement" (*WP* 1431; *SS* 7:353, emphasis added).

Tolstoy does not introduce the epiphanic image of the sphere or globe as explicitly into his discussions of historical pattern as he does in Pierre's dream, but implicitly the notion of the Newtonian earthly sphere pervades these historical discussions, which abound in references to Newton's laws of gravity. The "force of free will" is as subject to the "laws of necessity" as the "force of gravitation" is to "Newton's law" (*WP* 1450; *SS* 7:376). "As with the law of gravity," the "enormous mass" of the retreating French armies attracts "the discrete atoms [individual soldiers] to itself," thus ensuring its cohesiveness (*WP* 1228–29; *SS* 7:134). Commander Kutuzov knows it is pointless to pursue the French, for "the apple must not be picked while it is still green. It will fall of itself when ripe" (*WP* 1223; *SS* 7:129). Kutuzov, like Tolstoy himself, uses Newtonian metaphors to show his intuitive grasp of the laws of historical gravity.

These gravitational laws of our earthly sphere—laws central to Tolstoy's and Commander Kutuzov's shared epiphany of history—derive from God; they describe God's direction of history ("only the Deity . . . can by His sole will determine the direction of mankind's movement"). Platon Karatayev believes that "Man proposes, but God disposes": Platon's example provides Pierre with what is specifically labeled a "center of gravity," namely, a spiritual and psychological sense that he too, like Platon, has a "judge within him who by some rule unknown to him" decides "what should and should not be done" (*WP* 1158, 1324; *SS* 7:53, 239). The feeling of a center of gravity that Pierre acquires from Platon is a sense of contact with the "center" of our earthly sphere, that center that is God. God controls the laws of motion of our individual and collective life-sphere; indeed, as we learned from Pierre's dream, in a larger mystical or pantheist or epiphanic sense, God *is* the sphere. Tolstoy, as historian, likewise teaches that God controls the laws of motion of our life-sphere: "only the Deity . . . can by His sole will determine the direction of mankind's movement."

From Platon, Pierre learns the Tolstoyan lesson that only receptive, intuitive, or unconscious thought—wise passiveness—can put one in touch with the mystery at the "center of gravity" of our historical sphere. The laws of gravity that govern the movements of droplets and currents, of individuals and societies, are at bottom spiritual laws, beyond reason. But these spiritual laws of individual and social life share the inevitability of the laws of natural and even of divine life.

In sum, as presented to us by the unifying element-motion-shape pattern of *War and Peace*, Tolstoyan reality, in the realms both of personal epiphany and of historical epiphanic pattern, is a round and centered thing, composed of symmetrical, harmonious, mutually counterbalancing motions in accord with an inner law like the control of gravitational forces over water. People without awareness of holistic reality, people who feel no oneness with the great oceanic swells and lulls of our life-sphere (St. Petersburg nobles are good examples of such people), live in a world of unreality, "phantoms and echoes," "form" not "substance" (*WP* 850, 1117; *SS* 6:145, 7:7). Their thoughts belong to maya, illusion, not to the rounded, rhythmic reality of the encompassing ocean.

We have been led to an epiphanic justification of History's ways to humanity.[10] I would be tempted to call the total experience a theophany except that the element-motion-shape pattern seems much more deeply rooted in Tolstoy's imaginings than the very loosely defined "God" it is said to manifest. (In any case, I see a continuum leading from theophanies to epiphanies, and [as noted in my introduction] the distinction in any given case may be nearly impossible to make.) Spheres, pendular or symmetric motion of drops or tides or currents or waves, even of aery needlelike structures or musical sound waves—these have a hallucinatory force in *War and Peace*, a dreamlike power that carries conviction. Pierre Bezukhov's water-sphere dream and all the closely related epiphanies of Prince Andrei, Petya, Nikolai, Kutuzov, and Tolstoy himself express a serene and meditative calm that could hardly offer a more marked contrast to Carlyle's flaming Odin, a seer who in vision recreates himself as human-divine epiphany of eruptive, flashing Fire.

Yet Tolstoy and Carlyle are alike in that neither can escape the distortions, the hazards, of trying to force history into the bounds of an elemental epiphany. Carlylean heroes all emulate Odin, but Odin is an unhistorical imagining of Carlyle's; it turns out, moreover, that when we look at history we find Odin's would-be emulators to be rather poor copies, anyway—poorer and poorer as history proceeds. Teufelsdröckh reimagines the Odin-style fire force rather well, but he too fails to embody it in his own life story. Carlyle's epiphany-inspired theory of historical heroism is called radically into question by history—not just by history as *we* might see it, but even by history as Carlyle himself sees it. Tolstoy's problems as epiphanist of history are no less severe.

These problems are threefold. First, of course, the assumption that eastward and westward movements constitute the essential stuff of history is unproved, and many readers will doubt its validity. Second, it is unprovable that such movements are divinely caused, no matter how vaguely divinity is defined. And finally, even if God's purposes, as ultimate efficient and final causes of history's formal movements, are ultimately inscrutable, there is still the problem that these purposes come into open conflict with the Christian ethics Tolstoy would also like to teach. Tolstoy emphasizes that "with the standard of good and evil given us by Christ," we know that greatness requires "simplicity, goodness, and truth" (*WP* 1279; *SS* 7:190). Yet Tolstoy's God disregards these Christian criteria in appointing historical leaders, for Napoleon's "cruel, grievous, harsh, and inhuman role" was "predestined for him" when "providence" chose him specifically "for the deplorable ineluctable role of executioner of peoples" (*WP* 980–81; *SS* 6:293, 295). Dunnigan's translation is fairly accurate, but it is misleading to write "deplorable" (suggesting moral disapproval) where Tolstoy says merely "sad"—a word that indicates no moral judgment. The depressing bleakness of Tolstoy's utterance is inescapable: Napoleon is described as "prednaznachennyi provideniem na pechal'nuiu, nesvobodnuiu rol' palacha narodov"—literally, "pre-appointed by providence for the sad, unfree role of executioner of peoples."

It is astonishing that Tolstoy can bring himself to make such a claim as he does here: only his deep imaginative commitment to his epiphany of historical "currents" and "waves" can explain it. If Napoleon is but a drop in a divine historical current or wave, subject to those ineluctable laws of "gravity" that govern the movement of historical waters over the surface of our earthly sphere, then Napoleon's tragic actions may seem justifiable to Tolstoy (that is, providentially approved, divinely predestined) by the "logic" of the image pattern that Tolstoy invokes as an epiphany of history. But twentieth-century readers will have no less difficulty with this extraordinary providential or divine appointment of an "executioner of peoples" than did Tolstoy's nineteenth-century critics.

Tolstoy's totalizing tendencies get him into an unfortunate position—that of invoking an epiphany-based image of history whose implications conflict very disturbingly with the humane values we may legitimately derive from the equally epiphanic experiences of his privileged fictional questers. Morson's description of Tolstoy's novel as "a book with an absent center" cannot be maintained in view of our findings here, for the pattern uniting Tolstoy's own epiphany of history with the epiphanies of his fictional seers functions as a powerful—perhaps too powerful—unifying center of *War and Peace*.

EIGHT

Turning Stones to Fire

The Apocalypse According to
Barrett Browning

We all have a "sense of an ending"; we feel that the conclusion of any work, even a secondary or analytical work like this book, is meant to be a kind of climax, that whatever occupies the concluding portion has in some sense a privileged place. So in concluding the series of phenomenological case studies that constitute this volume with a neo-Bachelardian analysis of Barrett Browning's *Aurora Leigh*, I need to make my intentions clear. I do not wish to imply that *Aurora Leigh* is the culmination of an ascent; though my Barrett Browning chapter follows the one on Tolstoy, I do not expect the reader to infer that Barrett Browning improves on, or even equals, Tolstoy. Rather, she is the best subject for my "ending" chapter because of her own epiphanic focus on moments felt as apocalyptic, as the forcefully climactic, transformative endings of phases in life—though for Barrett Browning, as for Wordsworth in "The Pilgrim's Dream," apocalyptically imagined endings also mean beginnings.

Although I do not see Barrett Browning's verse narrative as any sort of grand climax, I want to make three claims for the work. First, *Aurora Leigh* is in my judgment one of the best epic poems of modern times—greatly underrated until recently and even now far less read than it should be. Second, the organizing principle of *Aurora Leigh* is the strategic placement of epiphanies, making it comparable in structure and design to Wordsworth's *Prelude* or Pater's *Marius*. By clarifying the individual epiphanies in Barrett Browning's masterwork, we can illuminate the central theme or subject of that work. For *Aurora Leigh*, like *The Prelude* or *Marius*, not only contains epiphanies but is fundamentally *about* epiphanies. My third and final point is that *Aurora Leigh* may be usefully juxtaposed to the epiphanic visions of Carlyle and Tolstoy because its epiphanies, like theirs, are visions of human action within a historical context, of people acting to shape and to transform history.

Barrett Browning's epiphanies might appear to be more modest than those of Carlyle since her envisioned protagonist is neither a world-historical personage (like Mahomet or Napoleon) nor a figure of national repute (such as Cromwell or Burns or Dr. Johnson). But Barrett Browning's epiphanies are every bit as fiery as Carlyle's, and in a way they are much more ambitious in their implications. For, unlike *Heroes* with its discouraging theme of decline and fall, *Aurora Leigh* does not offer a vision of historic entropy, a disappointing Carlylean epiphanic sequence of dimming glories, of diminishing returns. Instead, Barrett Browning presents fiery epiphanies that continue to have not only encouraging but startlingly affirmative results, epiphanies that can still *do* something in, and to, and for, the world. In contrast to Carlyle's fires, which forcefully flash out but then simply disappear, Barrett Browning's fires transform stone, making it crystalline, refulgent. The stone itself becomes fiery.

Like Tolstoy, Barrett Browning finds epiphanic power in the individual and private moment; she insists, as Tolstoy does, that individual moments of insight have a determining place in the larger divine scheme of human history. But she does not glorify passivity or serene acceptance; though her hero is a poet and not a warrior, that heroic poet is a warrior of spirit. Barrett Browning does not attain the greatness of Tolstoy as an imaginer of diverse human beings. But she is more coherent in presenting questions of human responsibility within history; for her, God does not "choose" executioners like Napoleon or "predestine" them for deplorable roles. Barrett Browning thinks that there is never any excuse for simply flowing with the historical tide.

Elementally, Barrett Browning is closer to Carlyle. I have noted that her fires irradiate and etherealize the stony objects of their combustion, unlike Carlyle's epiphanic flames, which for the most part simply erupt and flare amidst the surrounding darkness. But both seers are epiphanists of flaming glory.

Finally, in one crucial aspect, Barrett Browning relates interestingly to the Wordsworth of "The Pilgrim's Dream": I refer to the fiery apocalypticism of Barrett Browning's epiphanies. As Wordsworth shows a debt to the Book of Revelation in his "Pilgrim's Dream" vision of a world transformed, so too Barrett Browning quite clearly responded to Revelation intensely and with power—and far more often than Wordsworth ever did. Here we have one more instance, then, of a crucial intertextual determinant of epiphanic vision. Barrett Browning's apocalyptic conflagrations and eruptions, her world-altering transformations of rock into crystalline flame, reveal emphatically feminist fires. As such, Barrett Browning's epiphanies challenge all traditional mythic notions of womanly waters or masculine suns. Indeed, even when Barrett Browning envisions epiphanic androgynes (as we shall see below), these fiery gender-crossers may be viewed as feminist by implication, appropriating for the uses of feminist polemic the vir-tues (etymologically unfortunate term) of both sexes.

Because Barrett Browning's apocalyptic or spiritualizing or world-transforming fires are epiphanies of "endings," epiphanies of the kind associated with the end-of-the-world apocalypse presented in the end-of-the-Bible Book of Revelation, she reserves her paradigmatic epiphany for the end of *Aurora Leigh*. There, as we shall see, Aurora's lover Romney, a blind man who repeatedly likens himself to a *stone* ("as powerless . . . as a stone," "A mere bare blind stone in the blaze of day"),[1] attains a state of *crystalline* visionary purity ("eyes . . . unspotted in their crystals" [9.580–81]) that opens him up to the *fire*-engendering love of dawnlike Aurora ("two large explosive hearts . . . melted, in the fire" [9.718, 720]) and thus enables him, newly enlivened and refined by ardent flame, to feel the motions of the crystal skyey spheres and to see the crystalline fires of heavenly gems. Once Romney's own stoniness has turned to flame with the help of crystal vision, his transformed vision can project its own glory in an epiphany of yet more fire-filled crystal stones. (Romney's transformation, we will see, is shared, closely paralleled, and made possible by Aurora herself.) Such is the paradigm of all Barrett Browning epiphanies: *stone becomes fiery with the help of crystal.*

We will return to this climactic paradigm, of course, at story's end, where we can analyze it more deeply and enjoy it at more leisure, in its proper context. But the reader should keep it in mind at the start and throughout the chapter. Like the paradigmatic keys to epiphanic structure in Carlyle and Tolstoy, like the vision of fiery Odin in *Heroes* and the water-sphere dream of Pierre in *War and Peace*, Barrett

Browning's epiphanic paradigm is presented as a vision, a dreamlike apparition of exemplary, hallucinatory power. Like Carlyle and Tolstoy, Barrett Browning assists our neo-Bachelardian phenomenological venture by helpfully supplying the vivid paradigm we need as starting point for our study. She is exceptional only in placing this starting point at the apocalyptic ending of her epic.

Few fire epiphanists can ever have been so ambitiously apocalyptic as Barrett Browning. *Aurora Leigh* is no mere book of dawn, despite the plain meaning of its eponymous heroine's name; something more is meant than just the morning redness in the sky. We are intended to be present at an epiphanic reshaping of material history, a fiery spiritualization and transfiguring of the envisioned world. Though Aurora does try at times to admonish herself to limit her aspirations to a level more in keeping with her unassuming station and modest origins, her efforts at self-persuasion almost comically fail—because her fiery cosmic rhetoric is so appealing and unquenchable:[2]

> Aurora Leigh, be humble. Shall I hope
> To speak my poems in mysterious tune
> With man and nature? - with the lava-lymph
> That trickles from successive galaxies
> Still drop by drop adown the finger of God
> In still new worlds? . . .
> With multitudinous life, and finally
> With the great escapings of ecstatic souls
> Who, in a rush of too long prisoned flame,
> Their radiant faces upward, burn away
> This dark of the body, issuing on a world,
> Beyond our mortal? . . .
> Aurora Leigh: be humble.
>
> (5.1–6, 19–24, 42)

Aurora soon stops telling herself to be humble, knowing it won't work. She may have felt obliged (temporarily) to suppress her love for her condescending cousin Romney, yet she will not compromise, will not succumb to subordination, will not betray her poetic calling. "For the truth itself," she reasons, "That's neither man's nor woman's, but just God's" (7.752–53). In her fiery epiphanies, Aurora can embody this androgynous truth "without the approbation of a man" (5.63). Aurora's own androgynous imagination envisions, encompasses, and unifies what traditional typology would characterize as both the male (active) and female (passive) fires: lava-lymph trickling down God's finger, and ecstatic spirits burning up their bodies to issue forth into new worlds of responsive intensity.

Here it may be apposite to respond briefly to recent observations on Barrett Browning's androgynous imaginings. Tracing images of the hand and of the sun throughout the poet's career, Virginia Steinmetz says that although these images reveal Barrett Browning's "struggle to find an image of androgyny disassociated from the sun" in its male-biased interpretations, "all she discovered was an image of a woman as the passive vessel of the sun and an image of herself as the bold creature of the sun who would dare to use its energy to supersede it and fail in her own eyes."[3] But I would suggest that if we see the sun imagery as a subset of the larger epiphanic pattern of turning stones to fire, Barrett Browning as an elemental apocalyptist will not by any means be seen to have failed in her own eyes.

The unrelentingly apocalyptic fieriness[4] of Barrett Browning's elemental epiphanies means that, as a polemicist of new possibilities for female heroism at the present time,[5] the author of *Aurora Leigh* is a far more confident and unvacillating fire-seer than the Carlyle of *Heroes*,[6] with his nostalgia for a bolder, freer past. Barrett Browning attacks Matthew Arnold's classicizing nostalgia, too, as mere evasiveness: "The critics say that epics have died out / With Agamemnon and the goat-nursed gods; / I'll not believe it" (5.139–41). There are possible heroes in every age. "Ay, but every age / Appears to souls who live in't (ask Carlyle) / Most unheroic" (5.155–57). How, then, can one refute the skepticism of Arnold and Carlyle? How to answer the doubters who detect no heroic potential in the present time?

The best response, Barrett Browning feels certain, is not a discursive reply but an epiphanic one: to present a symbolic image of bold, active energy in an epiphany of *stone transformed by fire*. "Every age," Barrett Browning tells us, "Through being beheld too close, is ill-discerned / By those who have not lived past it" (5.166–68). Suppose that Xerxes had accomplished his plan of carving Mount Athos into the form of a man: peasants "gathering brushwood in his ear" would not be able to see the enormous statue. They would need to travel "five miles off" to view the huge stone man filled with sun-fire from the sky, sun-fire that has proved the food of inspiration, transforming the rocky man into a fiery poet of silence. The peasants would see

> Full human profile, nose and chin distinct,
> Mouth, muttering rhythms of silence up the sky,
> And fed at evening with the blood of suns;
> Grand torso, - hand, that flung perpetually
> The largess of a silver river down
> To all the country pastures.
> . . . Never flinch, [Barrett Browning tells the would-be poet]
> But still, unscrupulously epic, catch
> Upon a burning lava of a song,
> The full-veined, heaving, double-breasted Age:
> That, when the next shall come, the men of that
> May touch the impress with reverent hand, and say
> 'Behold, - behold the paps we all have sucked!
> That bosom seems to beat still, or at least
> It sets ours beating: this is living art,
> Which thus presents and thus records true life.'
> (5.171, 174, 176–81, 213–22)

Again Barrett Browning has envisioned her fiery Sublime Androgyne. As male, the godlike mountain-hero, nourished with sun-blood, his appropriate fiery ambrosia, flings down the largess of a silver river as God drops lava-lymph down from his finger. As female, the equally divine full-breasted hero-goddess conveys the sound of her heartbeat in the equally flaming ichor of the poet's lavalike music. This is heroism doubled: the spirit of the age captured by the singer of the age. And however androgynous the vision, it is of course a woman (Barrett Browning) who envisions it as prototype and program for another woman (the maturing poet Aurora Leigh).

What is more, in both heroic visions the same elemental epiphanic transformation occurs: stone becomes fire. Fed with fiery sun-blood, the stone statue, newly become poet, sings his silent rhythms to the sky: his rock-body is animated, metamorphosed, transfigured by the fire that has fed it and that now circulates through it as silent song.

And the epic poet's burning lava likewise brings alive the Great Mother of the present age; eruptive *stone* is molten into the *streaming fire* of song in order that her heartbeat may be heard.

Again we have seen the crucial process in Barrett Browning's fully developed pattern of elemental epiphanies throughout *Aurora Leigh*: turning stone to fire. The fire is felt as spiritual, the transformation as something miraculous, transcending Nature. Unlike Carlylean fires, which usually have only an inchoate or turbulent darkness to combat, Barrett Browning's spiritual flames work at enlightening, clarifying, sublimating (in an alchemical way) the solidest of all possible emblems of despair: rocks, metals, mountains. The image that connects the fires and the rocks is that of crystal. "Crystal" is a word that occurs almost as often in *Aurora Leigh* as "fire" and "stone," for in crystals rock becomes the conductor of fire: letting the flame enter, the rock is transfigured; and the fire, too, becomes seemingly supernatural, partaking of a jewellike permanence. Through the purifying medium of a crystalline awareness, metallic rock becomes transparent to spiritual fire.

As accords with the uncompromising nature of Barrett Browning's vision of heroic apocalypse, water—the element opposed to fire—is relegated to a lesser, mostly pejorative place. Indeed, in the traditional apocalypse to which Barrett Browning exhibits such a strong attraction, even though we see a "pure river of water of life, clear as crystal," we are also told that when "the first heaven and first earth were passed away" to make room for new ones, "there was no more sea" (Rev. 22:1, 21:1). So too in *Aurora Leigh*: occasionally we find some crystal-clear water, but mostly the water imagery is linked with seas or floods or drowning—and it is baleful.

In fact, there may be more than scriptural reasons for this. In his reading of Barrett Browning's correspondence with Robert Browning, Daniel Karlin explores psychological sources of the former's "morbid fear of the sea" and even "dislike of its sound": her brother Edward had died of drowning, having parted with Elizabeth after a quarrel.[7] Recurrent patterns of epiphanic imagery are overdetermined; psychoanalytic factors, though not sole causes, may be contributors. Here, as in my earlier remarks on Arnold, Tennyson, and Pater, I would stress the symbiosis of neo-Bachelardian phenomenology not only with psychoanalysis but with a host of other critical orientations.

In each of the epic's nine books there are at least two major epiphanic experiences relating to spiritual fire and usually also to its transformation of stone, its ability to transmute death into life, often with the help of crystal. Along with these fiery epiphanies, for instructive contrast, we usually discover as well a temporarily discouraging instance of the chaotic and inimical sea, or of threatening sealike waters. A sign of the eventual victory of transcendence, an emblem of the final victory of life over death, is afforded by timely appearances of crystal. Indeed, since the traditional image of the celestial spheres is sometimes introduced, I think it likely that the nine-part division of *Aurora Leigh* may well allude to these nine well-known crystal shapes. We begin the visionary epic with a spark of fire; we end it with jewel crystals; and in between we encounter many obdurate symbolic rocks to be transformed.

Aurora, whose Italian mother dies when the little girl is only four years old, describes her own life as "A poor spark snatched up from a failing lamp / Which went out therefore" (1.32–33). Her mother "was weak and frail," Aurora explains; "She could not bear the joy of giving life, / The mother's rapture slew her" (1.33–35). But this euphemistic "rapture" theory, evidently furnished by her helpful father, is not convincing to Aurora on the unconscious level, and she continues to envision herself as a fiery spark in lifelong need of redemption. The deep-rooted guilt she feels makes it difficult to distinguish heavenly fires from hellish or purgatorial ones as the poem proceeds—difficult, but all the more necessary. Apocalypses will appear to Aurora in forms that are hellishly distorted, or mockingly parodied. To help her make the needful distinctions, Aurora learns to trust the quiet but powerful and uncompromising kind of recurrent epiphany in which fire expresses itself as light: the dawning of the intuitive "still ray" that "Goes straight and fast as light, and high as God" (1.814).

Aurora's earliest questions in the First Book of *Aurora Leigh* focus on rocky nature, which always needs to be transformed, and on fiery poetry, which is the means of transformation. After her English father dies, young Aurora, taken from Italy to live in rural England with a

resentful aunt (who had jealously disapproved of Father's marriage
from the beginning), finds that in her new and alien country

> The skies themselves looked low and positive,
> As almost you could touch them with a hand,
> And dared to do it they were so far off
> From God's celestial *crystals*; all things blurred
> And dull and vague. Did Shakspeare and his mates
> Absorb the light here? - not a hill or *stone*
> With heart to *strike a radiant colour up*
> Or active outline on the indifferent air.
>
> (1.262–69, emphasis added)

This initial query is offered tentatively, with hesitation, disappoint-
ment, and unease. Yet the question is a rhetorical one, and Shakespeare provides the clearly implicit answer. The landscape need not
remain far off from God's crystals of star-fire. Hill and stone can indeed acquire the heart to strike up a radiant fire-color (as does the
stony hero-statue fed on sun-blood that we looked at earlier) if the
poet has but the heart to envision it. It will be up to Aurora to provide
the dawn in this dreary atmosphere by extending her vista. She will
need to hearten and elevate the prospects closed in both by the seemingly "low and positive" British skies and (as we shall see) by her
cousin Romney's equally lowering, leveling Comtean positivist philosophy—both blotting out celestial "crystals."

Fiery poetry is the radiant-making, transforming power. But poetry, like all human writing and speculation, is riddled with false
apocalypses, tragic fools'-fires. In the "world of books," the "wicked"
are "winged like angels; every knife that strikes / Is edged from elemental fire to assail / A spiritual life" (1.748, 750, 751–53). Indeed,
"many a seer pulls down the flaming heavens / Upon his own head
in strong martyrdom, / In order to light men a moment's space"
(1.763–65); this is a prophetic negative epiphany of self-destructive,
positivistic cousin Romney. A child like Aurora may well feel assailed
by fearful, unknown perils in the book world—as on a battlefield, or
in the catacombs, with "torch / Grown ragged in the fluttering air"
(1.776–77). Indeed (and here is our expected negative imagery of
sea-water), the seeker may well find herself praying to God to save
her from the "breakers," from the hazards of "hard swimming

through / The deeps," from "being dashed / From error on to error" (1.795–96, 798–99), till harbor is reached. But luckily, safe haven is in sight, or in prospect—because of the transformative, salvific power of epiphanic fire:

> . . . At last because the time was ripe,
> I chanced upon the poets.
>   As the earth
> Plunges in fury, when the internal fires
> Have reached and pricked her heart, and, throwing flat
> The marts and temples, the triumphal gates
> And towers of observation, clears herself
> To elemental freedom - thus, my soul,
> At poetry's divine first finger-touch,
> Let go conventions and sprang up surprised,
> Convicted of the great eternities
> Before two worlds.
>   (1.844–54)

Poetry is elemental, epiphanic, volcanic; it overthrows and annihilates stony temples, replacing stone with revelatory flame. Fiery poetry is not just priestly, or ministerial, but prophetic, overturning institutions of worship already established. The poet is convinced, and she convinces others, of the eternities that face us in this and the next world. But "Convicted" seems to mean more than just convinced; it hints at a sense of guilt underlying the fiery rebellious upsurge. So, as Barrett Browning continues her auroral epiphany of poetry's power, she emphasizes the need to transcend the personal, the subjective, the natural, in order to make possible a vision of fire that will go beyond the material sun, to become wholly of the spirit:

> . . . O delight
> And triumph of the poet . . .
> [Who] says the word so that it burns you through
> With a special revelation, shakes the heart
> Of all the men and women in the world,
> . . . .
> The palpitating angel in his flesh
> Thrills inly with consenting fellowship

> To those innumerous spirits who sun themselves
> Outside of time.
> . . . poetry, my life,
> My eagle, with both grappling feet still hot
> From Zeus's thunder. . . .
>   (1.901–2, 905–7, 912–15, 918–20)

Surely Aurora's querulous aunt was right to suppose that "souls were dangerous things to carry straight / Through all the split saltpetre of the world" (1.1034–35), though she drew a wrongly timid conclusion from her awareness of the perils of flame. Whatever risks our poetic task imposes must be taken: no poet is more valuable than the fiery tragic poet Keats, whose life, "Distilled to a mere drop," falls like a scalding "tear / Upon the world's cold cheek to make it burn / For ever" (1.1008–10). For our very soul is no positivistic *tabula rasa*, but a palimpsest concealing a potentially flaming apocalypse. Whoever says "The soul's a clean white paper" should rather say, "A palimpsest, a prophet's holograph" covered up by later monkish writing but still a fiery "apocalypse" with detectable strokes of the half-concealed "alpha and omega / Expressing the old scripture" (1.825–26, 828, 831–32). Though it is not yet clear how this composite fiery epiphany will ever make Aurora's restless spirit feel at home in her forbiddingly foreign new country, she ends her First Book with the assured assertion, "I learned to love that England" (1.1068). There must be some way to crystallize it into a gemlike New Jerusalem.

Book 2 teaches mainly by negative elemental epiphanies: here the stones are turned to fire over and over, but only in semi-parodic ways. On her twentieth birthday Aurora the aspiring poet, thinking herself alone, dares the experiment of trying on a wreath of ivy to see how a laureate might feel. When cousin Romney turns out to have been spying on her,

> . . . I stood there fixed, -
> My arms up, like the caryatid, sole
> Of some abolished temple, helplessly
> Persistent in a gesture which derides
> A former purpose. Yet my blush was flame,
> As if from flax, not stone.

> . . . The tide
> Had caught me at my pastime, writing down
> My foolish name too near upon the sea
> Which drowned me with a blush as foolish.
>   (2.60–65, 68–71)

Petrified with shame, Aurora finds her caryatidlike stony rigidity
made even more ludicrous by the flaming blush that turns the stone
to fire. But this is not the true epiphanic or crystal-pure apocalyptic
flame, for it is compromised by weakness, by the feeling of being
drowned in embarrassment, flooded by a sea (negative water-epiph-
any) of chaotic, unwilled, unpleasant feeling, the feeling of having
one's egotism discovered. Cousin Romney compounds the unpleas-
antness by advising Aurora, "Keep to the green wreath, / Since even
dreaming of the stone and bronze / Brings headaches, pretty cousin,
and defiles / The clean white morning dresses" (2.93–96). To this hu-
miliating admonition, Aurora replies that she "would rather take my
part / With God's [resurrected] Dead, who afford to walk in white /
Yet spread his glory" than "fear to soil my gown in so much dust"
(2.101–3, 105). Resurrection, apocalypse, remains her theme, resistant to anyone's parodies, or to her own embarrassments.

Romney makes an even more insistent attempt to parody both
Aurora's apocalyptic ideals and her epiphanic imagery later in Book
2, and again he fails. Romney has proposed marriage, and he has
been turned down, for as Aurora rightly observes, her cousin is already married: his "wife" is his Fourierian "social theory" (2.410).
But Romney makes a last-ditch effort to overturn Aurora's decision:
in a letter, he bequeaths to Aurora's aunt a large sum of money, so
when the aunt suddenly dies, Aurora finds that she has inherited
wealth, thanks to Romney. Generous Romney tries to impress Aurora
with her new indebtedness to him by insisting on the apocalyptic
finality, the absolute irreversibility, of her happy change in fortune:

> . . . 'As easy pluck
> The golden stars from heaven's embroidered stole
> To pin them on the grey side of this earth,
> As make you poor again, thank God.'
>   (2.1111–14)

What Romney satirically pictures here is a mock-epiphany, a ludi-crous way to turn earth's stony grey to golden flame, to bring God's stars down to earth as at the last Great Fire. Romney's final stratagem to parody the apocalypse is worthy only of contempt: Aurora rips up the letter. She has redeemed her earlier embarrassment, her flood of fiery shame: Romney, it now appears, was the truly misguided dreamer of untransfigured stone—or lurid metal: he cannot buy Aurora with coin.

As the plot thickens and miseries intensify throughout Book 3, the elemental anti-apocalypses become even more tormenting than were the mockeries of Book 2. Separated from Romney now as if they were "divided rocks" with an estranging, salt (and rather Arnoldian) "torrent-world" between them (2.1245–46), Aurora tries to subsist in London by her writing. But the wearying journalistic demands on her spirit, the torments of being confined (and professionally defined) by marketplace requirements, find expression in a striking fire-and-met-al image of constraint and compression, an anti-apocalypse:

> I worked the short days out, - and watched the sun
> On lurid morns or monstrous afternoons,
> (Like some Druidic idol's fiery brass
> With fixed unflickering outline of dead heat,
> From which the blood of wretches pent inside
> Seems oozing forth to incarnadine the air)
> Push out through fog with his dilated disk,
> And startle the slant roofs and chimney-pots
> With flashes of fierce colour.
>
> (3.170–78)

Fire cannot transfigure this metal; its heat remains dead, and it kills rather than resurrects. The Druid idol is society-as-God. Its burn-ing brass is the same as the "tormenting circle of steel" which every-one wears who seeks, for his or her own selfish sake, a "crown" of fame or glory (3.166). Aurora feels the divine "fire-seeds of creation held / In Jove's clenched palm before the worlds were sown," but the palm remains unopened and may yet become "charred," the spark "quenched" (3.252–53, 259). It is one more imprisoning, imprisoned form of fire that cannot find apocalyptic expression.

The story of Marian Erle, a poor, abused young woman whom Romney has rescued and now wishes to marry, offers another sad variation on elemental, apocalyptic epiphany, yet with some hope as well, for it is a story of escape, of refusal to succumb. As we hear Marian's tale, we see her first in her recollected childhood: though sickly, she can commune with nature and with the poems she reads in the intervals between sewing tasks, lyrics whose music is revealingly compared to that of a glass harmonica (made of crystal), and which contribute to her "crystal thoughts" (3.1017). But when Marian's mother later tries to sell her to a pimp, she tears her hands away

> Like lilies from the rocks, from hers and his,
> And sprang down, bounded headlong down the steep,
> Away from both - away, if possible,
> As far as God, - away!
> . . . Mad fear
> Was running in her feet and killing the ground;
> The white roads curled as if she burnt them up,
> The green fields melted. . . .
>
> (3.1066–69, 1073–75)

In this powerfully moving elemental epiphany of fiery desperation, we see Marian trying to escape the whole hellish world, to get to God's better one. As she runs, the earth seems to curl into ash as if incinerated, the fields melt from the same all-consuming flame, and finally, at the moment when Marian's heart swells as if to fill her whole body so that she is flooded with panic and knows she is about to collapse, she thinks, "And now I am dead and safe" (3.1087). The world seems to have been melted down, the *stony roads burnt up*. Marian is taken to a hospital, whose beds are "Like graves dug side by side" (3.1108): from fire, she seems to enter a world of deadness or stony immobility, a tomb-world. But she will be flamingly resurrected from these stony gravelike enclosures.

First, however, in the central section of Barrett Browning's epic (Books 4 through 6), things must get infinitely worse before they get better—though the increasingly overpowering negative apocalypses of Marian's life will be somewhat offset, in visionary terms, by the

countervailing positive elemental epiphanies still granted at intervals
to Aurora as narrator. Romney thinks he has rescued Marian from
despair through his magnanimous gesture of proposing to marry her.
But he does not love her as an individual person, only as a potential
collaborator in his Fourierian philanthropy, his utopian socialism. A
negative epiphany of water proves how uncritical Marian had been
in originally accepting his marriage offer:

> . . . Obviously
> She had not thought about his love at all:
> The cataracts of her soul had poured themselves,
> And risen self-crowned in rainbow: would she ask
> Who crowned her? - it sufficed that she was crowned.
>
> (4.182–86)

Marian's misty rainbow crown is no more rewarding than Aurora's
imagined crowns of stone or bronze or steel that we looked at before.
So it is ironically a good thing that Lady Waldemar, who jealously
wants Romney for herself, dissuades Marian from going through with
the marriage.

But Lady Waldemar waits till the very last moment before unleash-
ing the full ugliness of her jealous rhetoric, so Marian has no chance
to make known her change of heart before the very day of the wedding—which thus turns into a disastrous *negative elemental apocalypse*.
The crowd appears "A finished generation, dead of plague, / Swept
outward from their graves into the sun, / The moil of death upon
them" (4.548–50). It is no true fiery resurrection; Romney's magna-
nimity has worked no real change upon the poverty-stricken people
he has invited to the wedding, and when the bride fails to show up,
the mood turns hateful. The crowd appears a "dark slow stream, like
blood," or an apocalyptic monster composed of "bruised snakes":
"What an ugly crest / Of faces rose upon you everywhere / From the
crammed mass!" (4.554, 566, 569–71). Resentment, born of degra-
dation unredeemed as yet by any enlightened form of aid, turns the
apocalyptic or purgative fire back into the deadness of corrupted
earth: "fiery swirls of slime" (4.589). There is no stepping into the
sun. It is blotted out by the muddy whirlwind.

Romney can make no sense of this; he continues to criticize

Aurora's supposed impracticality in following her poetic (rather than philanthropic) calling—but when Aurora in exasperation asks him where he thinks humanity is going, his reply unwittingly helps provide just the epiphanic perspective we need at this point, as he shows us his *inability to transform stones to fire*:

> . . . 'Where?' he said, and sighed.
> 'The whole creation, from the hour we are born,
> Perplexes us with questions. Not a *stone*
> But cries behind us, every weary step,
> 'Where, where?' *I leave stones to reply to stones.*
> Enough for me and for my fleshly heart
> To harken the invocations of my kind,
> When men catch hold upon my shuddering nerves
> And shriek, 'What help? what hope? what bread i' the house,
> What fire i' the frost?' There must be some response,
> Though mine fail utterly. This social Sphinx,
> Who sits between the sepulchres and stews,
> Makes mock and mow *against the crystal* heavens,
> And bullies God, - exacts a word at least
> From each man standing on the side of God,
> However paying a sphinx-price for it.'
>
> (4.1174–89, emphasis added)

Romney has capitulated to the social sphinx, the strangler-monster that mocks the "crystal" heavens. He fails to realize that there is no need to abandon the spiritual, the poetic dimension of life, no need to pay such a "sphinx-price" for social betterment. Not poverty alone seeks amelioration; in Barrett Browning's view, the entire envisioned world needs to be spiritually redeemed, flamingly reshaped and transfigured through "crystal." "Stones" cannot be left to "reply to stones"; the human poet must reply to them, must "strike a radiant colour up" (1.268) from them, must turn them into fire-conductors through a crystalline awareness, seeing through the world (both natural and human), making it transparent to fiery, spiritual truth.

Aurora spells this lesson out for her own (and the reader's) benefit in Part 5, clarifying the role of crystal-making in turning dead graveyard rock into fiery-faceted elemental epiphany. The way to avoid writing "books as cold and flat as graveyard stones" (5.360) is for the poet to crystallize the insight arising concurrently from two sources: feeling and reflection, passion and "conscience" in the double sense of awareness and morality:

> . . . Does a torch less burn
> For burning next reflectors of blue steel,
> That *he* [the poet] should be the colder for his place
> 'Twixt two incessant fires, - his personal life's
> And that intense refraction which burns back
> Perpetually against him from the round
> Of *crystal* conscience he was born into
> If artist-born?
>
> (5.373–80, emphasis added)

The "round" of "crystal" conscience suggests that awareness of one's social surroundings is as crucial for Aurora as for Romney, though it is not enough, for it must not rule out spiritual fires arising from the "personal life" as well. But Aurora will not sell out to the wealthy any more than Romney will. Refusing Lord Howe's offer to introduce her to a rich patron, she can hardly disguise her dislike of that "sparkling brawling stream" (a characteristic little elemental allegory of baleful waters that would drown the apocalyptic fires) that constitutes London high society (5.985).

Knowing she will hardly advance toward crystalline awareness amid the falsely "sparkling brawling stream," the trivially witty combativeness, of the London rich, Aurora instead seeks truly fiery epiphanies in Italy, the land of her birth (and of her parents' death), which she addresses in strikingly apocalyptic terms, as if the land were filled with silenced spirits awaiting their liberating epiphanic resurrection from stony graves into fiery sunlight: "My Italy . . . Thou piercing silence of ecstatic graves, / Men call that name!" (5.1190, 1195–96).[8]

> My own hills! Are you 'ware of me, my hills,
> How I burn toward you? do you feel to-night
> The urgency and yearning of my soul . . . ?
> . . . Still, ye go
> Your own determined, calm, indifferent way

> Toward sunrise, shade by shade, and light by light,
> Of all the grand progression nought left out. . . .
>   (5.1267–69, 1273–76)

Aurora is like the dawn-light that burns toward the stony hills, yearning to transfigure them, to strike from them a radiant color, the hue of fire. But, as always, she refuses to allow herself to go too far toward what might become a worship of nature. Like the very hills themselves, she must not be overeager to complete her "progression"; she must not be impatient to hasten her spiritual progress toward the higher, stone-transforming spiritual fire that outshines the sun.

Aurora must unlearn another kind of impatience, too: overeagerness to judge—a self-righteousness that Barrett Browning parodies with a sardonic, caricatural version of her epiphanic theme of fiery crystals (here, the jewels of the New Jerusalem). When, in Paris, she encounters Marian, who is caring for a child, Aurora rashly draws conclusions about Marian's morals, and she is duly chided for being so righteously ready to utter a Last Judgment:

> " . . . Ah, Miss Leigh,
> You're great and pure; but were you purer still, -
> As if you had walked, we'll say, no otherwhere
> Than up and down the new Jerusalem,
> And *held your trailing lutestring up yourself*
> *From brushing the twelve stones*, for fear of some
> Small speck . . . the child would keep to *me*,
> Would choose his poor lost Marian, like me best. . . . "
>   (6.710–17, emphasis added, "me" emphasized in text)

Aurora is too self-righteous to touch the fiery heavenly gems, the envisioned crystalline "stones" of the New Jerusalem. Indeed, Barrett Browning's radiant epiphanic imagery ensures that Marian's child will remain proof against Aurora's ill-considered ire: to have looked at the child's smiling face is to have "watched a flame / And stood in it a-glow" (6.610–11). The judge is judged in the most elemental, epiphanic way. Aurora's initial error is purged as by spiritual, transforming fire.

The nadir of Marian's life, as she describes to Aurora the traumatic experience and suicidally tormenting consequences of having been raped in Paris (a source for the child's birth that Aurora had been incapable of imagining), is embodied in the most overpowering negative elemental epiphany in all of *Aurora Leigh*. Well-intentioned helpers tie a stone-heavy image of Virgin Mary around Marian's neck—

> How heavy it seemed! as heavy as a stone;
> A woman has been strangled with less weight:
> I threw it in a ditch to keep it clean
> And ease my breath . . .
> . . . my brain cleared presently;
> And there I sate, one evening, by the road,
> I, Marian Earle, myself, alone, undone,
> Facing a sunset low upon the flats,
> As if it were the finish of all time,
> The great red stone upon my sepulchre,
> Which angels were too weak to roll away.
>   (6.1257–60, 1268–74)

It is impossible for Marian to rid herself of the rocky weight of undeserved reproach. The "stone"-heavy image that Marian has cast off returns, in her waking nightmare, infinitely magnified and increased in oppressive heaviness, for the "stone" now assumes the very form of the sun itself, as if the entire earth were a tomb, the *fire-red setting sun* its tomb*stone*. The apocalyptic *turning of stones to fire*, elemental epiphany of Barrett Browning's poetic ideal as we have seen it embodied throughout the poem so far, is hellishly reversed here as the *sun's fires turn to stone*.

Though the pace of the plot slows down in Book 7 as Marian and her child travel with Aurora to Italy, this section of the poem is epiphanically rich, with three ingenious variants on the elemental paradigm: an all-too-human expression of resentful and frustrated feeling; an intimation of transcendence; and a brilliant lyrical set piece that seems to show us natural fires in the very process of transmuting themselves into spiritual ones. Aurora is now doubly frustrated: she is enraged at the trickery on Lady Waldemar's part whereby Marian, instead of being safely shipped to Australia, found herself foully deceived and marooned penniless in Paris. And Aurora is also trying, unsuccessfully, to stifle her jealousy of Lady Waldemar, whom she imagines Romney has by now married (Aurora's nightmare vision of

the wedding bells seems to come straight from the grisly "Bells" poem
by Poe [7.397–409]). So it is not hard to find both Aurora's accumulated outrage and her stifled but still active sexual feeling for Romney
expressed in an epiphany of a trip through a mountain tunnel transformed into a vision of the fiery *rock-piercing lightning* of Thor and the
buried but active anguish of a Titan (Vulcan, most likely, beneath his
smoldering volcano):

> . . . So we passed
> The liberal open country and the close,
> And shot through tunnels, like a lightning-wedge
> By great Thor-hammers driven through the rock,
> Which, quivering through the intestine blackness, splits,
> And lets it in at once: the train swept in
> Athrob with effort, trembling with resolve,
> The fierce denouncing whistle wailing on
> And dying off smothered in the shuddering dark,
> While we, self-awed, drew troubled breath, oppressed
> As other Titans, underneath the pile
> And nightmare of the mountains.
>
> (7.429–40)

I have called this projection of inner torment into a vision of rock-
piercing fire "all-too-human," but it is powerful. It is the adequate
elemental dramatization of a problem, even if, in Barrett Browning's
terms, it can offer no solution. For that, a more spiritual fire must
transform, not merely penetrate, the stone.

Nature itself provides no fire that can adequately transform stone;
indeed, in Barrett Browning's view, nature may be called the very
stone that needs spiritual or epiphanic transmuting. Any given natural scene or landscape is like the stone on which Jacob pillowed his
head while dreaming of God's providence manifested by the angels'
ladder; without Jacob's transformative dream the stone, the place, nature itself, means nothing:

> 'Tis only good to be, or here or there,
> Because we had a dream on such a stone,
> Or this or that, - but, once being wholly waked,
> And come back to the stone without the dream,

> We trip upon't, - alas, and hurt ourselves;
> Or else it falls on us and grinds us flat,
> The heaviest grave-stone on this burying earth.
>   (7.497–503)

In Marian's nightmare the sun itself turned into such a gravestone. But there exists a higher, immaterial fire, such as might be perceived in an epiphany—for example, in Marian's face when, recounting one of the few instances of goodness she experienced in her desperate journey, Marian "smiled beyond the sun" (7.114). This spiritual fire does more than pierce or penetrate stones; it alchemizes or transforms or crystallizes them into meaning.

Even in her transitional and still mournful mood Aurora seems to see a rivalry of upper and lower fires in nature, indicating a hierarchy or ladder of epiphanic fires and suggesting a corresponding process by which one ascends in perception from more mobile and local flames to those more comprehensive, more transformative, more *stone-melting,* more transcendent in their power. Aurora sees

> . . . butterflies, that bear
> Upon their blue wings such *red embers* round,
> They seem to *scorch* the blue air into holes
> Each flight they take: and *fire-flies,* that suspire
> In short soft lapses of *transported flame*
> Across the tingling Dark, while overhead
> The *constant and inviolable stars*
> *Outburn those lights-of-love.* . . .
> We tremble and are afraid, and feel as if
> The *golden flood of moonlight* unaware
> *Dissolved the pillars* of the steady earth
> And made it less substantial.
> . . . .
> And lizards, the *green lightnings* of the wall,
> Which, if you sit down quiet, nor sigh loud,
> Will flatter you and take you for a *stone,*
> And *flash familiarly* about your feet
> With such prodigious eyes in such small heads!
>   (7.1058–65, 1074–77, 1080–84,
>   emphases added)

Love's merely passionate fires seem outburnt by other, more exalted epiphanic flames. The stony "pillars" of the earth seem "dissolved" by the alchemy of fiery light—*stone into fire*. Even lizards tease our yet-unaltered stoniness with their flattering flashes. The whole epiphany of stone either potentially or metaphorically transformed to fiery light has a gentle, teasing quality; yet the larger elemental paradigm of Barrett Browning's universe is discernible, its meanings flashing through.

Romney arrives—a "sea-king" emerging from a valley drowned in shadows (8.60)—and although the "sound of waters" accompanying his arrival (8.61) gives the dubious epiphany of water something of the high prophetic tone of Revelation ("his voice as the sound of many waters" [Rev. 1:15]), Romney has a lot of explaining to do. He, after all, had disdainfully rejected Aurora's poetic vocation, leaving the both of them comparable to rocks divided by an estranging sea. But, as we discover, Romney dramatically progresses toward redemption through a tale of elemental transformation—not by water but by fire.

Romney's brief narrative in Book 8 is an epiphanic story of fire, stone, and crystal. The narrative attests to a twofold conversion, accomplished by Romney's own unhappy fate and by Aurora's later indirect influence. The participants in Romney's Fourierian phalanstery, his utopian social commune, egged on by resentful local clergy, had effected a negative apocalypse by burning down Leigh Hall, the manorial estate that Romney had charitably donated to house the project. The whole house, newly become "Leigh Hell," disappeared "In a mounting whirlwind of dilated flame," which "Blew upward, straight, its drift of fiery chaff / In the face of Heaven, which blenched, and ran up higher" (8.939, 989–91). What the apocalyptic flame has left is a relic of untransmuted stone:

> "You'd come upon a great charred circle, where
> The patient earth was singed an acre round;
> With one stone-stair, symbolic of my life,
> Ascending, winding, leading up to nought!"
> (8.1032–35)

But Romney himself—the internal man—is more significantly changed than any visible symbol of his former hopes. Even the physical blindness he incurred in trying to save Marian Erle's game-poaching father from death is judged, in the context of the poem, less deeply transforming than Romney's interior metamorphosis, his revolution in thought. Romney has returned to Aurora because "her *crystal* soul / Had shown me something which a man calls light" (8.1212–13, emphasis added), something expressed in her poems, which "moved me in secret as the sap is moved / In still March-branches, signless as a stone" (8.593–94). *Romney is the stone that has been infused with fire from the crystal*—from the crystalline, transformative, dawning awareness conveyed by Aurora's poetry.

Book 9, like Night the Ninth of Blake's *The Four Zoas*, is filled with climactic imagery of fiery judgment and phoenixlike resurrection. But since this concluding book of the epic is also the fullest expression of Barrett Browning's unique paradigm of elemental epiphany, she has made sure that the most powerful moment in Book 9's composite epiphany—already set forth as phenomenological paradigm at the beginning of this chapter—involves the transformation of stone, through crystal, into fire.

Romney's physical blindness is not at first evident: like Milton's "drop serene" (*Paradise Lost* 3.25), Romney's affliction allows his eyes to retain their normal appearance, for they still have a *crystalline* aspect that remains pure: "the outer eyes appear indifferent, / Unspotted in their crystals" (9.580–81). Yet Romney feels that, "though as powerless . . . as a stone" (9.598), he can still shelter Aurora. In the world of Barrett Browning's elemental epiphanies, a stone is not at all "powerless" if it be also "crystal" like the "unspotted" aspect of Romney's vision: such crystal, the redeemable or transformable aspect of stoniness, can be epiphanically changed into a blaze of light by inner, spiritual fire.

Aurora, too, has become more crystalline in her awareness, more reflective of, and more open to, the melting, heart-transforming power of a loved one's suffering. Aurora feels that she, by coming to understand Marian's trials and Marian's love for her child despite her trials, has learned to temper the initial arrogance that had made her so ready to place laurels on her own head and to despise Romney's type of philanthropic idealism. Romney's new crystalline awareness is mirrored in Aurora's. Indeed, Romney—"A mere bare blind stone in the blaze of day," as he calls himself (9.570)—and Aurora are equally transformed in their final love, which is an apocalypse of immaterial fire: "two large explosive hearts . . . melted, in the fire, - /

Embrace, that was convulsion" (9.718, 720–21). Romney is most obviously the epiphanic "stone" that has been molten down by convulsive "fire," but the formerly flinty pride of Aurora, too, has been effectively alchemized into flame.

As fire purges what had been rocky in the souls of the two epiphanic seer-lovers (the blind man and the sighted woman), crystal sounds are heard. "And, as we sate, we felt the old earth spin, / And all the starry turbulence of worlds / Swing round us in their audient circles" (10.838–40): these are musical motions of the crystal spheres, now first perceivable by the lovers whose stoniness has been purgatively transformed and molten by flame. Aurora is even requested, like the Angel Gabriel, to blow the Last Trump: "Now press the clarion on thy woman's lip," says Romney, " . . . And breathe thy fine keen breath along the brass, / And blow all class-walls level as Jericho's / Past Jordan" (9.929, 931–33). Philanthropy is not abjured; it becomes a practicable kind of historical heroism once the soul has crossed the Jordan, once the fire of crystal spirit has clarified and purged the clay, the earth, the stone. When the stoniness of obdurate pride has been molten down in both woman and man, when mutual love has crystallized the fires of passion into a clarity of insight born of mutual empathy, poet and philanthropist are alike ready to envision a leveling of class barriers. Finely imaged as stone walls of Jericho, these rocky social barriers—like the walls of individual incomprehension that had so long separated Romney from Aurora—can likewise be eventually demolished through the fiery power of spirit, here imaged as "spiritus" or breath, a woman's breath.

It is indeed a woman, Aurora, who sounds the symbolic trumpet of the apocalyptic Last Judgment. For it is she who represents Barrett Browning in her insistence on the primacy of poetic vision in guiding social change. Aurora, spokeswoman of the fiery dawn, heralds a vision that she herself was unable to embody with the requisite completeness until she had learned to love both Marian and Romney. Yet even during the time when Aurora's life had not yet yielded fully to the demands of her vision, that vision was expressing itself in her fiery poetry. The crystalline clarity and power of Aurora's verse won the heart of Romney despite his relative blindness—and in doing so, granted him new vision.

Aurora had been too eager to seize laurels before she had earned them, too eager to imagine herself as a laurel-crowned stony caryatid (revealingly untransmuted into crystal). Romney's pride had been even greater and more disastrous in its consequences. But his intentions, at heart, were good. Even in Romney's blindness, the "crystals" of his eyes and spirit remained somehow "unspotted," open to transformative, inward vision, to the epiphanic "light" shining through Aurora's "crystal soul" (8.1212–13) and embodied in the poetic flame of her perfected verse.

According to Barrett Browning, Romney's philanthropic impulse, like Aurora's poetic calling, *can* be a source of legitimate heroism in history at the present time. What the story of this woman and man is meant to show, through its many bold epiphanies, is that if the rocky barriers that constitute fallen social reality are to be purged by the crystalline clarity of heroic vision, zeal must combine with understanding, heat with light, practicality with poetry, in the fire of spiritual love. Some may find this prospect rather too grand. But it follows from Barrett Browning's recurrent epiphanic pattern of stones, crystals, and transformative fire. And it is due to Barrett Browning's remarkable resources as creator of elemental epiphanies that her social and poetic vision comes across as well as it does.

It is true that Barrett Browning gives the epic's final epiphany of fiery crystals to Romney, but it is Aurora who translates what she knows he is seeing into poetic speech:[9]

> . . . And when
> I saw his soul saw, - 'Jasper first,' I said,
> 'And second, sapphire; third, chalcedony;
> The rest in order, - last, an amethyst.'
> (9.961–64 [cf. Rev. 21:19–20])

All the consuming, transforming fires shine forth at last in crystal after crystal. The woman and the man see this epiphany together: their stoniness purged, molten, by crystalline vision into fiery enlightenment, they see a fire-crystal figuration of what they have themselves attained. It is the Apocalypse according to Barrett Browning, epitomizing an epiphanic pattern disclosed by neo-Bachelardian phenomenology.

Conclusion
Fifteen Theses

In this book I have offered a new method for the study of literary epiphanies. This method, applied in eight chapters of nineteenth-century case studies, has been based on a comprehensive rethinking, revision, and systematization of Bachelard's phenomenological approach.

To conclude, I propose fifteen theses to sum up the methodological principles and main findings of the book.

1. Epiphanies—literary moments that are felt to be exceptionally intense, expansive, and mysterious (I borrow these last two criteria from a fine book by Ashton Nichols)—are as worthy of systematic analysis as any other aspects of literary art. Fascinating and appealing in their own right, epiphanies offer an object of study that should interest critics of widely differing theoretical orientations.

2. An epiphany maker usually makes more than one epiphany. A writer's epiphanies will exhibit recurrent patterns.

3. A Bachelardian approach—focusing on recurrent elements, motions, and shapes—will disclose an author's chief epiphanic indicators.

4. Bachelardian phenomenology has to be revised to focus on epiphanic products rather than on supposed mental processes that went into their making. In this way, concrete literary data may be empirically observed without any of the dangers of intuitionism sometimes thought to beset rival phenomenologies such as that of Georges Poulet.

5. A further indispensable revision of Bachelardian method is to focus first on a given author's paradigmatic epiphany, the literary moment in which the characteristic epiphanic indicators are most clearly presented and fully elaborated. Then more fragmentary or attenuated variants may be readily recognized.

6. Surprisingly often, such a paradigmatic moment will be explic-

itly labeled "vision" or "dream" by its creator—a helpful indicator for the phenomenological analyst.

7. In many cases a recurrent epiphanic pattern, as marked most clearly by its paradigmatic form, will be a superb unifier of a writer's work. For example, Coleridge's paradigm of fitful motions and fragile forms in his abruptly interrupted dream-sonnet unifies all ten of his greatest poems. Tennyson's *In Memoriam*, *Idylls of the King*, many of his lyrics, and most of the chief dramatic monologues contain re-presentations of the aweful dawn-rose and the wheel, seen most completely in "The Vision of Sin." The red-yellow fire flower and dying white bird, epiphanic themes elaborated in the paradigmatic "Child in the House," appear everywhere in Walter Pater's *Marius the Epicurean*, *Gaston de Latour*, and the best of the *Imaginary Portraits*.

8. Since a given author's epiphanic paradigm is often a magnificent lyric or prose passage that has been neglected or ignored for any number of possible reasons, the study of epiphanic paradigms can bring to light new treasures. Nearly all the epiphanic paradigms studied in my book exemplify this thesis.

9. An unexpected richness of epiphanic production discoverable by neo-Bachelardian method may initiate a re-evaluation of the status of a writer, or may strongly contribute to a re-evaluation already underway. Examples: Pater, Barrett Browning.

10. The fact that phenomenologically discoverable epiphanies are intense, mysterious, and expansive suggests they are of deep concern to the given author and therefore also of psychoanalytical interest. Examples: the guilt-trauma paradigms of epiphany in Tennyson and Pater, and the guilt associated with Arnoldian epiphanic cities of the burning plain.

11. The fact that phenomenological paradigms are often strongly influenced or mediated means that phenomenological paradigm study is helpful in understanding intertext and influence. Examples: the effect of Revelation on Wordsworth and Barrett Browning; the use of the "sphere whose center is everywhere" by Wordsworth and Tolstoy; the influence of Coleridge on Pater's white birds.

12. If a writer plays two contrasting roles, for example, poet-critic or visionary-polemicist, a study of the writer's epiphanic pattern will show whether the two roles harmonize or not. If the poet-critic (Coleridge, Arnold) writes criticism whose founding metaphoric images do

not tally with the preferences implied in the poetic epiphanies, or if the visionary polemicist (Carlyle) writes polemics that do not square with the messages implied by the visionary epiphanies, then we have a key to the conflicted personality of the writer who plays the dual role.

13. The fact that attitudes toward air, earth, water, and fire are affected in western society by male-influenced tradition means that the extent of adherence to, or departure from, these constrictive norms will make the resulting epiphanic paradigm interesting to feminist criticism. Example: Barrett Browning.

14. The fact that an epiphanic paradigm is a unifying structure will give phenomenological students of epiphany an interest in the abiding, insistent, and central unities in an author's work. This, in turn, will counteract the limitations of the "decentered" approach, which because of its basic assumptions does not help us ask, for example, questions about epiphany patterns in Tolstoy's *War and Peace*. Current trends in criticism emphasize slippery signifiers, collapsing centers, carnivalesque heteroglossias—varieties of unruly heterogeneity. There is nothing wrong with this. But emphasis on such enduring unities as recurrent epiphany patterns may be a salutary corrective when the "decentered" approach proves insufficient.

15. New Historicists may well wish to take account of epiphany patterns in writers who offer broad-ranging visions of history— for example, Carlyle, Tolstoy, and Barrett Browning. Such findings show that far from being a philosophy oblivious of human history (as Eagleton averred), phenomenology can clarify the imaginative processes of historical imaginers. And all historians are historical imaginers.

Notes

Works Cited

Index

Notes

INTRODUCTION

1. Ashton Nichols, *The Poetics of Epiphany: Nineteenth-Century Origins of the Modern Literary Moment* 1–5.

2. Nichols, *Poetics of Epiphany* 28.

3. Paul de Man, "The Rhetoric of Temporality," *Blindness and Insight: Essays in the Rhetoric of Contemporary Criticism*, ed. Wlad Godzich, 2d rev. ed., 192–93, 211.

4. Frank Lentricchia, *After the New Criticism* 291–93.

5. Nichols, *Poetics of Epiphany* 5.

6. Martin Bidney, review of *The Poetics of Epiphany: Nineteenth-Century Origins of the Modern Literary Moment*, by Ashton Nichols, in *The Wordsworth Circle* 19 (1988): 205.

7. Morris Beja, *Epiphany in the Modern Novel* 16.

8. Robert Langbaum, "The Epiphanic Mode in Wordsworth and Modern Literature," *The Word from Below: Essays on Modern Literature and Culture* 40.

9. Beja 15–16.

10. Among Bachelard's essential element studies, two have still not appeared in English: *La terre et les rêveries du repos. Essai sur l'imagination de l'intimité* and *La terre et les rêveries de la volonté. Essai sur l'imagination des forces.* The 1960s saw the appearance of three translations: *The Poetics of Space*, trans. Maria Jolas (1964); *The Psychoanalysis of Fire*, trans. Alan C. M. Ross (1964); *The Poetics of Reverie*, trans. Daniel Russell (1969). *The Right to Dream*, trans. J. C. Underwood (1971), is the only English rendition to appear in the 1970s. Beginning in the 1980s, a new series of translations published by the Pegasus Foundation of the Dallas Institute of Humanities and Culture appeared; these now include *Water and Dreams: An Essay on the Imagination of Matter*, trans. Edith R. Farrell (1983); *Air and Dreams: An Essay on the Imagination of Movement*, trans. Edith Farrell and Frederick Farrell (1989); *The Flame of a Candle*, trans. Joni Caldwell (1989); *Fragments of a Poetics of Fire*, trans. Kenneth Haltman (1990). The same press has also reissued the Underwood translation of *The Right to Dream* (1989), and *Earth and Reveries of Will*, trans. Liliana Zancu, is scheduled to appear soon. Mary McAllester, ed., *The Philosophy and Poetics of Gaston Bachelard* concludes with a list of all Bachelard's French works and a bibliography of work in English on Bachelard. Roch C. Smith, *Gaston Bachelard*, contains an annotated bibliography of works on Bachelard in French and other languages. See also Smith's bibliography of Bachelard in *A Critical Bibliography of French Literature*, ed. Douglas W. Alden and Richard B. Brooks 1423–31.

Two excellent introductory works on Bachelard are *On Poetic Imagination and Reverie: Selections from the Works of Gaston Bachelard*, trans. and ed. Colette Gaudin; Mary McAllester Jones, *Gaston Bachelard, Subversive Humanist: Texts and Readings*.

11. Vincent B. Leitch, *American Literary Criticism: From the Thirties to the Eighties* 161.

12. Leitch 158.

13. Sarah Lawall, *Critics of Consciousness* vii.

14. J. Hillis Miller, quoted in Leitch 279.

15. Leitch 277.

16. Leitch 152.

17. Jay Clayton and Eric Rothstein, "Figures in the Corpus: Theories of Influence and Intertextuality," in Clayton and Rothstein, eds., *Influence and Intertextuality in Literary History* 4.

18. Terry Eagleton, *Literary Theory: An Introduction* 61.

19. Eagleton 58.

20. Paul Ginestier, in "Bachelard et ses lectures anglaises," *Revue de Littérature Comparée* 58 (1984): 177–84, finds few English examples; he finds the "Ophelia complex" with no quotations from Shakespeare (184). But John G. Clark, in "Gaston Bachelard devant la poésie anglaise" (*RLC* 58:185–96), says that meditations on intimate space in Bachelard's *Air and Dreams* and on alchemy in *The Poetics of Reverie* owe much to Shelley and Blake (188—Clark also finds Keats, Wordsworth, John Cowper Powys). Cf. Clark, "Cinq images de Shelley qui ont fasciné Bachelard," *Revue Internationale de Philosophie* 38 (1984): 287–314.

Bachelard is one of the finest Poe critics; see Bachelard, "Deep Waters—Dormant Waters—Dead Waters: 'Heavy Waters' in Edgar Allan Poe's Reverie," *Water and Dreams* 45–69. Michel Mansuy, in "Pour une étude comparée de la rêverie" (*RLC* 58:145–64), praising Bachelard as a wide-ranging comparatist, finds references to Byron, Shelley, Keats, Coleridge, Wordsworth, Swinburne, Meredith, Ruskin, Lafcadio Hearn, Hardy, Lawrence, and Woolf. In Bachelard's two earth-books Mansuy finds Gogol, Lermontov, Rozanov, Remizov, Esenin, Voloshin, Blok, and Biely (150).

21. *Amante marine de Friedrich Nietzsche*, by Luce Irigaray, published more than a decade ago, is the first book of a trilogy that also includes *Passions élémentaires* and *L'oubli de l'air chez Martin Heidegger*. Excellent applications of Bachelard may be found in the chapter "Elemental Reverie" in Jean Pierrot, *The Decadent Imagination: 1880–1900*, trans. Derek Coltman 107–37. The most ambitious Bachelardian study on a single English author is Bernard Brugière, *L'univers imaginaire de Robert Browning*. Roland Barthes' Bachelard-inspired *Michelet*, trans. Richard Howard, is one of his finest and least known works; epiphanies of "round, moist warmth" (203), of cosmic seas melding imagery of milk, blood, and salt, are as surprising as they are superbly evoked.

22. Bachelard, *Air and Dreams*, trans. Edith R. Farrell and C. Frederick Farrell, 127–60, 38–51. Bachelard also contrasts the silence and odorlessness

of Nietzschean air reveries to the music and perfumes of Shelleyan ones. I will say more later about such related features of elemental epiphanies.

23. For epiphanies of aromas and sounds see my "Parrots, Pictures, Rays, Perfumes: Epiphanies in George Sand and Flaubert," in *Studies in Short Fiction* 22 (1985): 209–17; "The Aeolian Harp Reconsidered: Music of Unfulfilled Longing In Tjutchev, Moerike, Thoreau, and Others," *Comparative Literature Studies* 22 (1985): 329–43.

24. Bidney, review of Nichols 205.

25. Geoffrey Hartman, in the same spirit as Nichols, considers Hopkins's characteristic epiphanies essentially "unmediated"; see *The Unmediated Vision: An Interpretation of Wordsworth, Hopkins, Rilke, and Valery.*

26. The unifying methodology of my book distinguishes it from compilations by several hands, e.g., Anna-Teresa Tymieniecka, ed., *Poetics of the Elements in the Human Condition: The Sea; From Elemental Stirrings to Symbolic Inspiration, Language, and Life-Significance in Literary Interpretation and Theory, Analecta Husserliana* 19; *Poetics of the Elements in the Human Condition: The Airy Elements in Poetic Imagination: Breath, Breeze, Wind, Tempest, Thunder, Snow, Flame, Fire, Volcano . . . , Analecta Husserliana* 23.

1. A PILGRIM'S DREAM OF APOCALYPSE

1. Geoffrey Hartman, *Wordsworth's Poetry: 1787–1814* xiii.

2. Hartman develops this thesis throughout; for the quoted phrases, see *Wordsworth's Poetry* 139, 122, 198. In *The Unremarkable Wordsworth* 24–25, Hartman elaborates on the "omphalos" theme in connection with the idea of geometry. In *A Mind for Ever Voyaging: Wordsworth at Work Portraying Newton and Science*, W. K. Thomas and Warren U. Ober provide valuable documentation of Wordsworth's mathematical and scientific interests, though in "Romantic Numeracy: The 'Tuneless Numbers' and 'Shadows Numberless'," *The Wordsworth Circle* 22 (Spring 1991): 124–31, Marilyn Gaull argues cogently that these authors overestimate the poet's esteem for Newton. She also rightly notes that the chapter, "Geometric Science and Romantic History: or Wordsworth, Newton, and the Slave-Trade," in Mary Jacobus, *Romanticism, Writing, and Sexual Difference: Essays on "The Prelude"* 69–93, does not deal directly with geometrical science as generally understood. Gaull's essay skillfully situates Wordsworth's thinking about science in the context of the history of mathematics during the period of *The Prelude*'s own history.

Of special interest in the phenomenological context of the present chapter is James A. W. Hefferman, "Wordsworth, Coleridge, and Turner: The Geometry of the Infinite," in *Bucknell Review* 29 (1984): 49–72, which includes a study of the boat-stealing and skating episodes in *The Prelude*. Hefferman's special interest in this wide-ranging and subtle inquiry focuses on a state of Romantic "sublime" awareness that is prepared by a consciousness of geometric forms in one's perception of nature, but in which a vertiginous feeling of supervening power transforms lines and shapes into figures of motion and force.

3. "The Pilgrim's Dream, or, The Star and the Glow-Worm" ll. 59, 61. All "Pilgrim's Dream" citations (hereafter *PD*, with line numbers in parentheses) refer to the "reading text" in William Wordsworth, *Shorter Poems, 1807–1820*, ed. Carl H. Ketcham.

4. Georges Poulet, *The Metamorphoses of the Circle*, trans. Carley Dawson and Elliott Coleman with the collaboration of the author; xxvii for the quotation, xi–xxvii for the survey of the *topos*.

5. "Of all the English poets, he on whom the theme of the circle has exercised the greatest fascination since Traherne, incontestably, is Coleridge" (Poulet, *Metamorphoses of the Circle* 103). Yet I would contest the assertion; Coleridge does not even begin to compare with Wordsworth as an epiphanist of circles.

6. Wordsworth, *Shorter Poems* 274 nn3,4.

7. *The Prelude* VII.41. All citations of *The Prelude* (hereafter *P*, with references in parentheses) refer to William Wordsworth, *The Prelude: 1799, 1805, 1850*, ed. Jonathan Wordsworth, M. H. Abrams, and Stephen Gill. All *Prelude* citations in my book refer to the 1805 version in this edition; since it is beyond the scope of my Wordsworth chapter to trace figures through successive drafts of *The Prelude*, I chose the version strongest in epiphanic power.

8. William Blake, *Milton* 20.19, in *The Complete Poetry and Prose of William Blake*, ed. David V. Erdman, 114.

9. Wet rocks are prominent in Wordsworthian epiphanies; see *P* VIII.565–77, VI.561–64.

10. "The Ruined Cottage," MS D. ll. 512–25. All references (hereafter by line numbers in parentheses) refer to William Wordsworth, *The Ruined Cottage and The Pedlar*, ed. James Butler.

11. I have in mind not only St. Paul but also Walt Whitman's stanza beginning "Swiftly arose and spread around me the peace and joy and knowledge that pass all the art and argument of the earth" and ending with "mossy scabs of the wormfence, and heaped stones, and elder and mullein and pokeweed"; see the originally untitled poem later dubbed "Song of Myself," *Leaves of Grass: The First (1855) Edition*, ed. Malcolm Cowley, 5.81–89.

12. It is true, as James M. Averill says in *Wordsworth and the Poetry of Human Suffering*, that Wordsworth in *The Prelude* presents his tendency toward such imaginings as to some extent "a youthful foible," and such a presentation is a mode of "distancing" (180). But this somewhat self-deprecating rhetoric on Wordsworth's part does not diminish the palpable epiphanic power of the account.

2. FITFUL MOTIONS, FRAGILE FORMS

1. James Engell, *The Creative Imagination: Enlightenment to Romanticism* 338.

2. Engell 339.

3. Samuel Taylor Coleridge, *Biographia Literaria* 2 vols., 2:258.

4. I cannot discover in the secondary literature any attempt to apply

Bachelardian phenomenological analysis to the epiphanies of Coleridge. Somewhat related to the present study is Arden Reed, *Romantic Weather: The Climates of Coleridge and Baudelaire*; though Reed expresses debts to Michel Serres and Earl Wasserman, to Derrida and de Man (75), his investigations seem to me partly phenomenological in technique and intent. Examples are Reed's explorations of the much-varied themes of "a mist that darkens the sky" and of "eddyings and vicious circles" in the poet's perceptions as well as in the obscure, circuitous, and divagating motions of the Coleridgean writing procedure itself (183). There is a distant parallel to my project in Edward Kessler, *Coleridge's Metaphors of Being*, but Kessler's interests are less phenomenological than ontological: since he is concerned to find metaphors for "Being" in Coleridge, the images he finds are usually half-conceptual in nature ("Phantom," "Limbo"). Kessler's "The Eddy-Rose" is a useful contribution to the total phenomenology of Coleridgean imagery, but that chapter is one of the book's briefest, and the only one of Coleridge's greater lyrics in which an eddy may be found is "Dejection." I find phenomenological interest in Jerome Christensen, "The Color of Imagination and the Office of Romantic Criticism," in *Coleridge's Theory of Imagination Today*, ed. Christine Gallant, 227–42.

5. In *Blake and Goethe: Psychology, Ontology, Imagination*, I noted Coleridge's "oscillation" between "solipsistic and dialogic perspectives," but I noted roughly the same contrast—between what Goethe calls our need "to selve" and our contrasting need "to unselve" (*uns zu verselbsten* and *uns zu entselbstigen*)—in Blake, Wordsworth, Shelley, and Keats as well; clearly it does not individualize Coleridge (*Blake and Goethe* 10, 6).

6. "Melancholy: A Fragment," 11.11–13. All Coleridge verse citations (hereafter by line numbers in parentheses) refer to Samuel Taylor Coleridge, *The Complete Poetical Works of Samuel Taylor Coleridge*, ed. E. H. Coleridge, 2 vols.

7. The revelatory significance of Sara's imagined reproof (she is not to be considered a bothersome scold: the poet partly identifies with her) is underlined by the fact that her putative rebuke ("And biddest me walk humbly with my God" [l. 52]) echoes Micah 6:8 ("and what doth the Lord require of thee, but to do justly, and to love mercy, and to walk humbly with thy God?"). This allusion is not noted in any edition I have discovered, but awareness of it is requisite for a full understanding of the poet-persona's conflicted state of mind: he imagines Sara (or at least Sara's glance) as implicitly *quoting God's prophet.*

8. Richard Holmes, *Coleridge: Early Visions* 184.

9. The phrase "velvet black" (l. 279) is odd, for "velvet" is an incongruous texture for a hairless, "glossy" snake (l. 279). Could this be a reminiscence of the "stranger" film from "This Lime-Tree Bower"? Films of soot are velvety-looking as well as black.

10. See M. H. Abrams, general ed., *The Norton Anthology of English Literature*, 4th ed., 2 vols., 2:352 n6. Coleridge was right to counsel us not to overemphasize the "moral": the seeming endlessness of the Mariner's prophetic purgatory, among many other nightmarish aspects of the story, makes the

narrative profoundly problematic as a "moral" tale. For more light, from a comparative perspective, on the ambivalent implications of the story and its epiphanies, see my "Beneficent Birds and Crossbow Crimes: The Nightmare-Confessions of Coleridge and Ludwig Tieck," in *Papers on Language and Literature* 25 (1989): 44–58.

11.   The ambivalence of all epiphanies in "Christabel" is clarified by study of their partial sources in certain scenes of Milton's *Comus*; see my "*Christabel* as Dark Double of *Comus*," in *Studies in Philology* 83 (1986): 182–200.

12.   Johann Wolfgang von Goethe, *Faust* in *Werke: Hamburger Ausgabe*, ed. Erich Trunz et al., 10th ed., 3:193.6271–72.

3. DUPLICITOUS WELCOMERS

1.   A. Dwight Culler, *Imaginative Reason: The Poetry of Matthew Arnold* 1–17 and *passim*.

2.   Alan Roper, *Arnold's Poetic Landscapes* 1–11 and *passim*.

3.   William A. Madden, "Arnold the Poet: (1) Lyric and Elegiac Poems," in *Writers and Their Background: Matthew Arnold*, ed. Kenneth Allott, 57–58.

4.   Matthew Arnold, "The Study of Poetry," in *English Literature and Irish Politics*, vol. 9 of *The Complete Prose Works of Matthew Arnold*, ed. R. H. Super, 161.

5.   Arnold, "The Study of Poetry," in *English Literature and Irish Politics*, vol. 9 of *The Complete Prose Works of Matthew Arnold* 187.

6.   J. Hillis Miller, in *The Disappearance of God: Five Nineteenth-Century Writers* 212–69, offers a phenomenological (Pouletian, not Bachelardian) study of Arnoldian space and time. Close in spirit to my argument here, though differing in method and central focus, is David G. Riede, in *Matthew Arnold and the Betrayal of Language*; instead of the duplicitous implications of elemental imagery, Riede concentrates on the Arnoldian problem of the duplicity inherent in traditional language.

7.   Madden 58.

8.   Culler in *Imaginative Reason* (8) notes that "in *To Marguerite—Continued* it is asserted that although on the surface we are islands, 'Surely once . . . we were / Parts of a single continent!' and this is further evidenced by the fact that underneath the sea the islands are connected with one another by a deep volcanic fire. So, too, in *Empedocles on Etna*, the Liparean islands are connected with each other and with Etna by 'sister-fires,' although on the surface they are connected only by 'a road of moonbeams.' " Culler mentions these scenes in discussing the reconciling sea. But the ambivalences I study here lead us to ask: Do we glide down from the burning plain only to encounter another burning plain beneath the sea? Is the first plain bad, the second good? Or is the mass of fire beneath the sea to be seen as another, fiery sea? Can a fiery sea be better than a watery one, if a burning plain is bad? The fiery underside to Arnold's water imagery (and vice versa) makes all value questions problematic, all levels of experience equivocal in meaning.

9.   I cannot find any detailed study of this poem. Park Honan, in *Matthew*

Arnold: A Life, thinks the travelers' progression from the "defeating spiritual present" to "release in a sea of death" shows "the fate of talented men who have knowledge but, being crippled by it, are powerless to act" (166–67). Nichols notes the epiphanic power of "A Dream" but does not analyze the poem (*Poetics of Epiphany* 118–19).

10. C. B. Tinker and H. F. Lowry, in *The Poetry of Matthew Arnold: A Commentary*, note that "Olivia and Martin, if they are real people, have never been identified" (45): the likelihood that they are not real seems to me increased by Arnold's pervasive strategies of doubling (to emphasize two-sidedness, ambivalence, duplicity) as both a psychological necessity and an imaginatively compelling technique throughout the poem (see remarks on doubling below).

11. "A Dream," ll. 1–19. All Arnold verse citations (hereafter by line number in parentheses) refer to Matthew Arnold, in *The Poems of Matthew Arnold*, ed. Kenneth Allott, 2d ed. rev. Miriam Allott. Note that in this section of the poem any subliminal hints of sadness ("umbrage," "pinings") are "Muffled," as the cottage walls by the climbing plants: the incantation of "golden gourds; golden" is like a spell meant to perpetuate the enclasping assurance of maternal comfort ("mountain-skirts," "warm scent"), of ontological roundness and repletion (ll. 4–5, 17, 18, 6–7).

12. The plain-as-punishment motif is strongly sounded in "Dover Beach," too, along with the theme of the burning plain as Hell. In "Of the Devil's Party: Undetected Words of Milton's Satan in Arnold's 'Dover Beach'," *Victorian Poetry* 20 (1982): 86–87, I noted the correlation of "neither Joy, nor . . . light" with the "darkness visible" and "torture without end" of Hell (*PL* 1.63–68) and the parallel of the "darkling plain" to that "dreary Plain, forlorn and wild, / The seat of desolation, void of light" (*PL* 1.180–81) where "Satan proposes that he and his fellow devils might do well to rest and lay their plans for further battle with the Almighty." Riede (200) cites some of my remarks, integrating them into his discussion of the duplicity of language in Arnold.

13. Such a hypothesis would also tie in with the pain caused to Sohrab, in Arnold's later epic poem, by Rustum's continually taunting him about his supposed effeminacy; for this motif in *Sohrab and Rustum* see my "Zhukovskij and Arnold: Two Mid-Nineteenth Century Versions of the Sohrab-Rustum Episode," in *Forum for Modern Language Studies* 25 (1989): 16–33.

14. Madden (57) writes that at the end of this poem, the apparently fatal river "is transfigured by the language into an image of tentative hope suggesting that, despite his present alienation, man may someday be at peace with himself and with the universe, the outward and inward Rivers becoming one in the process." But study of the subliminal implications of imagery suggests how the poet in Arnold subtly opposes the (undeniably effective) devices of the transfiguring rhetorician.

15. Arnold, *The Poems of Matthew Arnold*, ed. Allott, 279–80; Allott also gives the burning bush reference (Exod. 3:1–6) along with a useful Carlylean quotation on the fiery, divine "flashing-in" that Moses felt.

16. In "Accurate Construction in Arnold's *Sohrab and Rustum*," *Papers on Language and Literature* 14 (1978): 58, Mark Siegchrist writes that "Although the possibility of ironic contrast" between the river of Sohrab's "gushing blood" and the majestic river Oxus "must be considered, the coda is so thoroughly integrated into the poem that such an interpretation is not finally tenable." But although we should see more parallelism than contrast in these two images, irony is not absent from their treatment, or from our response to each. Both the blood-river and the Oxus river participate in the poem's ironic fire-water ambivalences.

17. Gaston Bachelard, *Fragments of a Poetics of Fire*, trans. Kenneth Haltman, 104 (and 103–6 for a fuller discussion of the play).

18. Kenneth Allott and Miriam Allott, in "Arnold the Poet: (2) Narrative and Dramatic Poems," *Writers and Their Background: Matthew Arnold*, ed. Kenneth Allott (see *The Poems of Matthew Arnold* 107), show that even the watery seas in *Empedocles on Etna* are treated ironically: they cite the "rolling flood / Of newness and delight" (youthful experience) changing to the life of middle age when "Experience, like a sea, soaks all-effacing in" (1.3.354–55, 201).

4. LOVE AND LIMINALITY IN TENNYSON

1. See Victor Turner, "Liminality and Communitas," in *The Ritual Process: Structure and Anti-Structure* 94–130, esp. 94–95: during the central or liminal phase of a rite of passage "the characteristics of the ritual subject (the 'passenger') are ambiguous; he passes through a cultural realm that has few or none of the attributes of the past or coming state"; "Liminal entities are . . . betwixt and between the positions assigned and arrayed by law, custom, convention, and ceremonial." Turner cites as his source for the concept of liminality Arnold van Gennep, *The Rites of Passage*, trans. Monika B. Vizedom and Gabrielle L. Caffee.

2. W. E. Fredeman, " 'A Sign betwixt the Meadow and the Cloud': The Ironic Apotheosis of Tennyson's *St. Simeon Stylites*," *University of Toronto Quarterly* 38 (1968): 71.

3. W. David Shaw, *Tennyson's Style* 101.

4. Christopher Ricks, *Tennyson* 111.

5. W. E. Fredeman, "One Word More—On Tennyson's Dramatic Monologues," *Studies in Tennyson*, ed. Hallam Tennyson, 180.

6. "The Vision of Sin," l. 1. All Tennyson verse citations (hereafter by line number in parentheses) refer to Alfred Lord Tennyson, *The Poems of Tennyson*, ed. Christopher Ricks, 2d ed., 3 vols.

7. Hallam Tennyson, *Alfred Lord Tennyson: A Memoir by His Son*, 2 vols., 2:475.

8. Ashton Nichols, "The Epiphanic Trance Poem: Why Tennyson is Not a Mystic," *Victorian Poetry* 5 (1986): 131–48; James R. Kincaid, *Tennyson's Major Poems: The Comic and Ironic Patterns* 12; A. Dwight Culler, *The Poetry of Tennyson* 25–28; Daniel Albright, *Tennyson: The Muses' Tug-of-War* 11.

9. Alan Sinfield, in *The Language of Tennyson's "In Memoriam,"* notes the

theme of "circles" in this section: "The last sections of the poem are bursting with circle imagery"; "The trance is itself described in terms of circles, suggesting that the poet at last manages to see all creation as part of one vast, harmonious movement" (149–50).

10. David Goslee, in *Tennyson's Characters: "Strange Faces, Other Minds,"* notes that Tennyson saves this image "from conventional necrophilia only by making the dead not the beloved object but the throbbing phallic speaker himself"(152). Yet the rescue is not accomplished "only" by this means but also by the resonance the image acquires through recurrent variants of the epiphanic fire-rose pattern in *Maud*.

11. See my essay, "Visions of Wholeness and Voices from the Deep: Kindred Wanderers in Byron's 'The Dream' and Tennyson's 'Ulysses'," *The Victorian Newsletter* 74 (1988): 41–45.

12. Such considerations add weight to the thesis argued throughout Herbert F. Tucker's *Tennyson and the Doom of Romanticism*, e.g., "From all available evidence it seems that the absence of Hallam made the opening of the self's casement less an admission of warm love than a traumatic wound" (165).

13. John D. Rosenberg, in *The Fall of Camelot: A Study of Tennyson's "Idylls of the King,"* says, "Allegorical interpretations of the *Idylls* obscure" the central "distinction" between "right versus wrong" and "right versus right" and "substitute didactic solutions for the moral dilemmas it poses" (24). But William E. Buckler, in *Man and His Myths: Tennyson's "Idylls of the King" in Critical Context*, convinces me that Rosenberg's anti-allegorical thesis is overstated (329–30).

14. Albright quotes this passage at length and treats its sources in some of Tennyson's earliest visionary poems; he notes that it shows the poet's wish to add to the *Idylls* "a fringe of the miraculous, the Romantically preposterous, as if a spirit of unearthly playfulness hovered at the edges of the tales. . . . One of the high muses in Tennyson's work—though certainly not the very most celestial—seems to be a muse who relishes marvels, Romantic unrealities" (72–74). I admit the playfulness of the passage, but I would also relate it to more serious epiphanic realities.

5. BEAUTY AND PAIN IN PATER

1. Walter Pater, *Collected Works*, New Library Ed., 10 vols., 1:236; all citations of Pater's works (hereafter by volume and page number in parentheses) refer to this edition. Volume 1 is *The Renaissance: Studies in Art and Poetry*; volumes 2 and 3 are *Marius the Epicurean: His Sensations and Ideas*; volume 4 is *Imaginary Portraits*, including "A Prince of Court Painters," "Denys L'Auxerrois," "Sebastian van Storck," and "Duke Carl of Rosenmold." The title *Imaginary Portraits* as used in this essay, however, must be understood as including also four additional portraits, which, as William E. Buckler notes in the preface to his edition of Walter Pater, *Three Major Texts: The Renaissance, Appreciations, and Imaginary Portraits* vii, Pater "thought of including in a sec-

ond series": these are "Hippolytus Veiled" from *Greek Studies* (volume 7) and "The Child in the House," "Emerald Uthwart," and "Apollo in Picardy" from *Miscellaneous Studies* (volume 8). Also cited in this chapter are *Appreciations, with an Essay on Style* (volume 5) and *Gaston de Latour: An Unfinished Romance* (volume 10).

2. The two passages studied by L. M. Findlay, in " 'This Hard, Gem-like Flame': Walter Pater and the Aesthetic Accommodation of Fire," in *The Airy Elements in Poetic Imagination*, part 2 of *Poetics of the Elements in the Human Condition*, ed. Anna-Teresa Tymieniecka, 102–13, are both from *The Renaissance* (one on Winckelmann, one from the famous "Conclusion"); Findlay's essay impressionistically celebrates Pater's achievement (212). In "Foreword: Fractal Pater," an introduction to Jay Fellows, *Tombs, Despoiled and Haunted: "Under-Textures" and "After-Thoughts" in Walter Pater*, J. Hillis Miller says that Fellows' method of analysis includes the "procedures of a kind of criticism now out of fashion: the 'criticism of consciousness' of Georges Poulet, Gaston Bachelard, and Jean-Pierre Richard, especially the latter two" (xi), but I find no Bachelardism in this book, unless Miller simply refers to Fellows' interest in Pater's occasional remarks on center and circumference, on centrifugal and centripetal motion. (In his chap. 3, Fellows develops the few Paterian uses of such terms into major metaphors of his own.) In any case, no red-yellow fire flowers or dying white birds are found in Fellows' study.

3. Cited in F. C. McGrath, *The Sensible Spirit: Walter Pater and the Modernist Paradigm* 92.

4. Cited in Jay B. Losey, "Epiphany in Pater's Portraits," *English Literature in Transition: 1880–1920* 29 (1986): 300. Looking at "The Child in the House," Losey mentions the hawthorn episode we will be examining but comments only on the persistency of associations (304).

John McGowan, in "From Pater to Wilde to Joyce: Modernist Epiphany and the Soulful Self," *Texas Studies in Literature and Language* 32 (1990): 425, argues convincingly that "Pater's inability to extend his extreme impressionism to account for the act of creation undermines his radical atomism and returns him to a more traditional, romantic use of epiphany."

5. Daniel T. O'Hara, *The Romance of Interpretation: Visionary Criticism from Pater to de Man* 51.

6. Gerald Monsman, in *Walter Pater's Art of Autobiography*, points to Pater's loss of his father at age 2 and of his mother at age 14 as belonging to a "pattern of psychological trauma" (82). This book extends the psychological explorations in Monsman's *Pater's Portraits: Mythic Pattern in the Fiction of Walter Pater*. Wolfgang Iser, in *Walter Pater: The Aesthetic Moment*, trans. David Henry Wilson, accounts for the early deaths of Paterian protagonists by supposing that the reality-defying stance of these aesthetes implies a negative outlook making life unbearable (168–69). Richard Dellamora, in *Masculine Desire: The Sexual Politics of Victorian Aestheticism*, describes a guilt-inducing social climate (which perhaps compounded the elements of remembered trauma that Monsman detects in Pater's imaginative life). Denis Donoghue,

in *Walter Pater: Lover of Strange Souls*, offers valuable cultural-historical context for Pater's aestheticism.

7. From Heraclitus, Fragment 30, in Harold J. Allen and James B. Wilbur, *The Worlds of the Early Greek Philosophers* 69.

8. Mary Moorman, *William Wordsworth: A Biography*, 2 vols., 1:348.

9. Linda Dowling, in "Nero and the Aesthetics of Torture," *The Victorian Newsletter* 66 (Fall 1984): 1–5, speaks of "the whimsically perverse humor, at times even verging on a delicate sadism, that runs throughout Pater's *oeuvre*" (4). Fellows speaks of a Paterian "incipient aesthetics of sadomasochism" (11). Carolyn Williams, in *Transfigured World: Walter Pater's Aesthetic Historicism*, speaks of "masochistic sexuality" as a "recurrent strain" in Pater's "romanticism" (255).

10. William E. Buckler, in *Walter Pater: The Critic as Artist of Ideas*, says, "The sketches of Ronsard, Montaigne, and Bruno are the finest literary harvest of *Gaston de Latour*. Of these, the sketch of Montaigne is the most critically satisfying" (284). These statements are true if you are interested in the critic as artist of ideas. But the sketch of Montaigne is very weak as a source of Paterian epiphany, and so is the sketch of Bruno. Ronsard alone, revealingly a poet rather than a philosophical essayist, inspires moments of outstanding epiphanic power.

6. EPIPHANIES FROM ODIN TO TEUFELSDRÖCKH

1. See introduction n21.

2. James Miller, *The Passion of Michel Foucault* 60–61; for the Ship of Fools as the "guiding image" of Foucault's book, see 100. Foucault, *Madness and Civilization*, trans. Richard Howard, is a greatly abridged version of *Folie et déraison*. Miller cites Foucault's introduction (61) to *Le rêve et l'existence* by Ludwig Binswanger: "No one has better understood the dynamic work of the imagination [than Bachelard]" (126). Miller analyzes Foucault's largely Bachelard-inspired "intricate aquatic reverie," showing "why the image of the ship setting sail is so well suited to evoke the *daimonic* forces at play in every person's life" (100).

3. Thomas Carlyle, *On Heroes, Hero-Worship, and the Heroic in History*, *The Works of Thomas Carlyle*, ed. H. D. Traill, 30 vols., 5.29. All *Heroes* citations (hereafter by page numbers in parentheses) refer to this volume.

4. Leo Tolstoy, *War and Peace*, trans. Ann Dunnigan, 733.

5. Chris R. Vanden Bossche, *Carlyle and the Search for Authority* 193 n11; for my article, see the acknowledgments in this book.

6. Robert W. Kusch, "Carlyle and the Milieu of 'Spontaneous Combustion'," *Neuphilologische Mitteilungen* 70 (1969): 339–44; "Pattern and Paradox in *Heroes and Hero-Worship*," *Studies in Scottish Literature* 6 (1969): 147–48.

7. G. B. Tennyson, *Sartor Called Resartus: The Genesis, Structure, and Style of Thomas Carlyle's First Major Work* 196–98 for light-dark, 198–99 for fire, 213–17 for water.

8. George Gordon, Lord Byron to Annabella Milbanke, 29 November 1813, in *Letters and Journals*, ed. Leslie A. Marchand, 12 vols., 3:179.

9. Eloise M. Behnken, *Thomas Carlyle: "Calvinist Without the Theology"* 52–71, lacks this awareness of decline: if Carlyle thinks civilization has "advanced a giant step" from Odin to Mahomet (59), why does Carlyle find "insupportable stupidity" in the Koran? (See below.)

10. Though he does not study Carlyle, Bachelard offers a brilliant exploration of phoenix epiphanies in "The Phoenix, A Linguistic Phenomenon," in *Fragments of a Poetics of Fire*, trans. Kenneth Haltman, 29–64.

11. In view of these problems, it is hard to see how "Carlyle's call for a rebirth of the spirit of hero-worship is . . . a call for resistance rather than for submission," as Philip Rosenberg avers in *The Seventh Hero: Thomas Carlyle and the Theory of Radical Activism* 199. Rosemary Jann, in *The Art and Science of Victorian History*, charitably grants that "the luminous clarity and insight of [Carlyle's] best passages more than atone for the intervening obscurity" (63), yet she notes the "serious drawbacks" of Carlyle's method: "Because his interest in events was essentially metaphorical or allegorical [my term would be "epiphanic"], he rarely gave them the close analysis that they demanded" (62).

12. Thomas Carlyle, *Sartor Resartus, The Works of Thomas Carlyle*, Ed. H. D. Traill, 30 vols., 1:56. All *Sartor* citations (hereafter by page numbers in parentheses) refer to this volume.

13. John D. Rosenberg, in *Carlyle and the Burden of History*, citing part of this *Sartor* passage on madness, says, "Sanity for Carlyle is not a natural condition but a fragile achievement, 'creatively built' and constantly imperilled. Madness . . . threatens to engulf us all" (13). But Carlyle's epiphany equates "madness" with flaming exuberance, not fragility or peril.

14. Anne K. Mellor, in *English Romantic Irony*, calls this an "oxymoronic conversion (through the union of fire and water)" (124). But Mellor's description of *Sartor Resartus* as a "self-consuming artifact" (131) is misleading. Unlike the metaphysical lyrics Stanley Fish characterizes in these terms, *Sartor* does not seek to cancel itself before an overpowering theophany—as might a lyric by George Herbert. The fire visions of *Sartor*, like those of *Heroes*, are nineteenth-century epiphanies, not seventeenth-century theophanies: intensity, expansiveness, and mystery are their sole guarantees of value.

15. Strictly speaking, it is inaccurate. "Nay, unless my Algebra deceive me, *Unity* itself divided by Zero will give *Infinity*," says Teufelsdröckh (153), but he's wrong: one cannot divide something into zero parts. But if we use zero as an asymptote, substituting for it a fraction indicating that which is infinitesimal, namely one over infinity, the equation will come out as Teufelsdröckh wishes, with Infinity as its result.

16. Compare the comments of George L. Levine, " 'Not Like My Lancelot': The Disappearing Victorian Hero," in *Perspectives on Nineteenth-Century Heroism: Essays from the 1981 Conference of the Southeastern Nineteenth-Century Studies*

Association, ed. Sara M. Putzell and David C. Leonard: " 'The first preliminary moral Act,' remember, is 'annihilation of self,' of the very self, apparently, that Teufelsdröckh labored to discover two chapters before." Carlyle "gives us a progress from nothing to nothing and locates somewhere in it the hero and all authority" (64–65).

17. Paul Jay, *Being in the Text: Self-Representation from Wordsworth to Roland Barthes* 107.

18. Peter Allan Dale, "*Sartor Resartus* and the Inverse Sublime," in *Allegory, Myth, and Symbol*, ed. Morton W. Bloomfield, 302.

19. Mellor 134.

7. WATER, MOVEMENT, ROUNDNESS

1. The number of questers or seers or seekers will depend on one's criteria for counting. I have included Platon Karatayev as a visionary on the assumption that if he *embodies* epiphanic truth (as he evidently does—we shall learn—through his metaphysical or ontological "roundness") he has presumably somehow "seen" that truth. Clearly, though, Platon is to be regarded as having basically found the truth he embodies (or else it somehow found him), so he is in that sense no longer a visionary seeker or quester—if indeed he ever was.

2. Gary Saul Morson, *Hidden in Plain View: Narrative and Creative Potentials in "War and Peace"*; see, for example, 205–10 on self as aggregate, 147–53 on "unnecessary" incidents and characters. In opposition to E. E. Zaidenshnur and R. F. Christian, who saw Tolstoy's creative process in producing *War and Peace* as fundamentally unified and coherent, and to Viktor Shklovsky and Boris Eikhenbaum, who viewed that process as conflicted and contradictory, Morson seeks to show that Tolstoy deliberately set out to discover the book's structure in the act of making it, to let the book "shape itself" as it was "being written" (see 173–82). "Round Table: Five Critiques and a Reply," an extensive discussion of Morson's work (critiques by Freeman Dyson, Alfred J. Rieber, Cathy Popkin, Carol Any, Anna A. Tavis, reply by Morson), appears in *Tolstoy Studies Journal* 2 (1989): 1–40.

3. Morson 143.

4. Morson 19. In Bakhtinian fashion, Morson argues that "there is no way to speak completely noncontextually in a novel," that since a novel is a dialogical form of literature, even a statement intended to be taken as absolute is contextualized, relativized by the reader who is cognizant of "novelistic tradition"; Morson calls this "metacontextualization" (19–20).

5. James M. Curtis, "The Function of Imagery in *War and Peace*," *Slavic Review* 29 (1970): 460–80, divides the imagery of the novel into "organic and inorganic—that is, images which refer to animals and plants and those which refer to machines and inanimate objects" (462). But the element-motion-shape pattern I discern in the book's epiphanies (water, symmetric or pendular motion, and the sphere) escapes both of Curtis' categories. Curtis sug-

gests that water "links the organic and inorganic similes" (470) he has studied, but the instances of water imagery he quotes are not analyzed, so their linkage value remains unproved.

Though I can find in the criticism no systematic phenomenological studies of the epiphanic pattern in *War and Peace,* there are certain phenomenological qualities in John Weeks, "Love, Death, and Cricketsong: Prince Andrei at Mytishchi," *In the Shade of the Giant: Essays on Tolstoy,* ed. Hugh McLean, 61–83, an attempt to account for Andrei's "extraordinary psychological state" prior to his death by looking at Tolstoy's use of "aural texture" (61).

6. Leo Tolstoy, *War and Peace,* trans. Ann Dunnigan, 1272; L. N. Tolstoi, *Voina i mir (War and Peace)* vols. 4–7 in *Sobranie sochinenij,* 20 vols., 7:181–82. All Tolstoy citations (hereafter *WP* and *SS* respectively with volume and page numbers in parentheses) refer to these editions.

7. Weeks speculates that an echo of this "piti-piti-piti" may be audible in the "regular tattoo of *ljubit'-ljubit'-ljubit'* " ("to love, to love, to love") that forms part of the sound texture of Prince Andrei's meditations later on in the passage (77).

8. Eliot gives it in Greek; see T. S. Eliot, *Collected Poems, 1909–1962* 175.

9. Weeks says since "Andrei and Petya are about to die" they are "given dispensation to hear the music of the spheres" (79).

10. For landmark discussions of Tolstoy on history from non-phenomenological viewpoints, see Boris Eikhenbaum, *Lev Tolstoi,* 3 vols.; Isaiah Berlin, *The Hedgehog and the Fox;* Paul Debreczeny, "Freedom and Necessity: A Reconsideration of *War and Peace,*" *Papers on Literature and Language* 7 (1971): 185–98; Edward Wasiolek, "The Theory of History in *War and Peace,*" *Midway* 9, No. 2 (1968): 117–35; F. F. Seeley, "Tolstoy's Philosophy of History," in *New Essays on Tolstoy,* ed. Malcolm Jones, 175–93; Andrew Baruch Wachtel, *An Obsession with History: Russian Writers Confront the Past* 88–122; Wachtel's dialogic and decentered approach, like Morson's in *Hidden in Plain View* and in his more recent *Narrative and Freedom: The Shadows of Time,* finds no epiphanic center in *War and Peace.*

8. TURNING STONES TO FIRE

1. Elizabeth Barrett Browning, *Aurora Leigh,* ed. Margaret Reynolds, 9.598, 570. All *Aurora Leigh* citations (hereafter with book and line numbers in parentheses) refer to this edition, which reprints the revised fourth edition of 1859; Reynolds' "Editorial Introduction" (78–156) is exemplary, and her "Critical Introduction" (1–77) is the best general preface to the poem.

2. In "Images of 'Mother-Want' in Elizabeth Barrett Browning's *Aurora Leigh,*" *Victorian Poetry* 21 (1983): 351–67, however, Virginia V. Steinmetz, basing her arguments in part on psychoanalytical object relations theory in the Kleinian tradition, identifies a pattern of regressive nostalgia for an absent mother, nostalgia not wholly mastered and recurrently embodied in idealized maternal portrayals. Steinmetz is building upon Barbara Charlesworth

Gelpi's study of Aurora's attempts to overcome inner ambivalences concerning her femininity in "*Aurora Leigh*: The Vocation of the Woman Poet," *Victorian Poetry* 19 (1981): 35–48.

3. Virginia Steinmetz, "Beyond the Sun: Patriarchal Images in *Aurora Leigh*," *Studies in Browning and His Circle* 9 (1989): 41.

4. The nature-transcending, world-transforming apocalypticism of Barrett Browning's epiphanic fires means that she never aspires to be a poet of nature in the Wordsworthian sense. So I cannot agree with Katherine Blake, "Elizabeth Barrett Browning and Wordsworth: The Romantic Poet as Woman," *Victorian Poetry* 24 (1986): 387–98, that Barrett Browning is involved in the same "romantic progression from human love to love of nature" as Wordsworth is in *The Prelude* (nor do I agree that "She must attempt to achieve at the end of her story the stage at which he starts" [see 394, 398]).

5. Marjorie Stone, in "Genre Subversion and Gender Inversion: *The Princess* and *Aurora Leigh*," *Victorian Poetry* 25 (1987): 101–27, suggests that Barrett Browning's subversion of traditional epic stereotypes in favor of a mixed genre that can deal in more modern mimetic ways with contemporary life is connected with her concomitant subversion of sexual stereotypes, in particular as she transgressively rewrites Tennyson. Dorothy Mermin, in "Genre and Gender in *Aurora Leigh*," *The Victorian Newsletter* 69 (1986): 7–11, also links changed concepts of gender to the evolution of *Aurora Leigh* as "novel-poem." Joyce Zonana, in "The Embodied Muse: Elizabeth Barrett Browning's *Aurora Leigh* and Feminist Poetics," *Tulsa Studies in Women's Literature* 8 (1989): 241–62, describes Aurora in strongly revised classical terms as muse, as goddess: "This goddess, unlike precursors in the poetry of men, is made of earth and committed both to living upon it and transforming it" (259). All these studies relate in various ways to the pioneering treatment of *Aurora Leigh* in Sandra M. Gilbert and Susan Gubar, *The Madwoman in the Attic: The Woman Writer and the Nineteenth-Century Literary Imagination* esp. 575–80, noting the "Romantic rage for social transformation concealed behind the veil of self-abnegating servitude [presumably Aurora as Antigone to a blinded oedipal Romney] with which *Aurora Leigh* concludes" (580).

6. But Barrett Browning, in her "Contributions Toward an Essay on Carlyle" in *Complete Works of Elizabeth Barrett Browning*, 6 vols., ed. Charlotte Porter and Helen A. Clarke, 6:312–21, quotes at length a characteristically effective Carlylean fire epiphany (317).

7. Daniel Karlin, *The Courtship of Robert Browning and Elizabeth Barrett* 32–33: Elizabeth seems to have felt deep guilt for having urged Edward to stay at Torquay longer than her father had wished, a guilt exacerbated by unacknowledged sibling rivalry.

8. Sandra M. Gilbert, in "From *Patria* to *Matria*: Elizabeth Barrett Browning's Risorgimento," *PMLA* 99 (1984): 194–211, explores the link between political and personal liberation, insurrection, resurrection, in Barrett Browning's evolving poetics.

9. Indeed, "The last lines of the poem show Romney in something of the attitude of the resigned, iconic woman, raising his head to gaze mutely toward the heavenly city, while Aurora looks on him and, like a mother interpreting the world to a child, names his unarticulated vision," as Dolores Rosenblum observes in "Face to Face: Elizabeth Barrett Browning's *Aurora Leigh* and Nineteenth-Century Poetry," *Victorian Studies* 26 (1983): 335.

Works Cited

Abrams, M. H., general ed. *The Norton Anthology of English Literature*. 4th ed., 2 vols. New York: Norton, 1979.

Albright, Daniel. *Tennyson: The Muses' Tug-of-War*. Charlottesville: Univ. Press of Virginia, 1986.

Alden, Douglas W., and Richard B. Brooks, eds. *A Critical Bibliography of French Literature*. Syracuse: Syracuse Univ. Press, 1980.

Allen, Harold J., and James B. Wilbur. *The Worlds of the Early Greek Philosophers*. Buffalo: Prometheus Books, 1979.

Allott, Kenneth, and Miriam Allott. "Arnold the Poet: (2) Narrative and Dramatic Poems." In *Writers and Their Background: Matthew Arnold*, edited by Kenneth Allott, 70–117. Athens: Ohio Univ. Press, 1975.

Arnold, Matthew. *The Poems of Matthew Arnold*. Ed. Kenneth Allott. 2d ed. rev. Miriam Allott. London: Longman, 1979.

———. "The Study of Poetry." In *English Literature and Irish Politics*. Vol. 9 of *The Complete Prose Works of Matthew Arnold*. Ed. R. H. Super. 11 vols. Ann Arbor: Univ. of Michigan Press, 1960–1977.

Averill, James M. *Wordsworth and the Poetry of Human Suffering*. Ithaca: Cornell Univ. Press, 1980.

Bachelard, Gaston. *Air and Dreams: An Essay on the Imagination of Movement*. Trans. Edith R. Farrell and C. Frederick Farrell. Dallas: Pegasus Foundation of the Dallas Institute of Humanities and Culture, 1989.

———. *Earth and Reveries of Will*. Trans. Liliana Zancu (forthcoming).

———. *The Flame of a Candle*. Trans. Joni Caldwell. Dallas: Pegasus Foundation of the Dallas Institute of Humanities and Culture, 1989.

———. *Fragments of a Poetics of Fire*. Trans. Kenneth Haltman. Dallas: Pegasus Foundation of the Dallas Institute of Humanities and Culture, 1990.

———. *On Poetic Imagination and Reverie: Selections from the Works of Gaston Bachelard*. Ed. and trans. Colette Gaudin. Indianapolis: Bobbs Merrill, 1971.

———. *The Poetics of Reverie*. Trans. Daniel Russell. New York: Orion Press, 1969.

———. *The Poetics of Space*. Trans. Maria Jolas. New York: Orion Press, 1964.

———. *The Psychoanalysis of Fire*. Trans. Alan C. M. Ross. Boston: Beacon Press, 1964.

———. *The Right to Dream*. Trans. J. C. Underwood. New York: Grossman,

1971. Reprint, Dallas: Pegasus Foundation of the Dallas Institute of Humanities and Culture, 1989.

———. *La terre et les rêveries de la volonté. Essai sur l'imagination des forces.* Paris: Corti, 1948.

———. *La terre et les rêveries du repos. Essai sur l'imagination d l'intimité.* Paris: Corti, 1948.

———. *Water and Dreams: An Essay on the Imagination of Matter.* Trans. Edith R. Farrell. Dallas: Pegasus Foundation of the Dallas Institute of Humanities and Culture, 1983.

Barthes, Roland. *Michelet.* Trans. Richard Howard. New York: Farrar, Straus, and Giroux, 1987.

Behnken, Eloise M. *Thomas Carlyle: "Calvinist Without the Theology."* Columbia: Univ. of Missouri Press, 1978.

Beja, Morris. *Epiphany in the Modern Novel.* Seattle: Univ. of Washington Press, 1979.

Berlin, Isaiah. *The Hedgehog and the Fox.* New York: Simon and Schuster, 1953.

Bidney, Martin. "The Aeolian Harp Reconsidered: Music of Unfulfilled Longing in Tjutchev, Moerike, Thoreau, and Others." *Comparative Literature Studies* 22 (1985): 329–43.

———. "Beneficent Birds and Crossbow Crimes: The Nightmare-Confessions of Coleridge and Ludwig Tieck." *Papers on Language and Literature* 25 (1989): 44–58.

———. *Blake and Goethe: Psychology, Ontology, Imagination.* Columbia: Univ. of Missouri Press, 1988.

———. "*Christabel* as Dark Double of *Comus.*" *Studies in Philology* 83 (1986): 182–200.

———. "Of the Devil's Party: Undetected Words of Milton's Satan in Arnold's 'Dover Beach'." *Victorian Poetry* 20 (1982): 85–89.

———. "Parrots, Pictures, Rays, Perfumes: Epiphanies in George Sand and Flaubert." *Studies in Short Fiction* 22 (1985): 209–17.

———. Review of *The Poetics of Epiphany: Nineteenth-Century Origins of the Modern Literary Moment,* by Ashton Nichols. *The Wordsworth Circle* 19 (1988): 205–7.

———. "Visions of Wholeness and Voices from the Deep: Kindred Wanderers in Byron's 'The Dream' and Tennyson's 'Ulysses'." *The Victorian Newsletter* 74 (1988): 41–45.

———. "Zhukovskij and Arnold: Two Mid-Nineteenth Century Versions of the Sohrab-Rustum Episode." *Forum for Modern Language Studies* 25 (1989): 16–33.

Blake, Katherine. "Elizabeth Barrett Browning and Wordsworth: The Romantic Poet as Woman." *Victorian Poetry* 24 (1986): 387–98.

Blake, William. *The Complete Poetry and Prose of William Blake.* Rev. ed. David

V. Erdman. Commentary by Harold Bloom. Berkeley: Univ. of California Press, 1982.

Browning, Elizabeth Barrett. *Aurora Leigh.* Ed. Margaret Reynolds. Athens: Ohio Univ. Press, 1992.

———. *Complete Works of Elizabeth Barrett Browning.* Ed. Charlotte Porter and Helen A. Clarke. 6 vols. New York: Crowell, 1900. Reprint, New York: AMS Press, 1973.

Brugière, Bernard. *L'univers imaginaire de Robert Browning.* Paris: Klincksieck, 1979.

Buckler, William E. *Man and His Myths: Tennyson's "Idylls of the King" in Critical Context.* New York: New York Univ. Press, 1984.

———. *Walter Pater: The Critic as Artist of Ideas.* New York : New York Univ. Press, 1987.

Byron, George Gordon, Lord. *Letters and Journals.* Ed. Leslie A. Marchand. 12 vols. London: John Murray, 1973–82.

Carlyle, Thomas. *The Works of Thomas Carlyle.* Ed. H. D. Traill. Centenary Edition. 30 vols. London: Chapman and Hall, 1896–99.

Christensen, Jerome. "The Color of Imagination and the Office of Romantic Criticism." In *Coleridge's Theory of Imagination Today,* edited by Christine Gallant, 227–42. New York: AMS Press, 1989.

Clark, John G. "Cinq images de Shelley qui ont fasciné Bachelard." *Revue Internationale de Philosophie* 38 (1984): 287–314.

———. "Gaston Bachelard devant la poésie anglaise." *Revue de Littérature Comparée* 58 (1984): 185–96.

Clayton, Jay, and Eric Rothstein. "Figures in the Corpus: Theories of Influence and Intertextuality." In *Influence and Intertextuality in Literary History,* edited by Jay Clayton and Eric Rothstein, 3–36. Madison: Univ. of Wisconsin Press, 1991.

Coleridge, Samuel Taylor. *Biographia Literaria.* 2 vols. Oxford: Oxford Univ. Press, 1907.

———. *The Complete Poetical Works of Samuel Taylor Coleridge.* Ed. E. H. Coleridge. 2 vols. Oxford: Oxford Univ. Press, 1912.

Culler, A. Dwight. *Imaginative Reason: The Poetry of Matthew Arnold.* New Haven: Yale Univ. Press, 1966.

———. *The Poetry of Tennyson.* New Haven: Yale Univ. Press, 1977.

Curtis, James M. "The Function of Imagery in *War and Peace.*" *Slavic Review* 29 (1970): 460–80.

Dale, Peter Allan. "*Sartor Resartus* and the Inverse Sublime." In *Allegory, Myth, and Symbol,* edited by Morton W. Bloomfield, 293–312. Cambridge: Harvard Univ. Press, 1981.

Debreczeny, Paul. "Freedom and Necessity: A Reconsideration of *War and Peace.*" *Papers on Literature and Language* 7 (1971): 185–98.

Dellamora, Richard. *Masculine Desire: The Sexual Politics of Victorian Aestheticism.* Chapel Hill: Univ. of North Carolina Press, 1990.

de Man, Paul. "The Rhetoric of Temporality." In *Blindness and Insight: Essays in the Rhetoric of Contemporary Criticism,* 2d rev., edited by Wlad Godzich, 187–228. Minneapolis: Univ. of Minnesota Press, 1983.

Donoghue, Denis. *Walter Pater: Lover of Strange Souls.* New York: Knopf, 1995.

Dowling, Linda. "Nero and the Aesthetics of Torture." *The Victorian Newsletter* 66 (Fall 1984): 1–5.

Dyson, Freeman, Alfred J. Rieber, Cathy Popkin, Carol Any, Anna A. Tavis, and Gary Saul Morson. "Round Table: Five Critiques and a Reply" [regarding Morson's *Hidden in Plain View,* see Morson below]. *Tolstoy Studies Journal* 2 (1989): 1–40.

Eagleton, Terry. *Literary Theory: An Introduction.* Minneapolis: Univ. of Minnesota Press, 1983.

Eikhenbaum, Boris. *Lev Tolstoi.* 3 vols. Leningrad: n.p., 1928–60.

Eliot, T. S. *Collected Poems, 1909–1962.* New York: Harcourt Brace, 1963.

Engell, James. *The Creative Imagination: Enlightenment to Romanticism.* Cambridge: Harvard Univ. Press, 1981.

Fellows, Jay. *Tombs, Despoiled and Haunted: "Under-Textures" and "After-Thoughts" in Walter Pater.* With an introduction by J. Hillis Miller. Stanford: Stanford Univ. Press, 1981.

Findlay, L. M. " 'This Hard, Gem-like Flame': Walter Pater and the Aesthetic Accommodation of Fire." In *Poetics of the Elements in the Human Condition: The Airy Elements in Poetic Imagination: Breath, Breeze, Wind, Tempest, Thunder, Snow, Flame, Fire, Volcano . . . ,* edited by Anna-Teresa Tymieniecka, 102–13.

Foucault, Michel. *Folie et déraison.* Paris: Plon, 1961.

———. Introduction to *Le rêve et l'existence,* by Ludwig Binswanger. Bruges: Desclée de Brouwer, 1954.

———. *Madness and Civilization.* Trans. Richard Howard. New York: Random, 1972.

Fredeman, W. E. "One Word More—On Tennyson's Dramatic Monologues." In *Studies in Tennyson,* edited by Hallam Tennyson, 169–85. Totowa, N.J.: Barnes and Noble, 1981.

———. " 'A Sign betwixt the Meadow and the Cloud': The Ironic Apotheosis of Tennyson's *St. Simeon Stylites.*" *University of Toronto Quarterly* 38 (1968): 69–83.

Gaull, Marilyn. "Romantic Numeracy: The 'Tuneless Numbers' and 'Shadows Numberless.' " *The Wordsworth Circle* 22 (1991): 124–31.

Gelpi, Barbara Charlesworth. "*Aurora Leigh*: The Vocation of the Woman Poet." *Victorian Poetry* 19 (1981): 35–48.

Gibaldi, Joseph, ed. *Introduction to Scholarship in Modern Languages and Literatures.* 2d ed. New York: Modern Language Association of America, 1992.

Gilbert, Sandra M. "From *Patria* to *Matria*: Elizabeth Barrett Browning's Risorgimento." *Publications of the Modern Language Association* 99 (1984): 194–211.

Gilbert, Sandra M., and Susan Gubar. *The Madwoman in the Attic: The Woman Writer and the Nineteenth-Century Literary Imagination*. New Haven: Yale Univ. Press, 1979.

Ginestier, Paul. "Bachelard et ses lectures anglaises." *Revue de Littérature Comparée* 58 (1984): 177–84.

Goethe, Johann Wolfgang von. *Werke: Hamburger Ausgabe*. Ed. Erich Trunz et al. 10th ed. 14 vols. Munich: C. H. Beck, 1974–79.

Goslee, David. *Tennyson's Characters: "Strange Faces, Other Minds."* Iowa City: Univ. of Iowa Press, 1989.

Hartman, Geoffrey. *The Unmediated Vision: An Interpretation of Wordsworth, Hopkins, Rilke, and Valéry*. New Haven: Yale Univ. Press, 1954.

———. *The Unremarkable Wordsworth*. Minneapolis: Univ. of Minnesota Press, 1987.

———. *Wordsworth's Poetry: 1787–1814*. New Haven: Yale Univ. Press, 1964.

Hefferman, James A. W. "Wordsworth, Coleridge, and Turner: The Geometry of the Infinite." *Bucknell Review* 29 (1984): 49–72.

Holmes, Richard. *Coleridge: Early Visions*. New York: Viking, 1989.

Honan, Park. *Matthew Arnold: A Life*. Cambridge: Harvard Univ. Press, 1981.

Irigaray, Luce. *Amante marine de Friedrich Nietzsche*. Paris: Minuit, 1980.

———. *L'oubli de l'air chez Martin Heidegger*. Paris: Minuit, 1983.

———. *Passions élémentaires*. Paris: Minuit, 1982.

Iser, Wolfgang. *Walter Pater: The Aesthetic Moment*. Trans. David Henry Wilson. Cambridge: Cambridge Univ. Press, 1987.

Jacobus, Mary. *Romanticism, Writing, and Sexual Difference: Essays on "The Prelude."* Oxford: Clarendon Press, 1989.

Jann, Rosemary. *The Art and Science of Victorian History*. Columbus: Ohio State Univ. Press, 1985.

Jay, Paul. *Being in the Text: Self-Representation from Wordsworth to Roland Barthes*. Ithaca: Cornell Univ. Press, 1984.

Jones, Mary McAllester. *Gaston Bachelard, Subversive Humanist: Texts and Readings*. Madison: Univ. of Wisconsin Press, 1991.

Karlin, Daniel. *The Courtship of Robert Browning and Elizabeth Barrett*. Oxford: Oxford Univ. Press, 1987.

Kessler, Edward. *Coleridge's Metaphors of Being*. Princeton: Princeton Univ. Press, 1979.

Kincaid, James R. *Tennyson's Major Poems: The Comic and Ironic Patterns*. New Haven: Yale Univ. Press, 1973.

Kusch, Robert. "Carlyle and the Milieu of 'Spontaneous Combustion'." *Neuphilologische Mitteilungen* 70 (1969): 339–44.

———. "Pattern and Paradox in *Heroes and Hero-Worship.*" *Studies in Scottish Literature* 6 (1969): 146–55.

Langbaum, Robert. *The Word from Below: Essays on Modern Literature and Culture.* Madison: Univ. of Wisconsin Press, 1987.

Lawall, Sarah. *Critics of Consciousness.* Cambridge: Harvard Univ. Press, 1968.

Leitch, Vincent B. *American Literary Criticism: From the Thirties to the Eighties.* New York: Columbia Univ. Press, 1988.

Lentricchia, Frank. *After the New Criticism.* Chicago: Univ. of Chicago Press, 1980.

Levine, George. " 'Not Like My Lancelot': The Disappearing Victorian Hero." In *Perspectives on Nineteenth-Century Heroism: Essays from the 1981 Conference of the Southeastern Nineteenth-Century Studies Association,* edited by Sara M. Putzell and David C. Leonard, 42–72. Madrid: Jose Porrúa Turanzas, S. A., 1982.

Lodge, David, ed. *Modern Criticism and Theory: A Reader.* London: Longman, 1988.

Losey, Jay B. "Epiphany in Pater's Portraits." *English Literature in Transition: 1880–1920* 29 (1986): 297–308.

Madden, William A. "Arnold the Poet: (1) Lyric and Elegiac Poems." In *Writers and Their Background: Matthew Arnold,* edited by Kenneth Allott, 39–69. Athens: Ohio Univ. Press, 1975.

Mansuy, Michel. "Pour une étude comparée de la rêverie." *Revue de la Littérature Comparée* 58 (1984): 145–64.

McAllester, Mary, ed. *The Philosophy and Poetics of Gaston Bachelard.* Washington, D.C.: Center for Advanced Research in Phenomenology; University Press of America, 1989.

McGowan, John. "From Pater to Wilde to Joyce: Modernist Epiphany and the Soulful Self." *Texas Studies in Literature and Language* 32 (1990): 417–45.

McGrath, F. C. *The Sensible Spirit: Walter Pater and the Modernist Paradigm.* Tampa: Univ. of South Florida Press, 1966.

Mellor, Anne K. *English Romantic Irony.* Cambridge: Harvard Univ. Press, 1982.

Mermin, Dorothy. "Genre and Gender in *Aurora Leigh.*" *The Victorian Newsletter* 69 (1986): 7–11.

Miller, J. Hillis. *The Disappearance of God: Five Nineteenth-Century Writers.* Cambridge: Harvard Univ. Press, 1963.

———. *Poets of Reality: Six Twentieth-Century Writers.* Cambridge: Harvard Univ. Press, 1965.

Miller, James. *The Passion of Michel Foucault.* New York: Simon and Schuster, 1993.

Monsman, Gerald. *Pater's Portraits: Mythic Pattern in the Fiction of Walter Pater.* Baltimore: Johns Hopkins Univ. Press, 1967.

———. *Walter Pater's Art of Autobiography.* New Haven: Yale Univ. Press, 1980.

Moorman, Mary. *William Wordsworth: A Biography*. 2 vols. Oxford: Oxford Univ. Press, 1957, 1965.

Morson, Gary Saul. *Hidden in Plain View: Narrative and Creative Potentials in "War and Peace."* Stanford: Stanford Univ. Press, 1987.

——. *Narrative and Freedom: The Shadows of Time*. New Haven: Yale Univ. Press, 1994.

Nichols, Ashton. "The Epiphanic Trance Poem: Why Tennyson Is Not a Mystic." *Victorian Poetry* 5 (1986): 131–48.

——. *The Poetics of Epiphany: Nineteenth-Century Origins of the Modern Literary Moment*. Tuscaloosa: Univ. of Alabama Press, 1987.

O'Hara, Daniel T. *The Romance of Interpretation: Visionary Criticism from Pater to de Man*. New York: Columbia Univ. Press, 1985.

Pater, Walter. *Collected Works*. New Library Edition. 10 vols. London: Macmillan, 1910.

——. *Three Major Texts: The Renaissance, Appreciations, and Imaginary Portraits*. Ed. Willam E. Buckler. New York: New York Univ. Press, 1986.

Pierrot, Jean. "Elemental Reverie." In *The Decadent Imagination: 1880–1900*, translated by Derek Coltman, 107–37. Chicago: Univ. of Chicago Press, 1981.

Poulet, Georges. *The Interior Distance*. Trans. Elliott Coleman. Baltimore: Johns Hopkins Univ. Press, 1959.

——. *The Metamorphoses of the Circle*. Trans. Carley Dawson and Elliott Coleman with the collaboration of the author. Baltimore: Johns Hopkins Univ. Press, 1966.

Reed, Arden. *Romantic Weather: The Climates of Coleridge and Baudelaire*. Hanover: Univ. Press of New England, Brown Univ. Press, 1983.

Richard, Jean-Pierre. *Poésie et profondeur*. Paris: Editions de Seuil, 1955.

Ricks, Christopher. *Tennyson*. New York: Macmillan, 1972.

Riede, David G. *Matthew Arnold and the Betrayal of Language*. Charlottesville: Univ. Press of Virginia, 1988.

Roper, Alan. *Arnold's Poetic Landscapes*. Baltimore: Johns Hopkins Univ. Press, 1969.

Rosenberg, John D. *Carlyle and the Burden of History*. Cambridge: Harvard Univ. Press, 1985.

——. *The Fall of Camelot: A Study of Tennyson's "Idylls of the King."* Cambridge: Harvard Univ. Press, 1973.

Rosenberg, Philip. *The Seventh Hero: Thomas Carlyle and the Theory of Radical Activism*. Cambridge: Harvard Univ. Press, 1974.

Rosenblum, Dolores. "Face to Face: Elizabeth Barrett Browning's *Aurora Leigh* and Nineteenth-Century Poetry." *Victorian Studies* 26 (1983): 321–38.

Schama, Simon. *Dead Certainties (Unwarranted Speculations)*. New York: Knopf, 1991.

Seeley, F. F. "Tolstoy's Philosophy of History." In *New Essays on Tolstoy*, edited by Malcolm Jones, 175–93. Cambridge: Cambridge Univ. Press, 1978.

Shaw, W. David. *Tennyson's Style*. Ithaca: Cornell Univ. Press, 1976.

Siegchrist, Mark. "Accurate Construction in Arnold's *Sohrab and Rustum*." *Papers on Language and Literature* 14 (1978): 51–60.

Sinfield, Alan. *The Language of Tennyson's "In Memoriam."* New York: Barnes and Noble, 1971.

Smith, Roch C. *Gaston Bachelard*. Boston: G. K. Hall, 1982.

Steinmetz, Virginia V. "Beyond the Sun: Patriarchal Images in *Aurora Leigh*." *Studies in Browning and His Circle* 9 (1989): 18–41.

———. "Images of 'Mother-Want' in Elizabeth Barrett Browning's *Aurora Leigh*." *Victorian Poetry* 21 (1983): 351–67.

Stone, Marjorie. "Genre Subversion and Gender Inversion: *The Princess* and *Aurora Leigh*." *Victorian Poetry* 25 (1987): 101–27.

Tennyson, Alfred Lord. *The Poems of Tennyson*. Ed. Christopher Ricks. 2d ed. 3 vols. Berkeley: Univ. of California Press, 1987.

———. *Tennyson's Poetry*. Ed. Robert W. Hill, Jr. New York: Norton, 1971.

Tennyson, G. B. *Sartor Called Resartus: The Genesis, Structure, and Style of Thomas Carlyle's First Major Work*. Princeton: Princeton Univ. Press, 1965.

Tennyson, Hallam. *Alfred Lord Tennyson: A Memoir by His Son*. 2 vols. New York: Macmillan, 1897.

Thomas, W. K., and Warren U. Ober. *A Mind for Ever Voyaging: Wordsworth at Work Portraying Newton and Science*. Alberta: Univ. of Alberta Press, 1989.

Tinker, C. B., and H. F. Lowry. *The Poetry of Matthew Arnold: A Commentary*. London: Oxford Univ. Press, 1940.

Tolstoi, L. N. *Sobranie sochinenij*. 20 vols. Moscow: Gosudarstvennoe Izdatel'stvo Khudozhestvennoi Literatury, 1960–65.

Tolstoy, Leo. *War and Peace*. Trans. Ann Dunnigan. With an introduction by John Bayley. New York: New American Library, 1968.

Tucker, Herbert F. *Tennyson and the Doom of Romanticism*. Cambridge: Harvard Univ. Press, 1988.

Turner, Victor. *The Ritual Process: Structure and Anti-Structure*. Ithaca: Cornell Univ. Press, 1969.

Tymieniecka, Anna-Teresa, ed. *Poetics of the Elements in the Human Condition: The Airy Elements in Poetic Imagination: Breath, Breeze, Wind, Tempest, Thunder, Snow, Flame, Fire, Volcano . . . .* Vol. 23 of *Analecta Husserliana*. Dordrecht: Kluwer, 1988.

———, ed. *Poetics of the Elements in the Human Condition: The Sea; From Elemental Stirrings to Symbolic Inspiration, Language, and Life-Significance in Literary Interpretation and Theory*. Vol. 19 of *Analecta Husserliana*. Dordrecht: Reidel, 1985.

Vanden Bossche, Chris R. *Carlyle and the Search for Authority*. Columbus: Ohio State Univ. Press, 1991.

van Gennep, Arnold. *The Rites of Passage*. Trans. Monika B. Vizedom and Gabrielle L. Caffee. London: Routledge and Kegan Paul, 1909.

Wachtel, Andrew Baruch. *An Obsession with History: Russian Writers Confront the Past*. Stanford: Stanford Univ. Press, 1994.

Wasiolek, Edward. "The Theory of History in *War and Peace*." *Midway* 9, No. 2 (1968): 117–35.

Weeks, John. "Love, Death, and Cricketsong: Prince Andrei at Mytishchi." In *In the Shade of the Giant: Essays on Tolstoy*, edited by Hugh McLean, 61–83. Berkeley: Univ. of California Press, 1989.

Whitman, Walt. *Leaves of Grass: The First (1855) Edition*. Ed. Malcolm Cowley. New York: Viking, 1959.

Williams, Carolyn. *Transfigured World: Walter Pater's Aesthetic Historicism*. Ithaca: Cornell Univ. Press, 1989.

Wordsworth, William. *The Prelude: 1799, 1805, 1850*. Ed. Jonathan Wordsworth, M. H. Abrams, and Stephen Gill. New York: Norton, 1979.

———. *The Ruined Cottage and The Pedlar*. Ed. James Butler. Ithaca: Cornell Univ. Press, 1979.

———. *Shorter Poems, 1807–1820*. Ed. Carl H. Ketcham. Ithaca: Cornell Univ. Press, 1989.

Zonana, Joyce. "The Embodied Muse: Elizabeth Barrett Browning's *Aurora Leigh* and Feminist Poetics." *Tulsa Studies in Women's Literature* 8 (1989): 241–62.

Index

MARTIN BIDNEY, a professor of English and comparative literature at the State University of New York at Binghamton, is the author of *Blake and Goethe: Psychology, Ontology, Imagination* and over fifty articles. He is currently at work on a sequel to the present volume, including more case studies of epiphany patterns in British and Russian literature.